RECLAIMING THE F WORD

ABOUT THE AUTHORS

CATHERINE REDFERN is founder of *The F Word* website. In 2002 the site was highly commended by Women in Publishing's New Venture Awards, and in 2003 Redfern was named by the *Guardian* as one of 50 'Women to Watch'. Now over twelve years old, *The F Word* (www.thefword.org.uk) is recognised as having contributed to a revived interest in feminism among younger women and men, and continues to provide a voice for the UK's feminist community today.

KRISTIN AUNE is Senior Lecturer in Sociology at the University of Derby, where she teaches on feminism, gender and religion. She has been involved in feminist groups for more than a decade and has published widely on gender, religion and feminism. Her books include *Women and Religion in the West: Challenging Secularization* (2008) and *Christianity and the University Experience: Understanding Student Faith* (2013).

RECLAIMING THE F WORD

Feminism Today

CATHERINE REDFERN

& KRISTIN AUNE

ZED

Reclaiming the F Word: Feminism Today was first published as
Reclaiming the F Word: The New Feminist Movement in 2010 by
Zed Books Ltd, The Foundry, 17 Oval Way, London SE11 5RR, UK.

www.zedbooks.net

This edition published in 2013

Typeset in Monotype Bulmer by Illuminati, Grosmont
Index by John Barker
Cover design by Alice Marwick

A catalogue record for this book is available from the British Library

ISBN 978-1-78032-627-6 pb

CONTENTS

ACKNOWLEDGEMENTS

THIS BOOK WOULD NOT EXIST if it weren't for the many hundreds of inspiring feminists who appear within it and who contributed in various ways.

Gratitude is due first to our survey respondents and those who were interviewed for the research.

The survey research was funded by the University of Derby, enabling Rose Holyoak to be employed as a research assistant. We are very grateful to Rose for her dedication to the project: for efficient administration of the survey, analytical skills and support on numerous research tasks. Helen Roberts also helped with data input.

We would like to thank our agent, Maggie Hanbury, and Gen Carden (formerly of The Hanbury Agency) for their interest in the manuscript and help in polishing the proposal and securing a publisher.

We are very fortunate to have Zed Books as our publisher. Throughout the process all the staff at Zed have been as supportive, helpful and enthusiastic as any authors could wish for. In particular, Tamsine O'Riordan's detailed and judicious comments on the manuscript helped us to produce a much better book; we are lucky to have worked with such a brilliant editor. Ruvani de Silva impressed us with her boundless enthusiasm and practical help in promoting our book. Kika Sroka-Miller produced a brilliant cover for the first edition, and her editorial work on the second edition was invaluable.

For reading and commenting on drafts of individual chapters, we are very grateful to Kim Allen, Louise Livesey, zohra moosa, Becky Barnes, Sonya Sharma and Jodie Mitchell. For sources and help with material for the second edition, thanks to Frauke Uhlenbruch, Sariya Cheruvallil-Contractor and Ebtihal Mahadeen.

For help with proofreading, thanks to Rosalyn Scott and, especially, to Rachel Haynes, whose eye for detail is incredible and who gave up much time and effort proofreading chapters.

For supportive and wise advice, we are grateful to Rachel Bell, Libby Brooks, Chilla Bulbeck, Deborah Cameron, Kira Cochrane, Katherine Rake, Yvonne Roberts, Katharine Viner, Natasha Walter and Imelda Whelehan.

Catherine would also like to thank Andrew Bowden for extensive support and encouragement, Jess McCabe, members of *The F Word* collective, contributors and readers, and baby Sam, who remained cheerful whilst the new preface was being typed out inches from his head.

Kristin would like to thank her friends, family and current and former colleagues and students for their inspiration and backing.

PROLOGUE

WE MET back in 2002. Catherine had just set up *The F Word* (www. thefword.org.uk) after identifying a gap for a UK-focused feminist website, whilst Kristin had just published her first book on women in the church, and was doing her Ph.D. while teaching part-time. Brought together through a shared interest in young women's attitudes to feminism and a passionate belief that feminism is as relevant as it ever was, in the last few years we have been excited by a vibrant feminist movement which seems to be growing exponentially.

Yet at the same time, we've been puzzled and disappointed by how feminism has been portrayed. It's as if we lived in a parallel universe. Article after article proclaimed that feminism was dead, and stated that young people in particular are uninterested in this once vital movement. We read columnists bemoaning women's lack of activism. We witnessed conferences host panel sessions entitled 'Is feminism dead?' or 'Do we need a new feminism?' Feminist academics appeared to overlook young people's involvement in feminism. We received emails telling us (hilariously) that 'all you feminists do is sit and slag off good entertainment and cry about how gingerbread men should be called gingerbread people.'

This simply didn't tally with what we had seen through our research and involvement with the feminist community.

Our aim in this book is to provide a whistle-stop tour of activity in the UK today and further afield. We will explain why feminism is still vitally important and introduce some of today's inspiring new feminists, describing what they want and what they are doing. We want to show feminism is liberating, diverse, challenging, exciting, relevant and inclusive, and we hope to offer inspiration for further involvement. In an increasingly global society, feminism transcends national boundaries, so we'll also showcase examples of feminist issues and activism beyond the UK.

In order to help us represent feminism fairly, over the course of a year we surveyed as many self-defined feminists in the UK as we could. We focused on the newer forms of feminist activism that had emerged since 2000 – groups, events, campaigns and individuals largely ignored by the mainstream media. We asked feminists about themselves, how they came to feminism, what issues were important to them and what activism they undertook. We asked their views on questions such as 'Can men be feminists?' and 'How do you define feminism?' The book includes quotes from people we interviewed,[1] as well as the words of writers, bloggers and researchers. The voices of contemporary feminists – younger ones especially – are often ignored, so we want to redress the balance.

Nearly 1,300 feminists replied, from across Britain, aged from 15 to 81. We believe it is the largest survey of feminists that has been undertaken in recent years. Whilst all surveys have their limitations, now we have evidence of what a large group of UK feminists think and want. And guess what? Gingerbread men weren't mentioned once.

Our survey shows that there are a large number of feminists active today who were not born during the heyday of 1960s' and

1970s' feminism, and who are working alongside older feminists. An amazing three-quarters of the feminists we surveyed were under 35. That's why we feel justified in proclaiming this as a new feminist movement – simply because many of the feminists themselves are new to feminism. And it's these newer feminists who are often derided and made invisible. You can read more about the survey's findings in the Appendix.

But first, let's get something straight. This isn't going to be one of those 'new feminist' books that reiterate negative stereotypes about 1970s' feminism and position younger feminists in opposition to it. We're not interested in pushing forward a hip, 'fashionable' kind of feminism. Whilst recognising that second-wave feminism wasn't perfect, in our experience younger feminists are quick to acknowledge their debt to older feminists. The attitude of P.J. Goodman, writing in *Pirate Jenny* zine (*c.* 2001), is typical:

> Let me have a moment here with those of you who have no idea the price your First and Second Wave Sisters paid so you could enjoy the benefits of saying you are not a feminist. Need I remind you that LESS THAN 40 years ago a woman could not get a credit card unless her husband cosigned for it. It has been LESS THAN 30 years since women have been admitted to graduate programs ... sister, someone cleared that path for you and paid dearly for it.... Do the right thing at your next gig, your next gallery show, your next art house screening, your next rock opera premier, the birth of your baby, or at the b'ris of your son and raise your fist, your glass, or your voice to the women who cut a swathe through this jungle for us so we could saunter along in their clear path and dare to say we aren't feminists.

We hope to prove that there is a large group of feminists reclaiming the 'f word' from those who trash it. No, it isn't as media-friendly as generations of feminists fighting like cats in a bag.[2] It's optimistic, rolling-your-sleeves-up-and-getting-things-done feminism.

PREFACE TO

THE NEW EDITION

FEMINISM TODAY

FOUR YEARS AGO, we wanted to shed light on the state of the feminist movement. We wanted to prove that feminists were still active, despite the mainstream media's claim that 'feminism is dead'. We wanted to show that young people were engaging with feminism afresh and we wanted to examine the issues feminists were dealing with and the activism they were engaged in. The result of that desire was *Reclaiming the F Word*.

Our book was unapologetically positive. Feminism today is diverse and vibrant, we argued, with something for everyone to get passionate about and a smorgasbord of opportunities for activism. Several years on, it seems a good time to re-evaluate. Some things have changed, others haven't. A global financial crisis and recession have hit. Many governments have changed, with some regimes buckling under public pressure during and after the 'Arab Spring'. These political and economic changes have provoked changes in culture and society and vice versa. Many feminist and political movements have evolved; others have kept beating the same drum.

This book's core argument – that there are serious gender inequalities in the world today and feminists are acting to challenge them – remains true. While some of the statistics cited for individual countries may have changed very slightly – for instance, pay gaps, rates of gendered violence or girls' educational achievements – they remain broadly accurate; we won't rehearse our evidence and arguments here. Instead, we'll focus on the changes that have occurred in the social context in which feminism takes place in society, on how some feminists have been engaging, and with what issues and effects.

Feminism back in the spotlight

It certainly feels that we have proved our point about feminists' existence. After a veritable drought in popular feminist publishing, our book emerged at the same time as several others (in the UK alone: Kat Banyard's *The Equality Illusion*, Ellie Levenson's *The Noughtie Girl's Guide to Feminism*, Caitlin Moran's *How To Be a Woman*, Laurie Penny's *Meat Market*, Nina Power's *One Dimensional Woman* and Natasha Walter's *Living Dolls*). Headlines announced feminism was alive again, a far cry from the 'feminism is dead' hand-wringing we reported on in our first edition.[1] Women's magazines jumped on the feminist bandwagon, with *Cosmo* launching a campaign to reclaim feminism in celebration of its fortieth birthday. Indeed, feminism is often presented as common sense and sexism as hopelessly old-fashioned: witness the public derision generated by Republican Mitt Romney's comment, during the second US presidential debate no less, that, in order to increase the number of women in his cabinet when he was governor of Massachusetts, he had asked his staff to bring him 'binders full of women'. Or think of the public approval (albeit mostly outside Australia) for the Australian prime

'We seem to be entering a new heyday for British feminism.' *Guardian*, 2010

'New feminism has started the fight-back at last.' *Evening Standard*, 2010

'Anyone can be a feminist.' *Times of India*, 2011

'Feminism: it's not a dirty word.' *Independent*, 2012

'We still need feminism.' *Stylist* magazine, 2012

'It's time for women to take back the word "feminism".' *Washington Post*, 2013

minister's public attack on sexism and misogyny in parliament in late 2012. Other research has picked up on this new 'wave' of feminism, and as we were writing *Reclaiming the F Word* others too were beginning to study the new feminist movement in the UK and beyond.[2]

Media scholar Kaitlynn Mendes, in her study of over 1,100 news articles in British and American newspapers, notices this growing press interest in feminism.[3] Yet in the articles she studied, discussions of feminism were often either 'defensive', designed to rescue feminism from 'negative stereotypes', or show a 'noticeable shift towards the "lifestyling" of feminism'; more focused on, say, whether botox or baking can be a feminist activity than on large-scale social or structural issues such as the economy or reporting on collective feminist activism. Indeed, we were regularly asked, can you be a stay-at-home mum; watch porn; wear heels; use lipstick; and be a feminist? A well-known women's magazine even hosted a debate for international women's day entitled 'I'm a feminist – can I vajazzle?'[4]

This defensiveness, boiling down to 'don't worry, you can be a feminist and still be "sexy"', in itself proves feminism is still needed. Having to shout 'I'm a sexy feminist' surely shows how pressurised our society makes women feel to fulfil a 'sexy' (to some archetypal heterosexual man) feminine ideal. Interviewing British and German women about their attitudes to feminism, Christina Scharff found that women often dissociate from the word 'feminist' in order to present themselves as heterosexual, not critical of men and happy to conform to conventional beauty standards.[5] Should feminists go along with this by insisting feminists are 'sexy' too, or should we challenge the pressures on women to see their worth primarily in their sexiness?

Debates like this show that the struggle is no longer to prove that feminists exist. It is now about what feminism means and requires of us.

So what is feminism today?

In this flowering of media attention, feminism is often presented as an identity label requiring no further action. One recent feminist book asserted 'being a feminist is what you want it to be'; another, called *Sexy Feminism*, was marketed as 'a girl's guide to love, success and style'.[6] One website renamed the movement 'FeMEnism', 'to reflect women's personal choice'.[7] Feminism's rehabilitation has also seen women on the political right explicitly identifying with the word, including American politician Sarah Palin, who opposes same-sex marriage and abortion even in cases of rape or incest, and British Conservative MP Nadine Dorries, who has regularly tried to bring anti-abortion bills to Parliament.

While there is no governing committee deciding who is 'allowed' to call themselves feminists, is it really the case that even someone whose views and actions are likely to harm the cause of women's rights can call themselves a feminist?

Certainly since we wrote our chapter on 'Liberated Bodies', it has become abundantly clear that reproductive rights need defending as never before. Abortion providers in the UK have seen an increase in vigils and protests taking place outside their clinics, perhaps encouraged by the attitudes of influential politicians like the British health secretary Jeremy Hunt, who reportedly favours reducing the abortion time limit to twelve weeks. In the USA, the rise of the extreme right-wing Tea Party and miscarrying women being arrested and charged with murder in some states makes Margaret Atwood's dystopia *The Handmaid's Tale* seem prescient. Restrictions on abortion have been proposed in Turkey and elsewhere, and Savita Halappanavar's death in Ireland after being denied an abortion caused outrage across the world.

But the fight for our bodies is not just about abortion. Women in Israel, Uzbekistan and South Africa have been forcibly sterilised or given contraceptive injections without their consent.[8] Hedva Eyal, author of the report into the case of Ethiopian Jewish migrants who were not allowed into Israel without submitting to these procedures, believes that 'it is a method of reducing the number of births in a community that is black and mostly poor'.[9] Transsexual men and women are also required to be sterilised in many countries in order to be legally recognised as their preferred gender identity.[10]

Choice and equality in the age of austerity

Feminism of course is about more than just reproductive rights and it has to be about more than just personal choice; after all, our 'choices' can never be completely freely made. Every decision we make is bound up in a whole package of social, cultural and historical expectations and legacies. Take, for example, increasing numbers of British students entering the sex industry to pay for university tuition,[11] or the decision to be a stay-at-home mum because of the prohibitive cost of childcare. Aren't these choices related to capitalism, patriarchy, heteronormativity (the view that heterosexuality is the norm, and/or ideal) and the state (often relegating women to unpaid domestic work or low-paid service-sector work, forcing them to depend on a male breadwinner, assuming there is a male breadwinner in the first place, cutting welfare benefits and public-sector jobs and raising tuition fees to the highest level in Europe)?[12]

The concept of 'choice' must be critiqued, so that we can understand and challenge our disadvantaged positions in a social system which is still structured by patriarchy and capitalism. And in the age of austerity – perhaps the most significant development since we wrote our 'Equality at Work and Home' chapter – this analysis is required more than ever.

The financial crisis is gendered. Its causes and impacts, and governments' subsequent policy decisions, are gendered. Governments have bailed out banks, reduced the tax payable by corporations, turned a blind eye to tax avoidance, and reduced the tax rate paid by the highest income earners, all actions mostly benefiting a small group of rich white men. At the same time, women have shouldered the lion's share of the budget cuts, despite being already in a disadvantaged position in the labour market, and despite the existence of European Union requirements that governments and public-sector bodies conduct equality-impact assessments of planned budget changes (an analysis to check whether any group is adversely affected by proposed changes, followed by actions to redress any negative impacts). In the UK the Women's Budget Group's investigation – incomplete because the government has neglected to break down all data by gender – concludes that 'Available evidence suggests that gender inequalities in the labour market will be worsened by the deficit reduction strategy.'[13] The Fawcett Society's analysis of the 2010 budget showed that women would shoulder 72 per cent of the cuts, due mainly to tax changes and benefit cuts. By 2012, after five government spending reviews, analysts revised this figure to about 75 per cent.[14] For Natalie Bennett, leader of the Green Party in England and Wales, the UK government's cuts demonstrate 'a gender bias that may be more extreme than anywhere else in Europe', with cuts to benefits and services, cuts to public-sector jobs, and increased care responsibilities as a result.[15]

This scenario is reflected globally, with women losing jobs in the public and private sectors and pay gaps widening in many countries as a result of the financial crisis and governments' austerity measures. In countries where people pay for health care and education, loss of income means that seeing a doctor or continuing a child's schooling can become unaffordable, as this and previous economic crises show. Cuts and job losses in affluent nations have a knock-on effect everywhere. In export-led, industrialised or industrialising nations, where women migrate from rural areas to work in manufacturing with the aim of sending money home to their families, loss of work means being unable to send money back, for instance for school fees. In times of recession, women sometimes take more paid employment when male partners lose their jobs. But, according to Jane Lethbridge, this work is poorly paid, 'degrading' and involves anti-social hours, and has led to girls being taken out of school to do the household tasks their mothers can no longer do. The rise in what Lethbridge calls 'vulnerable employment' (casual, badly paid and in poor conditions) is a concern for everyone, but it affects women more than men.[16]

In the USA, women's incomes still lag behind men's. But in the recession, American women fared better than UK women and have done better than men in the economic recovery. More jobs overall are done by men than women, but the gap between men's and women's employment pre- and post-recession has narrowed. Differences among women must also be examined. For instance, those who lost their homes due to the collapse of the subprime mortgage market were disproportionately women of colour. And, as in the UK, female-headed households, who are most dependent on welfare, have suffered most from cuts to welfare services.[17] The first phase of the US recession saw more men than women laid off, but in the second phase women lost more jobs because they were more likely to be employed in the government sector, where jobs were cut. Obama's 2009 stimulus package, the American Recovery and Reinvestment Act, is helping both men and women;[18] it may even, some argue, disproportionately benefit women (for instance, through tax benefits for low-income households).[19] Since the recovery has begun, at least as many – if not more – women have regained jobs, and women have done well because the sectors of job growth (including education and health services) are sectors where women are in the majority.[20] Yet any apparent gender convergence in the American economy is less about female gain and more about 'many of the precarious aspects of women's economic situation increasingly spreading to men', as economist Randy Albelda explains.[21]

In the UK, women make up 64 per cent of public-sector workers, so bear the brunt of public-sector job cuts. Those who remain employed in the public sector face pay freezes, and about three-quarters of those facing pay freezes are female.[22] Women, already living on little over half the income of the average man, are being made to suffer three-quarters of budget cuts – cuts made in response to the behaviour and culture of the (male-dominated) financial industries. Since benefits account for a fifth of women's incomes, in comparison with a tenth of men's, cuts to benefits will also disproportionately affect them.[23] Analysis by the Women's Budget Group – itself an excellent example of feminist activism in this area – points to single mothers not in employment and single female pensioners as worst hit.

With disability benefits slashed, disabled people's dependency on carers increases, and these duties fall predominantly to family members. As disability rights activist Emma Round points out, the family members burdened with additional caring responsibilities are mostly women, who at the most receive no more than a meagre carer's allowance (amounting to less than a quarter of the weekly minimum wage). For disabled women, increased dependence on partners unfortunately means that they are more vulnerable to abuse: more than half of disabled women suffer abuse at home, and disabled women are more at risk of sexual abuse and assault, partly because their disability can be taken advantage of through (non-consensual) fetishisation. It's also harder – if not impossible – to run away from unwanted advances.[24]

Public services are being cut and reorganised at such a level that, even when spending cuts are no longer needed, the infrastructure will have disappeared (or have been taken over by private and/or voluntary providers), and will be immensely difficult, if not impossible, to reintroduce. Austerity measures reflect a government preference for shrinking the state and expanding the private and 'voluntary' sectors. This restructuring, feminists fear, is ideological: it takes us back towards assuming a male breadwinner and female (unpaid) homemaker, increasing women's financial dependence on male partners and expecting women to take up the slack after public services like childcare centres or day centres for ageing or disabled relatives have been removed. Will new rights for sharing maternity leave between two parents, such as those introduced in the UK in 2011, be enough to counteract this threat to gender equality in parenting and care?[25]

What's more, the age of austerity has seen dramatic cuts to domestic violence services. Between 2010 and 2012 local authority funds to sexual abuse and domestic violence services fell by 31 per cent and specialist police domestic violence support was reduced by many police forces.[26] After protests from women's groups, planned cuts to legal aid for women in abusive relationships were, in part, shelved. With such a loss in support services, more women and children will have nowhere to turn to escape violent partners; these cuts, then, may literally kill women.

The changes brought about by governments since 2010 have hit women so forcefully that demands for 'equal pay for men and women' seem almost a minor concern. Equality in poverty is no equality at all.

Feminism and left-wing politics

As all the above shows, class-based or anti-capitalist arguments need a feminist perspective, and vice versa. But feminism's relationship to the left wing has been strained over the last few years, mainly over approaches to sexual violence.

Since we outlined the feminist demand 'An End to Violence Against Women' (Chapter 3) the gang rape of a student on a New Delhi bus provoked an international outcry at Indian police, legislation and public attitudes for not taking sexual violence seriously. There were allegations of sexual assault against Dominique Strauss-Kahn, former head of the International Monetary Fund. There were revelations about UK celebrity Jimmy Savile, described as 'a prolific, predatory sex offender', the case of gang rape of children in Rochdale, England, and the failure of public services and police to prevent these crimes. Shock, anger and disbelief have prompted anguished reflections on how these terrible events could happen. Unfortunately for feminists familiar with the scale of sexual violence, these revelations did not come as a surprise. Reports showed that in 2009-12, an average of 85,000 women and 12,000 men annually reported being victims of rape or sexual assault by penetration in the UK; only 15 per cent reported this to the police, and with only around 1,000 convictions.[27] And yet we've heard powerful people – mainly bungling politicians – excusing rape or downplaying its seriousness, referring variously to 'legitimate rape', 'grey rape', '"rape" rape', 'date rape', 'forcible rape', and even been told 'if it's inevitable, relax and enjoy it'.[28]

So the last thing feminists expected was to have to deal with rape apologism by people many of us consider our comrades: those on the left wing of politics. Prominent men's support of WikiLeaks founder Julian Assange over the alleged rape of two women in Sweden, and his refusal to be extradited for trial, caused anger among many. Socialist politician George Galloway, for example, stumbled into the row, claiming that Assange was only accused of 'bad sexual etiquette'. Naomi Wolf argued that the alleged victims should be named, and suggested that they simply had 'personal injured feelings';[29] Michael Moore called the case 'a bunch of hooey' (later clarified following a major feminist Twitter campaign).[30] Many women have experienced sexism and racism in the Occupy movement – from being propositioned at protest sites and objectified in the 'Hot Chicks at Occupy Wall Street' video, to being expected to take on the behind-the-scenes tasks while white men put themselves forward as the voice of the movement.[31]

The Socialist Workers Party, part of the UK's radical left movement, also faced charges of sexism. When a female party member accused a prominent committee member of rape, the party did not encourage her to report it to the police. Instead, party members who were friends of the accused conducted an internal investigation and then exonerated the accused. Failure to deal properly with allegations of sexual assault is not, Laurie Penny points out, peculiar to left-wing movements. But

> There is … a stubborn refusal to accept and deal with rape culture that is unique to the left and to progressives more broadly. It is precisely to do with the idea that, by virtue of being progressive, by virtue of fighting for equality and social justice, by virtue of, well, virtue, we are somehow above being held personally accountable when it comes to issues of race, gender and sexual violence.[32]

Concerns about the failure of some left-wing groups to take sexual violence seriously are not simply about the handling of a few distinct cases. Rather, they are symptomatic of a wider societal failure to challenge sexism and to create leadership structures that are truly democratic and gender-inclusive.

Feminism, politics and religion

To stand any hope of fighting back against these new changes and threats, feminists must be in positions of influence in political and religious institutions. This is something we discuss in Chapter 5. Since the first edition of this book, significant changes have occurred across the globe. The Arab Spring revolutions took place across the Middle East as people rose up to challenge regimes they saw as incompetent, autocratic, corrupt, or simply unable to feed their citizens or provide jobs, democracy and human rights. Likewise, the power of global, free-market capitalism continues to shape and compromise our livelihoods, politics, climate and very survival. Male domination in politics is as obvious as ever; in the UK, women's participation in politics and public life lags behind most of the rest of Europe and in certain areas (membership of the Cabinet, for instance) has actually fallen.[33] The USA, though with a slightly lower proportion of women in Congress than the UK, has seen a small improvement, with a record number of women (97 in 2013, nearly a fifth of the total) serving in the House and in the Senate.[34]

How did the 2011 Arab Spring uprisings across Tunisia, Morocco, Egypt, Libya, Bahrain, Syria and Yemen affect women? Women joined men in initiating the protests and, in some countries, were able to join the men on the streets, calling for improved human rights, better living standards and an end to unjust and dictatorial rule. Yet it quickly emerged that women were not safe within those spaces: like male protesters they faced arrest, torture and death at the hands of military forces and others opposed to their protest; but *unlike* them, they faced the further violence of rape, virginity tests and abduction. The new or reorganised governments established after the uprisings have an opportunity to improve women's participation. Yet the proportions of women in government or parliament before and after the 2011 revolutions have barely changed and in some cases (such as Egypt) have fallen.[35] With so few women elected and conservative religious factions prominent in many of the governments, it is difficult to challenge discriminatory laws restricting women's rights to child custody, divorce, inheritance and dowry, established to reflect various interpretations of, in this case, Islam in many countries worldwide. It is also hard to convince governments to ratify conventions like the international Convention on the Elimination of All Forms of Discrimination Against Women (CEDAW).

Human rights activists, like the International Federation for Human Rights, which is calling for governments to adopt '20 measures for equality', fear that the opportunities created by the uprisings may not come to fruition for women:

> The changes sweeping the region ... present real opportunities for women to push for their rights. Yet they also present risks of regression. Demands for equality are set aside while the efforts of protesters focus on bringing down regimes and dismantling oppressive state institutions. Recent history painfully reminds us that the massive occupation of public space by women during revolutions in no way guarantees their role in the political bodies of the regimes that follow.[36]

The connections between religion, politics and patriarchy were made visible by the trial and jailing of members of Pussy Riot for hooliganism motivated by religious hatred after they performed a 'punk prayer' in a Moscow cathedral. With lyrics such as 'Mother of God, chase Putin out', and 'Virgin Mary, Mother of God. Be a feminist',[37] the protest has been interpreted in different ways: as feminist challenge to a patriarchal state; as a protest against the Orthodox Church and its support for Putin; as anti-capitalist; and as anarchist critique of state authoritarianism.[38] As Katja Richters explains, the jailing of Pussy Riot was surprising, not only because Russia, as a secular state, would not usually intervene in such a case, but also because the reaction of cathedral clergy to the punk prayer was diverse and not uniformly condemnatory.[39]

Feminist groups in the former Soviet Union have also made the headlines. Ukrainian group FEMEN – whose topless protests highlighting their concerns with sex tourism and lack of abortion rights have brought them publicity and regular arrest in the Ukraine – were menaced and driven into the woods in nearby Belarus by the KGB when they mocked its president, thought by some to be 'the last dictator in Europe'.[41] In 2012, FEMEN joined forces with

> 'Many criticize us for our methods, calling them too extravagant and immoral... But we understand that this is the only way to be heard in this country. If we staged simple protests with banners, then our claims would not have been noticed.'
>
> FEMEN activist
> GALINA SOZANSKAYA[40]

Egyptian blogger Aliaa Magda Elmahdy in a naked protest against Egypt's planned constitution. With 'Sharia is not a constitution' scrawled across her body, Elmahdy stood alongside activists holding the slogans 'Religion is slavery' and 'No religion'.[42]

The increasing visibility of both religious and atheist feminism is also noteworthy. The campaign for women bishops – lost by a surprisingly small margin – saw egalitarians inside the Anglican church mobilise to argue the theological case for women in senior leadership. The UK also recently saw the launch of the UK-based Christian Feminist Network.[43]

There is increasing interest in, and involvement with, women's rights projects among Muslims too. Speaking to girls in schools,

Shaista Gohir, called 'Britain's most feminist Muslim' by *The Times*, realised most did not have role models of successful Muslim women, so she set up the website Big Sister. Big Sister showcases examples of pioneering and successful Muslim women in sport, the arts, politics, activism and history and provides leadership advice to younger women. National projects include Inspire, and there are others being established at a local level.

Yet for many Muslim women, feminism continues to be problematic because of its association with colonialist or 'Western' sentiments such as equating the wearing of the hijab with women's oppression – a view some Muslim (or formerly Muslim) feminists share. The young Muslim women interviewed by Sariya Contractor advocate for women's public role in education, employment, the family and the public sphere but speak of 'women's rights' rather than 'feminism'. They see those rights as being integral to Islam, properly understood.[44]

During group discussions I asked Muslim women, 'if not feminism, what would they call this movement?' In each case we brain-stormed for key-words that best described our struggles. The similarity of the words the women used was *not* surprising and the story the words told was intuitive – 'Islamic reawakening', 'Reviving Islam', 'Muslim women's rights,' 'Living Islam', 'Practising Islam' and even 'Muhajababes'!

... Finally the women concluded that maybe their struggle was not just about them as women, but was rather about initiating a revival of Islam as derived from the Quran and the *Sunnah* – the foundational Islamic texts – and not from Muslim's cultural practices. Some commentators may call this feminism; however for the Muslim women I spoke to this was a revival of that which had been lost to the culture as Islam had been diachronically propagated across diverse lands and peoples. Islamic feminism or not – it is important that this struggle is furthered and that its contributions are recognised.

SARIYA CONTRACTOR[45]

Sexism and social media

The Internet continues to be one of the most significant modern influences on our lives, and on feminism too, presenting new opportunities and new threats. From the use of social media during the Arab Spring, to increasing levels of online harassment of women writers (especially feminists),[46] feminist battles are increasingly influenced by the Internet, for good or for bad.

For example, in Chapter 2 we advocate 'Sexual Freedom and Choice'. Recently, publicly shaming women and girls for having sex (a trend feminists call 'slut shaming') has become more pernicious with the increasing use of social media, as sexualised photographs and videos of girls especially are circulated more easily. There is also a vigilante-style 'report a potential prostitute' website, which demands women pay to get their names removed from it.[47]

In the online world, it seems increasingly hard to promote the key feminist demand of consensual sex. A 2010 YouGov poll showed that one in three 16–18 year-old UK girls have experienced unwanted sexual touching at school.[48] Concern about the impact Internet pornography may have on children's developing sexuality (and, let's face it, porn is not exactly renowned for its depiction of realistic, consensual sexual encounters) have led to proposals for restricting access to online porn in some countries, including the UK and Iceland. The End Violence Against Women Coalition's new Schools Safe 4 Girls[49] campaign aims to make sex and relationships education a statutory part of the curriculum and educate young people to understand that violence in relationships is not acceptable.

The surprise self-published best-seller *Fifty Shades of Grey* has dominated discussions of women and sex in the last couple of years, with columnists wondering what made so many women identify with the masochistic heroine. But whilst the popularity of the book made women's sexual desire a mainstream topic, many pointed out that the book describes behaviours that are non-consensual and are in fact classic examples of partner abuse, rather than an accurate portrayal of a consensual BDSM relationship.[50]

Since we set out our demand for a 'Popular Culture Free from Sexism' (Chapter 6) the Internet has become even more influential in our cultural lives, with traditional media scurrying to catch up.

The Leveson Inquiry into press standards in the UK provided an opportunity for women's groups to highlight the treatment of women by the tabloids, covering issues such as paparazzi, sexism and objectification, but the Inquiry paid scant attention to how this plays out online. Yet statistics on women in the media demonstrate that men still dominate in new media as well as traditional journalism.[51]

On the positive side, a massive variety of feminist campaigners can be found causing ructions on Twitter, YouTube, Facebook, Pinterest, online petition websites and other forums, reaching a wider audience than ever before. For example, the 'No More Page Three' campaign gathered over 100,000 signatories to its 'Take the Bare Boobs out of The Sun' petition and used humour, videos, poetry and comedy to gather support.[52] The Everyday Sexism Project, too, won acclaim for documenting women's every-day experiences: from harassment in the street or the workplace, to sexism in adverts, the media or conversations. By using Twitter, the Project demonstrates with its relentless tweets – coming one after another – that what can seem to be insignificant isolated incidents are in fact a tsunami of daily discrimination. With almost 50,000 followers on Twitter and hundreds of daily posts, the Project regularly receives comments from men who say it has opened their eyes to the sexism women suffer.[53]

Feminism now:
action, controversies and disagreement

In our final chapter, 'Feminism Reclaimed', we sketch out what the feminist revival looks like. Is the picture any different now, and what have feminists been doing?

Feminists continue to organise with humour, vigour and passion, with tactics evolving in order to respond to the issues of the day. Pussy Riot's protest methods – the theatrical performance art, the colourful balaclavas, the manner in which their supporters mobilised using social media – typify those we now associate with younger, newer forms of feminist activism, while also reflecting their unique national, political and religious contexts. There are too many examples to detail in full, but we can mention a few.

In response to the '40 Days for Life' anti-choice protests outside some abortion clinics, feminists countered with '40 Days of Treats' in which staff at the targeted clinics were sent supportive gifts and messages. Activism about sexual violence has stepped up a gear. The recent Indian gang rape case, mentioned above, sparked incredible mass protests across Asia, some describing the response as a possible 'feminist spring'.[54] In response to comments about women 'dressing like sluts' from a Canadian police officer, the infamous Slutwalks – protest marches countering the blaming of victims of violence – spread like wildfire across the world, capturing the imagination of women who'd had enough of being told that what they wore could cause or prevent rape. In the UK, the marches were attended by both men and women, and were for many people their first mixed-sex feminist protest. And Eve Ensler's V-Day organisation against violence against women coordinated a 'One Billion Rising' worldwide global strike and protest event in 2013 to mark the grim fact that one in three women on the planet will be raped or beaten in her lifetime.[55]

Clearly, the old protest slogan 'whatever we wear, wherever we go, yes means yes and no means no' is in no danger of retirement.

Campaigns for same-sex marriage continue. Thirteen countries and nine American states now allow same-sex marriage; in the USA, 2012 saw the election of the first openly gay senator. In the UK, a bill to introduce equal marriage succeeded, and polls show wide support. Yet in many countries, such as Uganda, which recently threatened to introduce a law that could carry the death penalty for being gay, LGBTQI people are still struggling to simply exist.

Yet there is still disagreement about the best ways to create a feminist world. Many feminists are worried that 'popular feminism' has sold out to capitalism, heterosexuality and whiteness. Several high-profile feminists have been criticised for using discriminatory language about disabled or transgender people, or for seeming to downplay the importance of racism and class issues. In recent years, the term 'intersectionality' has gained prominence within feminist communities. 'Intersectionality' in this context means that oppressions and inequalities intersect: that it's impossible to understand gender without reference to differences of, and relationships between, age, sexuality, class, religion, ethnicity, disability or location. 'My feminism will be intersectional or it will be bullshit' – a declaration coined by Flavia Dzodan in a post critiquing the feminist community's response to a racist sign held at a Slutwalk march[56] – is frequently quoted, and there have been conscious struggles to be more attentive of intersectionality in some feminist conferences, writing, events and activism, such as at the GoFeminist and INTERSECT conferences in London and Bristol, respectively, in 2012.

Many younger activists perceive this as a generational difference, associating awareness of intersectionality with a younger generation. However, although the word may have been coined only in the last twenty years, the concept is much older, and similar debates occupied feminists from the 1970s, and especially during the 1980s.[57]

Black Feminists Manchester report 'a resurgence of politically black women's groups over the last 4 years, striving to raise consciousness of black identity for women and equally aiming to address issues faced by the whole black community'.[58] Black feminists have highlighted how they, and the issues they care about, are often marginalised or excluded within white-dominated feminist groups. Also, some so-called key feminist concerns, such as free, safe contraception and abortion, look entirely different from their perspective: black and ethnic minority women, poor women, disabled and immigrant women have had to fight instead against state-enforced sterilisation or contraception.[59]

Many feel that white, privileged, 'Western' feminists are guilty of talking about them, but of ignoring their own activism and opinions. For example, a group of Indian feminists reacted sarcastically to attempts by feminists at Harvard University to offer recommendations on gender violence in India and other South Asian countries, writing in an open letter:

> This is clearly something that we, Indian feminists and activists who have been involved in the women's movement here for several decades, are incapable of doing, and it was with a sense of overwhelming relief that we read of your intention to step into this breach.[60]

Pavan Amara, investigating working-class women's views of feminism, found a similar problem. One woman she interviewed commented:

> You hear talk of working-class women, but of the feminist conferences and meetings I've attended I've never seen them get a teenage mum up on stage or talk about why female crime is rising, or anything outside of that white, middle-class remit.[61]

Black Feminist Twelve Point Plan

1. WE WANT FREEDOM.
2. We want a reformation of the criminal justice system, the abolition of the prison industrial complex and the implementation of community based models of justice and accountability.
3. We want control over our reproductive health and believe it is essential to building and maintaining strong black communities.
4. We want an end to all forms of physical, emotional, and sexual violence against black children.
5. We want media to reflect the diversity of who we are, to include our voices, value our bodies and our stories.
6. We want an end to poverty and the development of an economy that benefits and provides for all people.
7. We want education for liberation that includes equitable distribution of funding, culturally relevant curriculum, community control of schools and an end to the school to prison pipeline.
8. We want access to secure, equal, safe, affordable and hazard free housing (public and private), community land rights, residencies of our choice and an end to homelessness.
9. We want to live in a society where we can feel safe and protected.
10. We want an end to invisibility, violence and homophobia towards LGBTQ people in our community.
11. We want a world where respect of the Earth's resources is central to every human society and economic system.
12. We want a black community free of sexism and sexist oppression, where Black Women can be self-determined members of their community.

BLACK FEMINIST WORKING GROUP, 2011[62]

Transgender feminism, often called 'transfeminism', which brings together feminism with trans approaches and concepts, continues to gain prominence. Transfeminism, some argue, shows just how far gender roles are socially constructed, rather than biologically driven. Yet within some feminist groups, especially those who advocate 'women-only' spaces, transsexual women have to struggle to be recognised as women and as allies in the struggle against gender oppression.[63]

In December 2011 the UN Human Rights Council released its first report about the progress of equality of LGBTQI citizens, with the high commissioner recommending that UN states 'investigate promptly all reported killings and other serious incidents of violence perpetrated against individuals because of their actual or perceived sexual orientation or gender identity... and hold perpetrators accountable, and establish systems for the recording and reporting of such incidents.' Although this is not yet a mandate, small steps are being taken to end discrimination and violence against individuals based on their sexual orientation and experienced or perceived gender identities, across the globe.

Feminism tomorrow

We have great reason to hope in the feminist movement, an international movement which has achieved – sometimes slowly and steadily, sometimes forcefully and sacrificially – incredible advances in the position of women the world over.

As Pamela Paxton, Melanie Hughes and Jennifer Green observe in their major study of women's political representation over the twentieth century, women's political representation has moved from being seen as unacceptable to being 'actively encouraged'. The responsibility for this success lies with the international women's movement, which 'worked to institutionalize women's equality in world society' and thus 'generated global pressure on nation states to incorporate women'.[64] Similarly, as the largest global study of violence against women to date found, it is feminist movements over the past four decades that have led the way in getting gendered issues taken seriously by governments, leading to improved policies and countless lives saved.[65]

Feminism continues to be claimed, reclaimed, expressed and lived out today, and this will continue tomorrow. We write this new Preface sobered by the powers of patriarchy, capitalism, racism, classism and homophobia under which much of the world toils. Even so, attempts to create new worlds through inspiring, creative, diverse and powerful acts of resistance give us all hope, again.

INTRODUCTION

Sometimes it's hard to be a feminist

IF YOU LISTENED to the myths circulating in the mainstream media, you'd have a fairly warped view of feminism. Feminism is pronounced 'dead' on a regular basis, especially by anti-feminist commentators eager to ram the final nail into the coffin, but also, sometimes, by established feminists. In recent years it's become routine for media stars to have a bash at feminism. From Bob Geldof and Fay Weldon to Doris Lessing and Patrick Moore, criticisms of feminism are gleefully reported in the press. Left-wing pundits use newspaper columns to bemoan the state of feminism among the youth of today, whilst right-wingers complain that 'feminism has gone too far'. It seems like everyone's talking about us, but not with us.

> 'I can now say, obviously I am a feminist ... the f-word is alive and dynamic ... we're not alone and that we've got no excuse for thinking so. Suddenly I can feel enfranchised and powerful – armed, loaded.' AMBER, 16, to *The F Word*, 2002[1]

A particular complaint of detractors is that no one appears to know what feminists want any more, that it has become vague and confusing. Even pro-feminist commentators seem to accept this idea of feminism's decline unquestioningly. 'Where have all the feminists gone?' asks Zoe Williams, 'And can we, in all conscience, celebrate the achievements of yesterday's feminists when we're making no effort to live up to them?'[2] Patricia Hewitt's somewhat disparaging comments at a Fabian Society conference in 2009 are typical:

> My experience of the 1970s was you had a very clearly definable women's movement. You had women in consciousness raising groups, political parties and in trade unions, critically, organising around a series of demands ... and I don't have that sense now that there is anything – well, there really isn't – anything which cuts across all of those different issues.[3]

Feminism's breadth and diversity are not considered strengths. The women's movement is too splintered to be of use, it is argued. It is as if people want to see a central organisation which issues certificates to 'real' feminists who agree on several unifying principles. Numerous commentators conclude that feminism has 'lost the plot'. 'Today's young women tend to be lazy, if not lapsed, feminists', we are told.[4] Meanwhile, all the feminists we know are dumbfounded, jumping up and down shouting 'We're over here! We've been marching in the streets, blogging, protesting, organising!' Or muttering 'Don't these columnists know how to use Google?'

Strangely, whilst being told they are as extinct as dinosaurs, feminists are simultaneously depicted as if they more or less rule the world. Depending on who you listen to, feminism has gone too far, is out of control, must be reversed, causes you to be unhealthy and makes you unhappy. Even stories that are *positive* about feminism have negative headlines. And the more these myths are repeated, the more they become accepted 'fact'. Feminism is dead. Young people aren't feminists. Feminism made women miserable. Feminism has gone too far.

In the popular imagination, feminists are sinister, mysterious figures, pitiable women clinging to outdated notions about men and women despite the evidence that the world is now an egalitarian paradise. Alternatively, they're actually the ones responsible for women's pressurised lives and today's overtly sexualised culture. Or they're ball-breaking, white, middle-class women who just want power and get it by making men's lives a misery. In this atmosphere, who, as the *Independent* asked, 'would want to call herself a feminist'?[5]

Unfortunately, the more we hear the 'fact' that people aren't feminists, the more it seems a self-fulfilling prophecy. Women and men who don't know much about feminism are put off it, and people who have feminist opinions are made to feel embarrassed about their beliefs. When Catherine set up the online magazine *The F Word* she was inundated with emails from women, especially young women, who were relieved and even shocked to find that

'Feminism: outmoded and unpopular'
Guardian, 2003

'Bra-burning feminism has reached burn-out'
The Times, 2003

'The Death of Feminism?'
BBC News, 2004

'Flower arranging will always trump feminism'
Observer, 2005

'Blind feminism has hurt our children'
The Times, 2007

'Feminism was a nightmare'
Paulo Coelho, *BBC News*, 2007

'How feminists tried to destroy the family'
Daily Mail, 2007

'Warning: Feminism is bad for your health'
Independent, 2007

'When feminism went nuts'
The Times, 2009

'Women less happy after 40 years of feminism'
The Times, 2009

'Has feminism turned women into wage-slaves?'
Daily Telegraph, 2009

'I was beginning to feel that there were no feminists alive today in Britain.' ANNE, to *The F Word*, 2002[6]

they weren't alone in having feminist views.

The negative coverage isn't that surprising; people have been saying that feminism is dead for years. It's a repetitive cycle that's been documented by writers like Susan Faludi in her seminal book *Backlash*.[7] But we should look beyond the superficial portrayal of feminism's demise and discover what is *actually* happening with feminists today. Yes, it's high time we reclaimed feminism from all this doom and gloom.

Beyond 'I'm not a feminist, but...'

Let's look at the UK as an example. Despite the hype, the truth is that – in terms of attitudes and expectations – the UK is more feminist than one might think. The refrain 'I'm not a feminist, but...' crops up curiously often. The mistake is to take at face value the first part of that cliché; the 'but' is the most important bit. Surveys consistently show that most people have feminist attitudes. A survey of 1,000 readers of *Cosmopolitan* magazine in 2006 found that 96 per cent believed a woman should receive the same pay as a man for doing the same job, 96 per cent thought women should have a right to a career as well as – or instead of – motherhood, and 85 per cent believed women should have the right to choose an abortion.[8]

There is widespread support for the principles of equal pay, equal opportunities in education, equal access to employment and political representation at all levels, shared housework and childcare, reproductive rights, and targeted welfare provision for survivors of domestic and sexual violence. Young people are more liberal than their parents and grandparents, and young women are especially supportive of equality and choice in parenting.[9] Most young people, then, are feminists without realising it. In theory at least, the principles of equality, fairness and non-discrimination are burned into younger people's brains.

But how many of them would call themselves feminists? The figures may surprise you. Whilst it's clear that the majority do not call themselves feminists, the numbers who do are sizeable.

The same survey of *Cosmo* readers asked whether they would use 'the F-word' to describe themselves. A quarter said yes. Several smaller studies of college students in the USA found that 10–25 per cent identify themselves as feminists.[10] Of Womankind Worldwide's cross-section of 500 British women questioned in 2006, 29 per cent considered themselves feminists.[11] There is some evidence that younger women are becoming *more* likely to identify as feminists. The first UK-wide survey of 3,200 members of Girl Guiding UK found in 2007 that *two-thirds* of 16–25 year-olds would be happy to call themselves feminists.[12] A 2008 poll of 1,000 readers of *Stella* magazine found that nearly 40 per cent called themselves feminists.[13]

It's incredibly encouraging that a quarter of British women – more, if we take an average of all the surveys – are happy to say they're feminists. Considering all the negative publicity feminism gets, this is a considerable achievement. Yet these surveys are invariably reported as a *failure* of feminism. Rather than thinking that feminism has failed because 'only' 25 per cent of women are feminists, we need to keep in mind that being an active feminist was never a popular choice, even in the 1970s.[14] And 25 per cent is a very good support base for a social movement.

What's putting people off?

Even if we accept that a larger proportion of society than ever use the feminist label, it's still true that most people shy away. Why?

There are a range of reasons. They may believe that only 'active' feminists have the right to adopt the label; they may be pro-feminist men who avoid the term out of respect for women. They may have encountered individual feminists whom they disliked or think that feminism is only about white, middle-class women's issues. They may just be averse to labelling themselves. Being a feminist can mean facing up to negative things in the world and trying to change them, which can be daunting, even dangerous.

However, the main reasons why some do not associate with feminism come down to the way feminism is defined, the idea that equality has already been achieved, and society's emphasis on individual gains at the expense of collective action.

Definitions of feminism

In an undergraduate class that Kristin has taught in two universities, students are asked anonymously to answer the questions: 'Would you consider yourself a feminist?' and 'What does feminism mean to you?' Reflecting the national picture, about a quarter respond that they are confirmed feminists, and nearly as many are certain they are not. The rest linger around the middle, giving 'Yes, but…', 'No, but…' or 'unsure' responses; the box on the left shows some of these.

How feminism is defined is crucial. When people say they are not feminists, it's often because they are using a narrow definition rather than a broad one. When asked, 'What does feminism mean to you?' the students whose definitions of feminism were most open were most likely to

> **Would you consider yourself a feminist?**
>
> 'In a way, yes. I believe that all people should be equal. As long as their abilities are the same, everyone should be treated the same.'
>
> 'Yes and no. I do believe in equality for both men and women, but I don't believe it should be something that is focused solely on one gender.'

identify themselves as feminists. In other words, if you think bona fide feminists go on marches, belong to 'official' feminist organisations, hate men and dress a certain way, you are less likely to identify with feminism. But if you believe feminism is about equality and freedom of choice for men and women, you're more likely to call yourself a feminist.

I'll be a post-feminist in the post-patriarchy

Research has found that women today often have feminist views, but may not take on the feminist label for themselves because they associate it with an image of 1970s-style feminism that they think is no longer relevant to their very different experiences of life in the twenty-first century.[15] Thirty-five men and women interviewed for the Equal Opportunities Commission's 2003 *Talking Equality* report believed that women's rights and equality needed to be promoted but felt that words such as 'gender equality' and 'feminism' were old-fashioned.[16]

The belief that feminism is no longer necessary since 'we're all equal now' is a major contributor to non-identification with feminism. Living in a 'post-feminist'[17] society basically

'Yes in the respect that I would like equality for men and women. However, if a woman wants to be a housewife that is also her choice.'

'Not entirely. I believe in equality but I'm not an active, loyal supporter and would never feel the need to rally etc.'

'Maybe. I believe men and women should have equal roles but men shouldn't be forgotten about – e.g. men are just as capable to look after children.'

'No, I don't feel oppressed by being a woman, though I believe there's a lot of sexism.'

'No. I'm very glad that last century there were women brave enough to fight for our rights and they have changed our lives. But towards the end of the century they screwed up a bit – for example, with the pill and work: now women work as well as have kids, clean and cook.'

means living in the period after the last major feminist movement in the West: 'women's liberation' or 'second-wave feminism'. That movement, which began in Britain in the late 1960s and stretched through the 1970s, was incredibly influential and achieved many successes: equal-rights legislation, welfare services for women, women's studies courses, to name but a few. But some of the gains were eroded by cuts to welfare spending under the 1980s' Conservative government and by a negative media backlash. Because of this, the common perception is that feminism was a movement of the past which was necessary at the time but which came to a definite end.

There have been dramatic changes in women's lives in recent decades. Women know about, and are grateful for, the opportunities feminism brought women, including the right to vote, equal opportunities in education, equal pay laws and rape crisis services. But women cannot always translate this historical awareness into concrete support for feminism, leading to older feminists complaining that feminism is taken for granted.

> **How do feminists define feminism?**
>
> 'Equality for all.'
> FEMALE, 46
>
> 'Feminism to me is about improving the lives of women, bringing about equality for all groups of people (such as LGBTQ). It's about celebrating differences and showing one size does not fit all.'
> FEMALE, 25
>
> 'Having a problem with the treatment you receive because you're a woman. Understanding that there are issues against fellow women, that there probably needs to be something done to remedy them.'
> FEMALE, 19
>
> 'A social and political movement which aims for the equality of the sexes.'
> FEMALE, 17

However, as we will explain in more detail in this book, feminism is still necessary. Women's *visibility* in popular culture doesn't mean women are *valued*, safe from violence or equal.

While images of empowered young women are frequently portrayed in culture, images of troubled young women are also in view: the young woman with an eating disorder, the teenage mother, the binge-drinking 'ladette'. These representations of females in crisis are often unsympathetic: in an individualistic culture, young women are often blamed for the difficult situations they find themselves in. And for men and boys, the difficulties they suffer in modern life are frequently exacerbated by sexist stereotypes about what men are and should be like.

The cult of the individual

Our culture's focus on the individual can obstruct us from giving feminism (which, after all, is about collective gains) our whole-hearted support. The UK, like many other Western nations, upholds the individual as the primary social unit. In the 1980s, Prime Minister Margaret Thatcher famously asserted: 'There is no such thing as society: there are individual men and women, and there are families.'[18] It's up to the individual to decide how to live: to work hard, take risks and hopefully thrive. Those who don't manage to climb the ladder of success are looked down upon as individual failures. The philosophy that we'll all succeed in the race of life if only we try hard enough doesn't take into account the fact that we start running from different places: our ethnic and economic backgrounds are just two of the factors that make it hard for some to achieve the same level of success as others. But since this is how our society currently works, it can be hard for individuals to mount the kind of collective challenge that feminism involves.

In an individualistic culture, it's almost as if, to demonstrate the empowerment and success expected of them, women have to dissociate themselves from feminism: they're empowered, so they no longer need it.

Reclaiming the f word

Now for the good news: despite all this negativity about feminism, there is a thriving movement active today and a large number of people are reclaiming feminism. Since the start of this millennium, a staggering number of feminist organisations and campaigning groups have formed in the UK.

A name has even been coined for all this new activity: 'third-wave feminism' (in fact this term has been used in the USA since 1992).[19] Whilst there is some disagreement about the usefulness of a 'wave' metaphor, or what this represents, the very fact that the term 'third wave' exists adds weight to the argument that there are a growing number of active feminists. We've watched this new feminism grow and have been involved with it over the last decade and know this is not a 'flash in the pan'.

If today's feminism is this hot, why haven't we heard about it?

There are some who will still be sceptical. If feminism was alive and vibrant, wouldn't we hear about it? If there are new organisations, festivals, websites and networking groups, why aren't they more widely known?

We believe there are some explanations for this curious blind spot. First, established and older feminists lack knowledge of new feminist activities; second, comparisons with the 'golden age' of 1970s' feminism; and third, people don't always appreciate that in a new context some feminists will do feminism differently.

Lack of recognition by established feminists

Infuriatingly, today's feminism is still under many established feminists' radar. Young women particularly are frequently dismissed as insufficiently political, as being interested more in shopping than in social change. This happens more or less wherever young feminism flourishes. In the USA and Canada, young feminist writers often complain that their activities are ignored or criticised by older activists.[20]

At one academic conference on third-wave feminism held in the UK, the two (younger) organizers later described encountering 'raw anger from some Women's Studies scholars when organising the conference – largely directed towards the very notion of the "third wave", as if it somehow stood for the outright demise of second wave feminism'.[21] But missing from this conference, and the ensuing book,[22] were young British feminists' voices and experiences. Several young feminists who tried to book were turned away because the places – which cost double the weekly income of a typical student – had been filled by conference speakers, generally older and in secure academic positions. The week after the conference, at the monthly meeting of the London Third Wave feminist group, a feminist journalist who attended expressed disappointment: it was talking about young women, but not to or with them. Even worse, she said, people were talking about 'historicising the third wave' while in the UK it was gathering speed. This mixture of denial ('no young feminists have emerged') and burial ('the third wave is already over') was, she said, bizarre.[23]

When the Equal Opportunities Commission released its *Talking Equality* report, it sparked an avalanche of negative headlines about feminism's reputation among young people. Older feminists like Germaine Greer and younger ones like Zoe Williams defended feminism, but in rather vague terms, not mentioning any actual feminist activity. Feminism, argued Williams, 'was as noble and important as any other civil rights movement, and yet we seem to take no pride in it. We are crazy to disown it like some kind of embarrassing old aunt.'[24] What she is saying is true, but the use of the past tense to describe feminism is striking. A representative from the Older Feminist Network wrote to the *Guardian*, advising 'those bright young women with their high heels and fancy clothes' to pay attention to pay issues or they would regret it in later life. Whilst the advice was sound, it painted young women as superficial. Another correspondent seemed to think young women would only be attracted to feminism if 'Topshop or FCUK [would] emblazon the word on a pink, belly button-baring T-shirt.'[25] Can we not give young women a bit more credit than this?

Even when established feminists become aware of new feminist activities, they are cautious about whether these new feminists are 'proper' feminists, whether they are sufficiently collectively political, or whether, in the current climate, reclaiming feminism is really possible.[26]

Obviously these criticisms don't apply to all older feminists, journalists or academics. Many established feminists encourage and support new feminists' work and are eager to find out what they think, involve them in their work and work with them on new projects. They understand that we can have a common cause and different methods; that we can be equally committed to gender equality without doing everything the same.

Comparisons with the feminist 'golden age'

Feminism is generally considered to have been at its peak in the UK during the mid- to late 1970s. In many people's imaginations, this was a glorious, never-to-be-repeated age in which women marched in their tens of thousands through the streets and the plume of smoke from the mountain of burning bras could be seen from the moon. Charismatic feminist leaders directed troops of dungaree-wearing, passionate women in protests and campaigns, and national women's organisations attracted hundreds of thousands of members. The measly efforts of today's feminists surely don't compare, do they?

Consciously or not, many people are stuck on this view of the golden age of feminism. But it isn't helpful. If the 1970s is always going to be used as some kind of benchmark of feminism's success against which newer feminists are found wanting, we need to get some perspective.

It's undeniable that for the women involved during that time, the era was exciting and ground-breaking, with its development of new ideas, the publishing of polemical books and the feeling of being part of something fresh and new, as many of the participating women have testified.

However, when this period is overemphasized as the defining point of 'true feminism', it's problematic. New feminists are left with a feeling of disappointment and frustration, despite all the amazing things that are going on today; that 'I wish I lived in the 1970s feeling', as one reader of *The F Word* website put it in 2002. We need to remember that criticisms of today's feminism as lacking in some way often stem from an idealised image of 1970s' feminism that isn't necessarily accurate. In addition, this view of feminism is a very Westernized view of the movement, neglecting feminist activism that has occurred since the 1970s and in non-Western countries and the global South.

Feminists today are not necessarily going to come up with dramatic new feminist theories, and a lot of the issues that were current then are still with us now. Women are still being raped, paid less than men, and access to abortion is restricted. Thus, new feminists are not heard because the messages they're putting forward seem not as radical or new as they were then.

Doing things differently

The third reason why today's feminists are not always recognized is because some of them do things differently from the 1970s. Some issues are different; even where concerns are similar, feminism might take contrasting forms. To see the changes, we can look back briefly at the 1970s to see how the world, and therefore feminist engagement with it, has changed.

In 1970, 600 women from across the UK converged at Ruskin College, Oxford, under the banner of Women's Liberation. They met again each year, sometimes several times, up to 1978. During their heated and passionate gatherings, they debated and gradually formulated a set of seven agreed demands; on the first International Women's Day in 1971 several thousand women marched to hand the first four demands to the prime minister.[27]

Today, some of these demands have been partially achieved: women and men are legally entitled to equal pay for equal work; legislation prohibits sex discrimination in employment and education; and women can take out mortgages alone. The NHS offers the contraceptive pill and free abortion (subject to various conditions). Access to free round-the-clock nurseries remains elusive, although the state provides some funding for childcare. Civil partnerships and new laws

> **The seven demands of the 1970s' women's liberation movement**
>
> 1. Equal pay
> 2. Equal education and job opportunities
> 3. Free contraception and abortion on demand
> 4. Free 24-hour nurseries
> 5. Financial and legal independence
> 6. An end to all discrimination against lesbians; a woman's right to define her own sexuality
> 7. Freedom from intimidation by threat or use of violence or sexual coercion, regardless of marital status; and an end to all laws, assumptions and institutions which perpetuate male dominance and men's aggression towards women

against discrimination on the grounds of sexuality, achieved in the early years of the twenty-first century, are bringing the sixth demand closer to fulfilment. Women today have many, mainly legal, improvements to be thankful for, so some of the women's liberation movement's demands are less pertinent. But since the 1970s new issues have emerged. Also, while laws against domestic and sexual violence have improved, this does not mean that women are no longer attacked and intimidated, or that institutions, like the judiciary, are free from sexist assumptions which affect how rape is treated. In sum, then, legal gains don't necessarily translate into substantial advances in women's lives. For women's lives to improve, not only laws, but also men's and women's thoughts and behaviour, have to change.

Partly because of these new issues, the form feminism takes has, to some extent, changed. The problems we've identified can't all be solved by simple legislative changes or increased funding. In many cases we're looking at nothing less than the need for a massive long-term change in society's attitudes. But that's what's so inspiring about feminists: they're ambitious, think big and take action, both individually and collectively. Feminist activism takes many forms, and popular cultural activism is as common as lobbying or protest marches. The Internet is a major area for activism today; 70 per cent of feminists we surveyed agreed that 'the Internet has been instrumental to today's feminist movement.'

We thought about our own survey research. If we could summarise what the diverse feminist community wants in this day and age, what would the key issues be?

Based on our knowledge of the feminist movement today, the responses to our survey, thousands of blog posts and articles, and attending meetings and festivals, we attempted to group together the information we had amassed into seven themes (a tip of the hat to the original seven demands). We expected that some of the original demands remained unfulfilled and would still be important. Indeed 85 per cent of our survey respondents think that the important feminist issues today are 'quite similar' or 'very similar' to those of the 1970s. But what had changed or what was new?

What do today's feminists want?

There are many differences among today's feminists. Heated debates occur over issues like pornography, the sex industry and men's role in feminism. Not everyone will agree on the issues we've highlighted, and everyone will prioritise them in different ways. Even if you are a feminist, you certainly won't agree with everything you read here.

Different kinds of inequality – ethnicity, sexuality, class, age, (dis)ability and religion – affect, and sometimes exacerbate, the disadvantages women face. The different social situations and identities of the women and men involved in today's feminism make contemporary feminism necessarily diverse. There are differences too in style and substance, with some organising protests through major cities and others dedicating themselves to activism and subversion online.

As Germaine Greer wrote in *The Whole Woman*, it is the job of each generation to 'produce its own statement of problems and priorities'.[28] As the women's liberation movement did a generation ago, we have come up with seven key themes or demands that we hope fairly represent the – frankly huge – range of activity and desires of UK feminists today.

As the list shows, feminism touches almost every aspect of our lives. As the chapters work through our seven themes, we move gradually from the personal to the public sphere, starting with the most private aspect, a woman's relationship with her body; we then proceed to sex and relationships; violence; education and work; politics and religion; culture; and, finally, feminism itself.

Feminists want:
1. Liberated bodies
2. Sexual freedom and choice
3. An end to violence against women
4. Equality at work and home
5. Politics and religion transformed
6. Popular culture free from sexism
7. Feminism reclaimed

The following chapters explore each theme. We'll show why feminism is still necessary and explain what concerns, hopes and dreams feminists have. Because we want to highlight the vibrancy of the movement today, each chapter features examples of inspirational activism and makes suggestions of things to do and read. We've included examples from the UK and around the world. Whilst we can't be certain that all of the individuals in every example call themselves feminists, we would definitely consider their actions feminist (it would be wrong to exclude such people from an overview of feminism simply because they may not have decided to pull on a Fawcett Society 'This is what a feminist looks like' T-shirt). With so many organisations and campaigns to choose from, we only regret that we couldn't mention everything.

If you're curious about feminism, we hope that after reading this you'll have a better idea of what feminists are concerned about and what they are doing. If you're a feminist already, we hope you'll be re-inspired and learn something new about other aspects of the movement. Consider this a celebration of everything you are and do.

Welcome to the new feminist movement.

1

LIBERATED BODIES

IMAGINE A WORLD where losing sleep over one's weight or obsessing about wrinkles isn't considered integral to being female, where women and men can wear whatever they want without ridicule or reprisals, where women and girls are healthy and happy with themselves and their bodies. Sadly, our world is not like this.

Our bodies are the only thing we truly own in life. Inhabiting our bodies joyfully and deciding what happens to them *should* be human rights. The women we talked to during our research wanted this. Yet female bodies are battlegrounds; the world is full of people and institutions that tell us how we should feel about our bodies and what we should do with them.

Compared to the 1970s, when the last wave of feminism was at its peak, younger women's lives are better in many ways. But where the body's concerned, things are much worse. Twenty years ago, Naomi Wolf pointed out that just as women were gaining economic power, the beauty backlash emerged to counter their gains. For her, as for radical feminists Susan Brownmiller and Sheila Jeffreys before and after her, beauty ideals are patriarchal

– they are a means by which men (or at least some men) control women. 'The beauty myth is not about women at all', Wolf writes, 'It is about men's institutions and institutional power.'[1] Other feminists rightly countered that adornment can be empowering, and racist, classist and ageist beauty ideals exist alongside patriarchal ones. But Wolf's argument still resonates. Older feminists' protests against bras and high heels seem tame compared to today's pressures: girls' self-esteem has hit rock bottom; eating disorders have mushroomed; media images of female bodies are thinner and less achievable; women have cosmetic surgery not out of vanity but to feel 'normal'; and younger women feel under pressure to remove their body hair in a manner once peculiar to porn stars.

If women in affluent nations are under such strain, the global outlook is worse. In developing countries, over half a million die each year during pregnancy and childbirth because of inadequate medical care.[2] Two million women in Africa, Asia and the Middle East live with the debilitating stigma of fistula (a hole in the birth canal that develops during a prolonged labour without medical intervention).[3] Lack of access to reproductive and health-care services is the major contributor to the rising rates of HIV among poor young women. Young women are now more often HIV positive than young men, since they are unlikely to be educated about prevention and, without economic assets, lack the ability to demand that their male partners use condoms.[4] Female genital mutilation (FGM) is an established practice in more than thirty countries, and increasingly emerges in Western countries with immigrant populations from FGM-practising regions. Many women worldwide suffer enforced sterilisation. Two-thirds of the world's blind are women and girls.[5]

From plummeting body image to fights over abortion, from childbirth to the freedom to dress as they choose, feminists want to see women's bodies liberated from negative attitudes and control by others. No one should make us feel bad about them, keep us ignorant about them, or force us to do things with them that we don't want. And that includes feminists too.

So our first demand is for liberated bodies. Liberated *from* an oppressive, negative culture of body hatred; from fear, shame and ignorance. And liberated *to* adorn and express them, however we choose, and to decide what happens to them.

Beauty ideals and real women's bodies: the growing gap

Unilever beauty brand Dove commissioned two global surveys about women, beauty and body image in 2004 and 2005, launching its 'Campaign for Real Beauty' off the back of the first. The 2005 survey of 3,300 women aged 15–64 in ten countries reveals depressing evidence about women's body image and the 'appearance anxiety' created by beauty ideals. Only one in ten women reported being happy with the way they looked. Seven in ten avoid everyday activities including socializing, going to work or school, or going on dates, because they feel badly about their looks. Beauty ideals begin affecting women in early adolescence, with 13 being the average age at which young women reported becoming concerned about their appearance *and* the average age at which women started their beauty regimes – which suggests that the two are connected. When asked what influenced their self-image, the most common influences were family members (especially parents), the media and romantic partners. The UK

> 'The ... project of femininity is a "setup": it requires such radical and extensive measures of bodily transformation that virtually every woman who gives herself to it is destined in some degree to fail.' SANDRA LEE BARTKY[6]

results were some of the worst, especially for younger girls; British women came next to bottom (above Japan) in rates of body satisfaction and the likelihood of having dieted. Some 95 per cent of British women want to change something about their physical appearance, most commonly their body size. And the white bias of globalised beauty ideals was clear from some of the responses by women from Asia, South America and the Middle East. A desire to change one's hair, eye colour or shape, or skin colour (presumably to resemble more closely the Caucasian ideal) was mentioned more frequently by women living in these regions.[7]

Self-esteem and body satisfaction are linked – if you're happy with your body, you're happy in yourself. But countless studies find that women's self-esteem is much lower than men's and that disordered eating and low body image frequently stem from women comparing their bodies to idealized images that appear in the media and are endorsed by peers and family members.[8] A German study found that body dysmorphic disorder (a distressing condition whose sufferers are preoccupied with small or imagined defects in their appearance) is 'relatively common'. It was found to be experienced by 1.4 per cent of men and 1.9 per cent of women, and associated with a risk of suicide attempts seven times greater than that of non-sufferers.[9]

Women's magazines regularly conduct surveys on women's body anxiety. In 2006 *Grazia* questioned 5,000 women in twenty British cities. They found that the average British woman worries about her size and shape every fifteen minutes, that only 2 per cent are happy with their body, and that 71 per cent believe that 'their whole life would improve greatly if they had a good body'. A 2007 reader survey commissioned by *New Woman* magazine revealed that 97 per cent thought size 12 was fat, and a further six out of ten women considered 'size zero' (a UK size 4) attractive.[10] Before we're all tempted to feed the latest *Cosmo* to the paper shredder, it's worth bearing in mind that readers of women's magazines aren't representative of women in general, so these statistics can't be quoted as *the* truth about British women's self-image problem. (And, as we'll discuss, the exceedingly low self-image revealed by readers of women's magazines points to problems with the magazines themselves.)

It hasn't always been like this. Comparing changes in images of women in popular culture with changes in real women's bodies, the gap between the ideal and the real is growing. Images of female bodies are getting thinner and larger breasted, while real women are getting heavier, so achieving the ideal is increasingly difficult.[11] In the 1970s, the average weight of models was 8 per cent less than the average woman, but by the late 1990s models weighed 23 per cent less. Since 1951, because of changes in lifestyle and food consumption, British women have put on an average of 7.5 lb (3 kg) in weight, 1.5 inches (4 cm) on their height and on their hips and 7.5 inches (16 cm) on their waists. Weighing all this up, the anthropologist Kate Fox estimates that the current desirable look is achievable for less than 5 per cent of the population.[12] But we're still crippling ourselves trying.

Causes of eating disorders are numerous; it's young women who mainly fall victim to them (nine out of ten sufferers are female, and the most risky age group is 14 to 25), and it's undeniable that society's beauty ideals are a contributory factor. According to *beat* (formerly the Eating Disorders Association), over a million Britons are affected by eating disorders. In the USA, during their lifetime an estimated 0.5–3.7 per cent of females suffer from anorexia and 1.1–4.2 per cent from bulimia. Finland has a lifetime prevalence rate of 2.3 per cent for bulimia, less than a third of which is recognised by health-care professionals.[13] Eating disorders – including anorexia, bulimia, binge eating and compulsive overeating – are linked to low self-esteem.

They often develop as ways of coping with difficult emotions or experiences. Campaigners express concern about the rise of pro-anorexia groups on social networking sites.

Beauty ideals are growing ever more extreme. So are the beauty practices that stem from the anxieties beauty ideals provoke. These include 'designer vaginas', popular with women who consider their genitals unattractive or want to be 'tightened up' after childbirth (one response, perhaps, to the pressure on mothers to 'get back in shape' soon after giving birth). In the USA, one of the latest operations is known as the 'pink-ectomy': women are reportedly paying good money to have their little toes amputated to fit better into the latest Jimmy Choos. Less extreme versions include toe tucks and collagen injections into the ball of the foot. Why? To make wearing high heels more comfortable. (A top female British lawyer admitted paying a US surgeon $23,000 for a complete 'foot lift').[16]

The British spend more on make-up, cosmetic surgery and non-surgical treatments (like Botox and chemical peels) than anywhere else in Europe. Worldwide, the beauty industry is worth $160 billion per year.[16] The cost to our wallets of appearance obsession should make us pause for thought. Can we really afford it, or are we being persuaded to sacrifice money – and time

> **Voices of eating disorder sufferers**
>
> 'I had a "voice" in my head that shouted at me. It told me I was fat and worthless and that I was not allowed to eat because I did not deserve food. I thought I was in control of my eating but it got harder and harder to ignore the voice.'
>
> 'Having suffered from anorexia from the age of 11 (I'm now 23 and recovering) I find it difficult to define what is a normal female body shape when I see women in magazines and in the windows of shops looking so willowy. What therapists tell me is normal is contradicted every time I see models and celebrities being praised as beautiful when they weigh less than me for my height.'[14]

– to the beauty industry that would be better spent elsewhere? When you think that the typical woman survives on only 54 per cent of the average man's income and has managed to put away that same proportion less in investments and savings,[17] you begin to question whether 'because I'm worth it' might be better applied to savings accounts than to make-up.

Men and boys are increasingly subject to pressures and self-esteem issues too; indeed, as Atkinson discovered from interviewing Canadian men, men are using procedures like breast reduction and hair transplantation for 're-establishing a sense of empowered masculine identity'.[18] Yet women are hit hardest and go to greater extremes. Over nine out of ten cosmetic surgery procedures in the USA and UK are carried out on women.[19] While only about 2 per cent of British women have had cosmetic surgery to enhance their looks, 23 per cent told the Dove survey researchers that they would consider it (27 per cent in the 15–17 age group); another survey put that figure at 44 per cent.[20] Currently, the top choice is breast augmentation. But since fashions change and writers were lamenting the popularity of flat chests only twenty years ago,[21] one wonders if the women having implants will ask their surgeons to take the silicone back in another decade's time.

This is body fascism. True respect for one's body will happen when stretch-marks, floppy stomachs, freckles, wrinkles and non-symmetrical breasts are accepted and embraced as part and parcel of human diversity.

Why should anyone care about this? If women choose to have breast implants, is it anyone else's business? Well, yes, because the cause of all this angst is a profound cultural devaluation of women's bodies, in fact of women themselves. Many cultures now assume that something is fundamentally wrong with the natural female body and that women are duty-bound to reshape ourselves. This needs to change.

The limitations of the beauty ideal

Being 'beautiful' or 'attractive' shouldn't have to be anyone's most important concern. Isn't it unfair that 'attractive' job applicants stand a better chance of being hired and receiving higher salaries? Is it right that, in jobs where women are told to wear heels and make-up, they are required to incur extra expense and discomfort, and put in extra time at the beginning of each day's work (with no extra pay!). And why should 'attractive' people be less likely to be found guilty of crimes and more often receive shorter sentences?[22] Yet even this might not be so infuriating if the definition of beauty was a bit less restrictive and elitist. For women, being attractive is still linked with being able-bodied, young, white and 'feminine'. Anyone who doesn't meet these criteria, by choice or design, is not considered by mainstream society as beautiful or even, frankly, acceptable.

Criteria for beauty also reflect other inequalities in women's lives. Women's beauty is associated with youth, whilst men continue to be considered attractive as they age. Despite the fact that women live longer than men, and we have a rapidly ageing population, older women are practically invisible in the media (think of all the older male presenters paired with twenty-something women on television shows). Cosmetic companies encourage us to despise ageing. It's little wonder we don't want to get old when ageing is depicted as a kind of disease rather than a new stage of life with its good as well as bad points. For the beauty companies, ageing only brings dullness, unevenness, blotches and wrinkles. So their foundation promises 'younger looking skin', and this, it follows, 'helps you stay beautiful'.

Older women's invisibility links in with their general low status in society. As Marianne, 55, explains:

> We do not have a proud tradition of elder respect or a good record of caring for our elders. Significant numbers of older women

live on the poverty line and therefore their health is at serious risk, never mind their quality of life ... Older women suffer from double and triple jeopardy, which is both sexist and ageist, and in the case of ethnic minorities, racist.

To address this we should start by supporting [campaigns] to reform the pensions system through arguing that it should place women and carers at its heart. We should fight [ageist] stereotyping as we fought sexism and racism. We should raise the status of the caring professionals and train our social workers intensively. Ageing is a non negotiable aspect of all our lives – it is in everyone's interests to fight the prejudice.

Similarly, positive representations of women of colour and disabled women are rare. Women of colour zohra moosa explains

are generally brought into images in racialised ways: they are pictured in images to reinforce or remark upon their race in some way. For instance, they are often featured to sell or dress in 'tribal' motifs, 'exotic' scarves and 'ethnic garb'. Or they are incorporated to make a pronounced statement about race, such as in the July 2008 Italian issue of *Vogue* which featured only Black models.

Sometimes women of colour are even deliberately invoked at the same time as they are actively excluded and made absent, such as [October 2009's] French issue of *Vogue*... rather than hire a Black model, white skinned Dutch model Lara Stone was blacked up in four pictures of a thirteen-page spread styled by the magazine's editor.[23]

Cosmetic procedures women choose are often based, disturbingly, on white, Western ideals. An estimated half of all Korean schoolgirls are having procedures to Westernise their eyes. Meanwhile, Susie Orbach reveals,

Poorer girls and women in Chinese cities are creating sticky plasters to tape on their eyelids to duplicate the look of an open, western eye. The young woman may carry several homemade eyelid openers and go to the bathroom mirror hourly to replace

her makeshift 'remedy' while her male friends may stuff socks into
their shoes to create extra height. It is up to each person to fix
their own body as though it were in need of a redesign.[24]

It's all about conformity. Television makeover programmes
offer to transform a 'frumpy' woman's appearance and bring
her confidence and success. Yet, to achieve this, the woman
has to put up with cruel mockery from the makeover gurus
– whose documented insults include 'Your teeth are yellow, have
you been eating grass?' and 'Oh my God ... she looks like a
German lesbian!' (homophobic – check; xenophobic – check)
– and 'correct' her body to achieve a more 'approved', 'sexy'
shape.[25] At the end of the process, known as 'the reveal', the
woman is thinner, tanned, Botoxed and heavily made up. 'Excess'
body hair or spots have gone, her breasts have been pushed up
and out, her hair has been dyed and fashionably cut, and she is
wearing the latest fashion 'must have'.

She may look good, but she's a copy of the prescribed image
of the moment, a mock-up of the white, affluent, heterosexual
makeover gurus. Differences of income, ethnicity and religion
are airbrushed away in the advice given to women. So what if
you don't want to 'accentuate your curves'? So what if you can't
afford a new wardrobe because you're a single mum juggling
three low-paid jobs with caring for your kids? Changing yourself
is still the only answer.

Is it all the media's fault?

In a media age, images of women are more significant shapers
of young people's identities than in the 1970s. Celebrity culture
plays a major role, with a profusion of celebrity magazines that
call stars 'fat' and 'anorexic' in alternate measure and offer readers
diets so they can emulate their chosen role model; Beyoncé's
Maple Syrup Diet, Liz Hurley's Kids' Cutlery Diet and the Baby

I'm Mrs 'Lifestyles of the
rich and famous'
I'm Mrs 'Oh my God that
Britney's Shameless'
I'm Mrs 'Extra! Extra!
This just in'
I'm Mrs 'She's too big
now she's too thin'
BRITNEY SPEARS,
'Piece of Me', 2007

Food Diet (devotees are rumoured to include Reese Witherspoon and Jennifer Aniston) are just a few.[26]

And lest we think that if we meet our culture's beauty standards, we'll be judged acceptable, look at the way women who spend more money on their appearance than most of us will ever possess are criticized for it: think Katie Price, Victoria Beckham or Britney Spears. Women who fail even slightly to achieve body perfection face levels of scrutiny and ridicule that would have been unimaginable a decade ago. They may be airbrushed in the approved shots, the mags say, but we have zoom lenses – you can't fool us! Woe betide a woman in the public eye who has a hair out of place, hair in the 'wrong' place, cellulite, or even 'wrinkly knees'.

Paula Black has studied why women go to beauty salons. She says:

> Women find themselves in a no-win situation. In order to appear fully feminine and reap the rewards of male approval (or at least avoid male disapproval) they must learn the skills of feminine bodily comportment and appearance. However, by being associated with such trivialities, women are unable to achieve power or status.[27]

Women can't win, because the female body itself is second class.

Perhaps we're painting too pessimistic a picture of the media's influence. Women can and do reject media images. Some women have high enough self-esteem to absorb endless images of women in popular culture without being affected; indeed, for some (bloggers, for instance), criticising the media is a pleasurable spectator sport. But for many of us, although we see the problems, the media have some impact despite ourselves. Many research studies get young women to look at images of women in magazines, then measure their body satisfaction. Generally, these show that the more exposure women have to these images the unhappier they are with their own bodies. Studies of women watching television makeover shows find that the more they watch, the more likely they are to be dissatisfied with their bodies and contemplate cosmetic surgery.[28] The high rates of body dissatisfaction among readers of women's magazines may explain why readers in the *Grazia* and *New Woman* surveys had such a distorted view of women's bodies: generally, reading women's magazines is bad for your self-esteem. Perhaps, like cigarettes, they should come with health messages: 'Warning: reading this magazine could seriously damage your health.'

Clothes and fashion: the illusion of choice

Women are buying twice as many clothes as a decade ago.[29] Women's magazines have expanded their fashion pages, offering the more cash-strapped of us advice on where to acquire high-street versions of designer outfits. As shopping has become the key female leisure activity, a new weekly, *Look*, has emerged to advise the so-called 'decadent generation' for whom buying a new outfit is a Saturday ritual.

Fashion is a Jekyll and Hyde industry. It offers women creativity, freedom, affordability and a democratic space where we can create our individual identities (and it *is* women who are targeted as the primary consumers of fashion; men's clothes are uniforms by comparison). Yet, as fashion scholar Elizabeth Wilson puts it, its 'glamorous façade continues to conceal a life of corrosive toil' for the factory workers (who are predominantly female) making the clothes.[30]

In the last few decades, we've become disconnected from how the clothes that appear on the stores' gleaming rails are actually made. Production has moved to the developing world because it's cheaper. Able to pay workers far less while spending obscene amounts on branding, companies rake in profits and stimulate demand by offering us cheap clothing. As we'll explain in Chapter 4, while we glory in 'retail therapy' the women making our jeans pay for our choices.

In addition to clothing production, feminists take issue with society's attitudes to clothing generally. From reality shows like *Extreme Makeover* to criticisms of our clothing choices, women are bombarded daily with messages on how they should dress. Religious and working-class women fare especially badly. Women wearing religious clothing and the binge-drinking 'ladettes' featured on programmes like *Ladette to Lady* experience similar moral censure about their attire. When nearly a quarter of people think that a woman would be partially or totally responsible for being raped if she was wearing sexy or revealing clothing,[31] and women wearing the hijab are spat on and harassed, our clothing 'choices' are not as free as they might appear.

In 2007, Manal Omar, director of the NGO Women for Women International, went swimming as usual in her five-piece Islamic-style swimsuit at her local fitness club. She was publicly humiliated by a man who objected to her costume and demanded to speak to the manager. The anger, prejudice and sexism revealed by this man and others in subsequent press articles and blogs were vicious; Omar's swimming costume was taken as an opportunity to unleash a diatribe of insults against Muslims, women, immigration and multiculturalism. When finally allowed to give her own account, Omar commented, 'It strongly disturbs me that I was disregarded as an individual, and demeaned to a one-dimensional stereotype. For many of those involved in the debate, the fact that I covered my head and my body seemed to make them forget that I had a brain.'[32]

Men and boys also have some way to go before they can experience freedom of dress. Growing up, boys learn to dissociate themselves from femininity. If a boy shows interest in clothes, he's laughed at for being 'gay' or a 'girl' (as if these were bad things). Unless men enter a profession where aesthetics is important, they have to suppress their creativity to fit a bland model of dress. Occasionally, society goes through periods of allowing men to break free from confining modes of dress (think glam rock in the 1970s, androgyny in the 1980s and the 1990s' media-coined 'metrosexual'). Yet these phases never last. 'Real' men are defined by work, not by what they look like, while a woman's identity resides in her appearance. 'Women can dress down in the office but men can't' goes the grumbling complaint from men in the papers every summer. Isn't it a little ridiculous that in the twenty-first century we're still talking about what men and women are 'allowed' to wear?

Menstruation

It's not only love and acceptance of female bodies that feminists want, it's also knowledge about menstruation and reproduction, since many women are still subjected to fear, shame and ignorance about these.

In some countries such as Zimbabwe, basic sanitary protection products are considered a luxury, so women are forced to use newspaper, rags or even leaves, which can lead to infections and serious health risks. Caroline Glasner, who volunteers at a London drop-in for destitute asylum-seekers, launched an appeal for donations:

> The women who attend have fled traumas such as torture, rape, separation from their children or murder of family members. Month on month, I've seen dozens of these women plead for

sanitary towels... It is humbling and heartbreaking knowing these basic necessities are unaffordable. It is shocking they have to resort to newspaper and rags.[33]

Cultural attitudes to menstruation need addressing too. Take PMS. Although the idea that women's hormones make them more emotional is an old one, premenstrual syndrome was 'discovered' and popularized by Katharina Dalton in the 1950s (the very decade when attempts were made to return women to domesticity). Dalton believed that women were depressed and unstable in the week before and during menstruation, due to a fall in hormone levels. She advised women to avoid taking exams, going to interviews, planning dinner parties or making hair appointments and to stay in bed for as much of the premenstrual week as possible.

There are obvious objections to this. For one thing, imagine asking your boss if you can take one week in every four off to lie around contemplating your menstrual flow. Second, research on the effects of hormones on women's behaviour is more ambiguous.[34] And third, PMS has a feminist case to answer. Feminists have seen PMS as a 'weapon for putting women in their place', as Sophie Laws puts it. She writes:

A woman who expresses anger or admits to be feeling under stress will often be asked, pityingly or aggressively, if it is 'that' time of the month...

The menstrual cycle has now been transformed by the medical profession into something only experts can tell us about. Women are supposed to be at the mercy of it, and our hopes for release depend upon doctors gaining a full understanding and finally control of it. The medical description of the menstrual cycle is taught to women, rather than women's own versions of their experiences being listened to: if you deviate from their norm, you need treatment. PMT is part of this medical model, not an ideal that came from women.[35]

While it's true that there are hormonal changes involved in menstruation and these impact women in different ways, there's no reason why the impacts should always be seen as negative. In fact, authors Delaney, Lupton and Toth got so fed up with hearing about surveys on 'menstrual distress' that they invented one for 'menstrual joy'.[36] Yes, some women suffer emotional and physical symptoms associated with menstruation, and this should be acknowledged. But PMS mythology isn't empowering for women.

Before writers like Naomi Klein (in *No Logo*) highlighted the disturbing power of large corporations in schools, many girls were – indeed still are – educated about one of the most important changes of their young lives, menstruation, by multinational sanitary corporations. As found in Diorio and Monro's study of menstruation education in New Zealand, menstruation tends to be presented negatively (periods are messy, stressful and to be reluctantly dealt with by the individual girl) and in a purely reproductive framework.[37]

Delegating responsibility for communicating such important messages to capitalist companies is surely robbing girls of a positive and empowering learning experience. The largest UK-based website for girls to learn about menstruation is www.beinggirl. co.uk, a site run by Proctor & Gamble to promote their products. Alongside advice on periods and tampons, girls are advised that 'Unfortunately, unwanted hair is an inevitable part of becoming a woman' and told to 'Work that body…. Create an exercise plan that lasts more than a week!!!!!!' In response to a girl's worry that 'everyone's crazy about boys (except me)', they tell her unhelpfully: 'chances are, the boy bug will bite you at some point.'[38]

Where can girls get positive advice about being a woman, unbiased advice that accepts diversity? The effect of websites like this is surely to make girls into conventional, compliant heterosexual consumers. Girls remain ignorant about alternative, environmentally friendly and economical menstrual products like washable pads, silicone or rubber cups and sponges.

Contraception and sexual health

As for contraception, life today is easier for younger women. Sixty years ago, the main method was coitus interruptus (withdrawal) and the pill hadn't been invented. In the last decade emergency contraception (misleadingly called the 'morning after pill'), which can be taken up to three days later, has given a second chance at preventing pregnancy to those whose condoms have broken or who didn't use contraception. Contraception is more easily available and working better. But there's still a need for more men and boys to take responsibility for contraception, and since no pill can protect you against sexually transmitted infections, the pill's never going to be the panacea we'd like it to be. We'll talk more about sex and relationships in Chapter 2, but for now let's think about how women fare when it comes to choices about whether, when and how to have children. Women need education, good reproductive services and choice about which of these to use. It sounds simple, but on all counts we've got some way to go.

Britain has the highest rate of teenage pregnancy in Europe, three times more than France and five times the rate of the Netherlands. Half of the population have had unprotected sex without knowing their partner's sexual history,[39] and those with a younger than average age of first sex, a greater number of sexual partners and without experience of formal sex education were particularly likely to have done so.[40]

For many of us, formal sex education consisted of a video in a science lesson and a brisk demonstration on how to put a condom on a banana (with no practice required, nor discussion of how to negotiate this faced with a real-life penis). Yet amidst all the laughter and embarrassing antics, we don't seem to be able to talk sensibly about sex: to say what we do and don't want and demand that our partners don't take risks with our health or get us pregnant when we don't want to be. We need to teach young people more about sex, earlier and in a more discursive, practical manner to remove the taboo and the titillation that leaves us acting like adolescents far later than we should.

Objectors will say that talking to children about sex early makes them more aware, and thus more likely to have sex earlier. These fears don't seem to be borne out by evidence from countries with early, more explicit, sex education. The notoriously liberal Netherlands gives more sex education at an earlier age, yet has a later average age of first sex (17.7 compared with 16 in the UK), lower rates of unplanned pregnancy and sexually transmitted infections, and less abortion.[41] Additionally, evidence shows that when young people aren't given much information and sex education is just abstinence education – which often applies to young people from religious families – this rarely stops them having sex; it just makes sex more risky when they do have it. One recent survey of 3,000 London pupils aged 15–18 found that although the religious students were less likely to have had sex than the non-religious, the religious students had lower levels of knowledge about sex education and were more likely not to have used contraception when they did have sex.[42]

Sexism still causes problems when it comes to contraception. When talking to young people about contraception, researchers have found that there are often gender-related taboos about negotiating condom use. A girl doesn't want to be known to carry condoms in case she's seen as a 'slut', and doesn't want her partner to think she's accusing him of having a sexually transmitted disease. This was two young women's way round this problem: 'Rather than saying "will you wear something, because I don't want to get AIDS?" which sounds really bad, doesn't it, we would say "you'll have to wear something because I'm not on the pill."'[43] A good solution, perhaps, but should girls really have to tie themselves in linguistic knots just because they don't want to get chlamydia?

Men should be taught to take more responsibility. When asked why so many men are bad at using condoms, John Guillebaud, Emeritus Professor of Family Planning and Reproductive Health at University College London, responded: 'Clearly, it has a lot to do with themselves not getting pregnant!'[44] This isn't good enough. In the media, teenage boys are portrayed as driven by their sexual urges, so *girls* are tasked with managing 'how far to go'; men can't be trusted with such a responsibility, apparently.[45] This one-dimensional view of men persists despite the worthy attempts of sex educators to make contraception the concern of males and females equally. The Family Planning Association found that 94 per cent of men aged 18–45 agreed that using contraception is the joint responsibility of men and women.[46] Fantastic! But when lads' mags seem more interested in getting readers to rate girlfriends' sexual technique than in helping them avoid pregnancy or infections, educating men and boys more effectively about contraception is an urgent priority.

Abortion

Contraception doesn't always work, and, for a range of reasons (including coercion, male reluctance and the 'you can't get pregnant the first time' myth), not everyone uses it when they should. With half of all pregnancies unplanned,[47] an estimated one in three women find themselves in a situation where they want or need an abortion.[48] This may not be ideal, but it's a reality we have to live with. Illegal or botched abortions account for around 68,000 deaths worldwide each year.[49] However much some people dislike abortion, preventing it by legislating won't stop it happening – it'll just lead to more women dying from unsafe abortions. Desperate people seek desperate solutions, and despite the (in some ways laudable) attempts of organisations to offer women options to carry the baby to term if she prefers, if a woman feels she can't go ahead with the pregnancy she won't, even if it puts her life at risk. Few people who are aware of the damage caused by unsafe abortions would want to remove the hard-won right to abortion granted to women by the 1967 Abortion Act.

Sarah B, 25, attended a panel discussion celebrating the fortieth anniversary of safe, legal abortion. She explains how significant it was for her:

> This panel discussion was one of the most inspiring feminist moments of my life, as women who had campaigned at the time of the first Abortion Act stood up to passionately impart their stories of the world before the act. They stressed the immense importance of not losing any more of the ground that we have previously had to fight so hard for.
>
> I'm a young feminist, and at pro-choice protests I shout 'pro-life – that's a lie, you don't care if women die' along with the rest of the crowd. But, up until that panel discussion, my cries had seemed almost theoretical because I hadn't experienced a world in which women had no choice but to seek illegal back-street abortions. I also couldn't fully imagine that people would really rather women endure that existence than live with the freedoms they have now.

Surveys have shown that around 80 per cent of British people support a woman's right to make her own choice about abortion.[50] Feminists in the 1970s believed that the right to choose should mean free abortion on demand. This demand, however, is still undelivered. The proportion of abortions provided free on the NHS in England and Wales has improved, from 67 per cent in 1994 to 80 per cent a decade later (Scotland comes out better at 99 per cent).[51] Most of these are performed before thirteen weeks of pregnancy, and waiting times have also declined. But there are geographical variations, and women are woefully dependent on the ethical predilections of individual doctors. In Britain, for abortion, *unlike every other medical procedure*, a woman has to persuade *two* doctors to support her decision; this bureaucracy can lead to delays or obstructions. The Royal College of Obstetricians and Gynaecologists supports easier access to abortion and the removal of the requirement for two doctors' signatures.[52]

In Northern Ireland, along with many countries in Africa, the Middle East, South America and Southeast Asia, women still lack the right to legal abortion. It's time this changed and women were given full control over their own bodies, no matter where they are. Even in countries where abortion is legal (or legal under certain conditions), this doesn't always mean abortion is available; reduced availability of services and practitioners (often due to death threats and harassment from anti-choice activists) and lack of money to pay for the procedure or travel to a clinic can restrict access.[53]

In the 1970s feminists wanted to make access to abortion easier. So do today's feminists. Yet we're also fighting attempts to turn the clock back. Over the past few years, resurgent anti-abortion campaigners have been attempting to chip away at our right to decide when or if we give birth. One pro-choice campaigner cites the complacency of young women, who have grown up taking legal abortion for granted and don't realise it could be threatened, as his greatest fear.[54] But as our survey demonstrated, threats to the availability of abortion is one of the galvanising factors for a revitalised feminist movement.

Pregnancy and childbirth

A few years ago, Naomi Wolf's book *Misconceptions* revealed the negative impact of contemporary birth practices on women. Childbirth, she argued, isn't seen as a natural event in a woman's life, but instead as pathological. The medicalisation of childbirth has had innumerable benefits, saving thousands of women each year from dying while giving birth. But once doctors took over, they had to run the show. Clock-watching began, with birth speeded up by interventions that many argue are unnecessary. Births are induced more often than is desirable. Women are made to give birth lying horizontally (hardly the best position for gravity to kick in), aided by anaesthesia and episiotomies (cutting the perineum) instead of patience.[55] But feminists and other mothers' groups are raising concerns that doctors have taken away control or choice from women and do not deliver the level of service needed for such an important event. In the last thirty years, the UK Caesarean-section rate has trebled to nearly a quarter of all births and the increasing medical interventions have side effects (such as infertility risks in the case of Caesareans) about which women don't always receive sufficient warning.[56]

'For too long, severe sexism and cultural preudices have restricted mothers and mothers-to-be, particularly in areas relating to pregnancy, birth and infant feeding. Informed consent and freedom of choice are two essential components in combating nearly all areas of ante- and postnatal discrimination. Ensuring women are actively involved in managing their health and that of their foetus[es] and are provided with evidence-based holistic care both before and after the birth is absolutely crucial to not only improving maternal and infant mortality rates, but giving more women an empowering experience of motherhood.' AMITY R, 30

A lot of this is down to funding. The UK government has announced plans for midwife-led maternity services; for individualized

Obstetric skills are valuable in high-risk births, when used with discretion. They can be life saving. But the technocratic management of childbirth combining technology, critical observation (often by complete strangers), intrusive monitoring and constant interruptions disturbs the flow of natural hormones that reduce pain and stimulate pleasure and excitement, blocks the spontaneous physiological process, traumatises women and often leaves them not only physically but emotionally damaged. Every intervention, even apparently minor ones, such as rupturing bulging membranes, talking during a contraction, getting a woman up on a bed and encouraging her to push when she has no urge to do so, introduces the need for further interventions, artificial uterine stimulation, painkilling drugs, instrumental delivery or Caesarean section which increases the possibility of haemorrhage, pelvic infection, a newborn who is admitted to the intensive care nursery, post-natal physical exhaustion, difficulties in breastfeeding and post-traumatic stress disorder.

SHEILA KITZINGER, *Birth Crisis*[57]

services offering options about where to give birth. These, however, vary by area, and critics are concerned that 'midwife-led' is a synonym for 'cheaper'. Different perceptions of ethics and morality also play a role in policy debates. Battles continue to rage about giving infertility treatment to those outside traditional families. We'll talk more in later chapters about the options women want when it comes to sex, partnership and family life.

Cutting through the body hatred: the feminist response

Feminists are fighting body hatred, ignorance and fear in myriad creative and inspiring ways. Here's how.

Sending positive messages about women's bodies

Nearly forty years after feminists flour-bombed the 1970 Miss World contest in London, young feminists disrupted the 2008

Miss University of London contest with placards and chants. On stage at Ladyfest London in 2002, two young feminists jumped and shouted through their 'radical cheerleaders' routine about body acceptance and resistance to mainstream beauty standards. Bowled over by the flurry of bright pink pom-poms and the sheer exertion of the performance, the crowd gave them a standing ovation. At a slam poetry reading in the USA, spoken-word artist C.C. Carter wowed the crowd as she challenged them:

> Perhaps you question the size of my hips –
> the second largest continent in the world sired these hips
> of course they would be as large –
>
> The oldest civilization on earth gave birth to these hips
> of course they would be as wide –[58]

At 'Unskinny Bop' club nights organised by fat activists, women and men can shake their booty in a non-judgemental atmosphere. Others publish the zine *Big Bums*, organise fat-positive events and campaigns, and run a blog called *Obesity Timebomb* that analyses media attitudes to fat issues.

Teenage feminists are drawing strength by sharing their intimate body worries in photocopied zines or blogs. Actions like these can seem unconnected, but together they are creating a culture of body acceptance which may filter into mainstream culture.

Jumping off the beauty treadmill

Individual actions make a difference. Take the multiplying acts of self-perfection we're engaging in that are raising the bar on female beauty. The

'Since giving diets the boot, I've developed thoughts from a feminist view point... I have so much love for myself because my body is me. I will never put up with the slightest comment or sneer. Nobody has the right to put someone else down... now I give off so much attitude that people wouldn't dare.' CLAIR, *Riot Grrrl London* zine 1, *c.* 2001

'I just realised that it's a year now since I stopped shaving my armpits; over 14 months since I last shaved my legs, and in my eyes that's call for a celebration, even if it does make one of my good friends retch! ... I chucked my razor away and persevered, wearing sleeveless tops on nights out and forcing myself to dance with my arms in the air. I got some funny looks, which amused me more than anything else, and eventually I grew to love my hairy armpits, I grew to love myself, to accept my grown woman's body and, more than anything, to love the freedom I discovered when I no longer had to waste time and money preparing my supposedly unacceptable body for the outside world.'

LAURA WOODHOUSE,
The F Word blog[59]

more women opt for Botox, the older women with wrinkles look. The more women remove 'unsightly' birthmarks or moles, the uglier women who don't remove them are made to feel. We have to question whether striving to fit the ideal is doing anything but harming other women. Some people may feel brave enough to challenge the accepted gender boundaries; some may not be ready for that yet. Either way, we need to try to make choices that won't hurt other women. Those who are brave enough to stand out from the crowd deserve applause.

Challenging the messages in the media and advertising

About Face is an organisation that addresses body image in advertising in the USA. Their website hosts pictures of the '10 worst offenders' as well as advertisements that show women in a positive light. During summer 2009 the About Face team undertook a 'covert dressing room action', in which teenagers stuck positive body messages onto changing-room mirrors, and organised a public information stall about body image in a busy San Francisco street.

For Londoner Kristin Smith, the straw that broke the camel's back was a series of 'before/after' cosmetic surgery ads on the Tube. Her Facebook group, 'Somewhat Strident', attracted over a thousand members, all keen to challenge the sexism in advertising and counter it with positive messages about body image and self-esteem. The group documented the (illegal) stickering of the ads by angry feminist commuters with smart comments like 'Comes with free lobotomy', 'Warning: reading may cause self-hatred', and 'You are normal, this is not'. These may be 'small steps', Jane Collins admits in *Electra zine* (issue 3), but 'defacing these posters, ripping them down and boycotting companies' products all add up to letting them know we're not happy with their exploitation of us.'

The organisation AnyBody was founded in 2003 by a collective of women in psychotherapy, media, fashion, law and research to 'give women a voice to challenge the limited physical representation of females in contemporary society'. They aim to change cultural attitudes towards food, eating and the body, and run a website with a regular blog about body issues. They're also lobbying the government and working with public organisations on campaigns and conferences about body issues.

One of the encouraging findings of the 2005 Dove survey was that young women want a world with a wider definition of beauty, would welcome more discussion of beauty pressures at a younger age, and want women to be more supportive of each other. Beauty, they believe, comes in different sizes, shapes and colours.

Ethical consumer choices

Clothing is another area where we need to exercise responsibility alongside choice. With women responsible for 80 per cent of consumer decisions,

> 'The implant ads on the Tube are beyond parody. I'd really like to put a large sticker on the "after" poster saying "Beachball Baps: So much more thrilling than equal pay, proportional government representation, affordable childcare, freedom from sexual violence and harassment and a partner with an IQ in excess of single digits who doesn't get wood for plastic".'
> MARINA T, 'Somewhat Strident But Who Cares' messageboard[60]

we're powerful and can change things. The UK ethical fashion market grew to £172 million in 2008 – more than tripling in two years – and charity shops, clothes-swapping parties and vintage clothing fairs are coming alive again. As it becomes cool to care, and we refuse to buy clothes that aren't ethically produced (warning: you'll need to avoid most stores in our high streets and shopping malls), showing responsibility and compassion to other women can become part of our daily lives. And with boycotts of stores that don't clamp down on sweatshops costing UK retailers a reported £384 million a year, loss of revenue might just prompt them to clean up their acts – and their clothes.[61]

Educating others about menstruation and fertility

There's a significant feminist focus on menstruation too. In Aberdeenshire, Lucy runs her Moonrabbits company selling alternative menstrual products. Such products, including washable pads, silicone or rubber cups and sponges, are often cheaper, environmentally friendly and free from the risks of toxic-shock syndrome associated with conventional tampons. From her Newcastle home, 'Silvertree' promotes 'menstrual activism', encouraging others to learn about sexual and menstrual health. This includes posting on discussion boards, stickering women's toilets to promote alternatives, and giving talks on positive visions of menstruation and fertility. Jadea Faith runs a Menstrual Activism group on Facebook, which offers 'education over myth, facts over sugar coating, alternatives and action to take our health into our own hands' and 'a space to rant about the about menstrual products and our experiences with them.'[62] ACTSA's 'Dignity – Period' campaign address global issues like female genital mutilation and the lack of access to sanitary products by women in developing countries. And Chella Quint and her friend Sarah Thomasin developed the tongue-in-cheek zine *Adventures in Menstruating* and a sketch show based on it, to challenge taboos and have a good laugh along the way.

Defending and extending reproductive health-care

Feminists are flocking to join pro-choice groups such as the UK's *Abortion Rights,* and there is a demonstrable surge in participation in active protests and campaigning around this issue in response to increasing attempts to reduce access. Campaigns in the UK and elsewhere collected women's personal experiences of having an abortion; these stories help people understand the real reasons women have abortions and counteract sensationalist media portrayals.

Feminists are fighting for women's health issues to be taken more seriously worldwide. Female genital mutilation (FGM) is being countered by groups like FORWARD, who campaign for more effective legislation against the practice, better health care and specialist services for girls and women affected by FGM, and for it to be seen as an abuse of human rights and a child protection issue. Fistula, a result of prolonged and obstructed labour, leaves many sufferers incontinent and socially excluded, and the Campaign to End Fistula is working hard to address this.

Feminists are continuing the work of pioneers like Wendy Savage and Sheila Kitzinger, along with organisations like the National Childbirth Trust. The NCT is working to improve parents' experiences before, during and after birth. It wants breastfeeding to become an attractive option, neither sneered at by the childless public nor marketed as inconvenient by businesses seeking a profit from formula milk and breast pumps. Other groups promote cultural acceptance of breastfeeding. When Facebook removed breastfeeding photographs from its website, the group Hey Facebook, Breastfeeding is Not Obscene! attracted almost 250,000 members.

Conclusion

Feminists want an end to global inequalities which mean many women lack the basic health care that women in other countries take for granted. We want our media, fashion and cultural industries to embrace diversity, not uniformity. We also want women to take stock of our own beauty practices: to evaluate how liberating they are to others as well as to us, and how they support or subvert mainstream representations. We want businesses to take social responsibility seriously, to think about people as well as profits, and to recognise that women at the bottom of the hierarchies of clothing production are worth more than subsistence-level wages. We want consumers to take action on a larger scale on environmental, fair trade and ethical issues. We want education, information and real choices about menstruation, contraception, abortion and childbirth. We want government support for these demands, which means money, public debate, policies and organised implementation of decisions taken. And we want women to take hold of these issues, afresh and again, and with humour and creativity. If our bodies are battlegrounds, it's time to call off the war.

In the next chapter, we'll discuss why what people *do* with their bodies – their intimate relationships and sexual choices – is a feminist issue.

Take Action!

1. Challenge advertising that promotes an unhealthy body image: write to the companies involved, slap humorous stickers on offensive ads, or insert feminist messages into magazines.
2. Boycott clothing stores without a proven commitment to ethical working practices (find out more about these from the Labour Behind the Label campaign).
3. Get involved with groups like Abortion Rights, AnyBody, or FORWARD.
4. Lobby for better fertility, family planning and sex education in your school.
5. Challenge your boundaries by doing something that doesn't conform. If you normally wear make-up every day, try not doing so. Let boys wear pink. What's the worst that could happen?

2

SEXUAL FREEDOM AND CHOICE

WHAT HAPPENS in women's sexual lives, many feminists contend, is as important as equal pay or political equality. Feminists have different priorities: some want to see women freed from guilt and embracing sexual pleasure, while others worry about sex that is unwanted, about women and girls being pressured to have sex, in circumstances not of their own making. Feminists' attempts to improve women's sexual lot vary too: some use 'traditional' tactics like lobbying their MPs and responding to government consultations, while others write erotic blogs and sell sex toys online.

In this chapter we'll cover sex education, double standards, pornography, homophobia, weddings, divorce and sexual bullying. We'll look at both sides of the coin: the ability to say yes or no to sex and be heard and respected. We'll look at discrimination suffered by people who fall in love with people they're not 'supposed' to be attracted to. We'll see how feminists are rejecting or redefining traditional models of relationships. Finally, we'll look at how women across the world suffer the consequences of their society's attitudes to sex and gender.

This chapter explores what prevents women from exercising free sexual choices, what needs to be done to improve our sexual lives and what feminists are doing to make this a reality. It looks at intimate relationships and sex for love and/or pleasure; sexual violence and sex work are covered in Chapter 3.

What prevents women from making free choices?

People should be free to make, and then enjoy, their own sexual decisions without interference from other people, the state, religion or wider culture. Sex should be freely chosen, pleasurable, safe, uplifting and fun! As feminists, we're concerned that sex is still fraught with inequality, double standards and sexism, with women and girls particularly feeling the brunt of inequality in the bedroom.

What is free choice? Arguably, no choice anyone makes is completely free from historical, social, cultural, economic and other influences. But it's important to understand the factors involved in our sexual decisions, to ensure that we are striving for genuine freedom of choice, and that the forces that push and pull us to make disempowering sexual choices are lessened.

Take some examples of sexual choices that are not freely made: a woman consents to sex with her abusive husband because she's afraid of what might happen if she refuses; a young man initiates sex with his girlfriend because he's being bullied at school for being a virgin; someone says no to a relationship with a man she loves because he's from a different religion and her parents wouldn't approve; someone agrees to a sexual practice they dislike because they're afraid of their partner leaving them if they don't. So something that can seem a free choice may actually be occurring for reasons that may not be immediately obvious. Feminists want to expand the range of information that people have about sex, so that their range of options are widened and their unique desires respected.

In expanding the sexual options available to women and men, feminists want to avoid limitations on what's considered appropriate behaviour for each gender. We believe human sexuality and relationships are varied, unpredictable and exciting. We don't believe that men always want X and women always want Y in bed. Sure, some may want X, but some might want Y, Z or even Q.

Having and exercising choices about sex isn't enough, though. This is where we get into the tricky issue of how our actions affect others. What feels good for you may not feel good for your sexual partner, so choice will always – rightly – be constrained by people who our choices impact upon. In a feminist context, our sexual choices shouldn't cause harm to anyone.

There are several issues which we believe hinder women from making their own choices about sex and relationships. These are sexual double standards; objectification and 'raunch culture'; pressure to have sex before they're ready; unhelpful education about sex; homophobia; and restrictions on leaving relationships.

Sexual double standards

Earlier feminists identified the 'double standard' of sexual behaviour for women and men. Going back at least a couple of centuries, Western capitalist societies – and others too – have believed that men have such strong biological sexual urges that they have a right to sex when the urge takes them. Sex is considered a natural aspect of their masculinity. Women, conversely, are seen as less sexually motivated than men; until relatively recently, 'respectable' women 'lay back and thought of England', while their husbands exercised their marital 'rights'. But at a time when men married late, it was considered acceptable (though rarely discussed) for single men to take lovers or consort with prostitutes, to 'sow their wild oats' before marriage. In nineteenth-century Britain, women were often stereotyped as virgins or whores. Women in poverty were especially vulnerable to the sexual advances of men, who regarded them as 'fallen', crucial sexual outlets but inferior to the 'respectable' 'pure' women they would marry. Meanwhile, middle-class women had to safeguard their reputations by resisting, and taking responsibility for, men's sexual advances until the time came to marry.

While things have moved on, these ideas endure. Women who have sex outside committed relationships are still judged more harshly than men, and working-class young women are more likely to be portrayed as lacking sexual respectability.[1] Words like 'dirty', 'filthy', 'slut' and 'slag' are used to denigrate sexually active women.

In her book *Promiscuities*, Naomi Wolf describes the impact of this on young women's developing sexuality. Young women like her had sexual desires, but received no help in expressing these positively. Discussing the messages given in the sex education textbooks in the 1970s, she writes:

> We were depicted as civilized, rational beings compared to the boys, who were so deranged by their sex drive that it was up to us to fight them off. No one said to us: 'Your dreams are so intense; your impulses are so profound; but you won't die of it.' Actually, the message was just the reverse – your impulses are not especially noticeable, and yet, if you act on them, you might die of it. The boys were physical, it was understood; we were emotional. So, because the dominant sexual story was teaching us to feel the opposite of what we felt, the intensity of our physical wishes made us fear, on an unacknowledged level, that we must be sluts.[2]

Today, among some social groups the prevailing culture persuades people to have sex before they're ready. In others, there's the opposite problem: a repressive culture prevents women from expressing their sexuality. Educational settings affect this: schools that only teach abstinence spread messages of shame and guilt about sex, and brand girls who have sex as 'sluts'. In such places, as this zine contributor recounts, acting upon desires can bring opprobrium on women to which men are rarely subject.

> They called me a bitch and a slut and worse and they told the rest of the school and they called me a bitch and a slut too. Only two people still talked to me except to hurl abuse. Boys told me dirty stories about what I was supposed to have done. Girls pushed me off my chair in assembly and threatened me. I hated myself. I started to cut myself every night. I never got over it. They never said anything to the guy. (*Who's That Bitch?* zine 3, 2003)

These two extremes – do it/don't do it – often combine within a single society, so that it becomes difficult to discern your desires among the clamour of voices telling you what you should be feeling and doing, even what you should find a turn-on. A girl can't win. If she doesn't portray herself as 'sexy' and desirable, she's called frigid. Yet if she's sexually active, she's a slut. The ability for women to say yes to sex without getting punished is therefore a key goal of feminists today.

Objectification and 'raunch culture'

In many societies, women are seen to embody the concept of sex. Think about how the phrase 'sex sells' is used to defend marketing a product with images of naked women. Think about how sex toys and erotica are marketed (whether aimed at men or women, they tend to have naked women on their packaging), and how women are encouraged to express their sexuality predominantly through display and exhibitionism (for example, in pole dancing), when men aren't. Consider countries where women are forced by law to cover their bodies to protect men from temptation. Or think of western countries where women can wear more or less what they want, but are thought culpable in their own rape if they are attacked wearing a short skirt or low-cut top. The same idea lies behind all of this: that women embody sex, 'own' sex and are therefore responsible for it (and for men's behaviour towards them).

What we see as 'sex' and 'sexy' has been filtered through the eyes of heterosexual men for hundreds of years. Under the sexual double standard, men's supposedly irrepressible sexual needs were uppermost, so women learned to see themselves as sexual objects, not sexual subjects: grateful for male attention, focused on pleasuring men, but not in charge of their own sexual journeys. As Wolf remarks,

> What little girls learn is not the desire for the other, but the desire to be desired. Girls learn to watch their sex along with the boys; that takes up the space that should be devoted to finding out about what they are wanting.... Both men and women ... tend to eroticize only the woman's body and the man's desire.[3]

But with the rise of women-produced pornography and Lily Allen singing about dumping a man because he was no good in bed,[4] surely women are no longer considered sexual objects? Unfortunately this doesn't seem to be so.

Ariel Levy and Rosalind Gill are feminist writers who have picked up on the phenomenon of women apparently getting sexual pleasure from their own objectification. Levy is bothered by the way women's sexual behaviour is becoming like men's. Women are going to strip clubs, watching porn, buying Playboy merchandise, but it's not clear whether these activities are really pleasurable for them or whether they are just simulating desire because the media tells them it's what men find sexy.[5] We inhabit a society whose media images persuade us that, as Gill puts it, 'young women should not only be beautiful but sexy, sexual knowledgeable/practised and always "up for it."'[6] For women who aren't in relationships (for whatever reason), as well as those who are and just don't feel *that* 'up for it', it's hard not to feel condemned by these messages.

Objectification keeps reinventing itself as empowerment (but never for men). New forms of female exhibitionism, like burlesque and indie-porn site Suicide Girls, market themselves as liberating and 'alternative'. Jess Smith, assistant editor of feminist magazine *Subtext* (who applied to be a Suicide Girl but changed her mind), and writer Laurie Penny (who spent a while as a burlesque dancer), have taken forays into these worlds and found them wanting. Reflecting on it several years later, Smith explains: 'Suicide Girls is like the middle-class version of a reader's wives feature, which I find sad – the concept of a perceived middle-class, seemingly "better", less sleazy way to be objectified by men.'[7] Penny agrees:

> Burlesque serves up misogyny in a tasteful package of feathers.... The burlesque striptease makes explicit what push-up-bras and sticky lipgloss only promise: a passive, faux-naive, peek-a-boo sexuality that has little to do with real female pleasure and everything to do with mimicking whatever we are told is 'sexy'.[8]

The right to say no

Elizabeth Morgan and Eileen Zurbriggen interviewed seventy-nine 18- to 23-year-olds in the USA about the messages they received about sexuality from their first dating partner. First dating partners often have more influence over young people's decisions than, say, the media or their families. Some interesting findings emerged. First, it was sexual intercourse that was talked about; other expressions of sexuality were ignored. High male sexual interest was the second theme; boys said sex was very important and the girls accepted that as part of their masculinity. In the women's accounts, this led their boyfriends to pressurise them to sleep with them, with varying degrees of coercion (four of the forty-eight women were raped). There were some exceptions – boys reluctant to have sex due to religious reasons, and girls who wanted to. But, generally, what seems to happen is that young women tend to have sex before they really want to, as opposed to young men, who generally don't.[9]

Feminist Sarah B, 24, describes this atmosphere as 'compulsory sexuality'.

> You can open most women's magazines and find tips for women on how to give their male sexual partners blowjobs. The word 'job' already implies that this is a chore, not a pleasurable way of interacting, and then there might be an article on 'working' on your relationship. Everyone admits that sexual interactions are more like going to work than having fun. Then you can open a contemporary feminist journal and find articles on sado-masochism, pornography, gender roles, etc. They are all about work as well – working through oppressive power dynamics with sadomasochism, working through patriarchy by complicating gender roles, using pornography to reclaim sexual power.... Nobody is talking about why you can't seem to get away from the sex. Apparently it's compulsory.

Some feminists fear that this 'compulsory' approach is leading to the medicalisation of female sexuality, in which Viagra-type pills or collagen injections in your G-spot are increasingly seen as a solution to some women's 'lack of desire'.[10] In many Western countries, pressures on teenagers to have sex are strong. This can take the form of bullying for being a virgin, backed up by negative attitudes towards virginity and voluntary celibacy. Countless children have emailed sex-education websites such as Channel 4's *Sexperience* with worries about virginity and peer pressure: 'im 15 and still a virgin but im being pressured every day by people making fun of me but i want it to mean something. wat should i do?'[11]

In films and television programmes like *40 Days and 40 Nights* (2002) and *No Sex Please, We're Teenagers* (BBC2, 2005) people take up the challenge to abstain. According to the advertising for *40 Days and 40 Nights*, 'One man is about to do the unthinkable. No sex. Whatsoever.' *Unthinkable*? Would they have said the same for a female protagonist? While these programmes do some good (for instance in building young people's self-esteem), they can't quite seem to shake the implication that *not* having sex is what's strange.

When not having sex becomes 'unthinkable', especially for men and boys, there's a dangerous inference that if someone doesn't want sex, something must be wrong with them. It also helps maintain the concept of men as ravenous sexual beings who 'need' sex, and whose 'need' is (a) more intense than women's and (b) likely to erupt in sexual violence against women if not satisfied. As feminists have pointed out, this view of male sexuality is incredibly insulting.

This idea of men as the pursuer appears in a whole range of self-help books about how to attract men. Regardless of how they feel as individuals, women and men are encouraged to act out roles which may directly contravene their true feelings. Women are encouraged to act aloof and uninterested, even if they aren't. Men are supposed to initiate everything. It's exhausting – and slightly creepy and dishonest. The male pursuing the female and pressuring her until she gives in is so common to our understanding of sex that this is even considered romantic. Is it any wonder that many people misinterpreted 'Every Breath You Take' as a sweet romantic song, or that lyrics like this are in mainstream pop songs?

> If you say that you dont want me
> thats OK I'm gonna get you anyway
> if you think you can avoid me
> that's alright 'cos i dont mind a little fight
> V, 'Blood Sweat and Tears', 2004[12]

Neither is it surprising when we read reports like this one:

> A study of sexual attitudes among 14- to 16-year-olds found teen-age boys thought it was acceptable to pressure girls into sex and to use alcohol to get them into bed.... 'The young men ... appeared to follow behaviour patterns that included pressuring girls to have sex, often with the use of alcohol ... they suggested that a girlfriend who slept around would probably pay a physical price and that using tactics like getting a girl drunk were acceptable.' Dr Hayter said: 'In one of the boys' focus groups there was even a suggestion that it was OK for a boy to force his girlfriend to have sex and the group started trying to differentiate between "just a bit of pressure" and "proper rape".'[13]

Amidst all these conflicting messages about what's appropriate, girls and boys need to have confidence to discern their *true* feelings, and, above all, to say no if they want to. It's important that feminists promote secular solutions that empower young people to say no to sex in the face of peer pressure; religious abstinence programmes shouldn't have the monopoly on giving kids the confidence to say no. Children and teenagers should be supported to wait until they are ready to make their own decisions, and tackling sexual bullying in schools needs to be a high priority.

For adults also, remaining single or not partaking in sexual activity should be accepted as a valid choice. Some people consider themselves asexual; others choose to be celibate for different reasons. Being single is not just better than bad sex; it's a valid, potentially empowering, state.

How we learn about sex

Another feminist concern is how we are educated about sexuality, and whether the messages we receive are helpful and healthy. Our society has a major influence on what we find sexy, so our sexual attitudes, feelings and behaviour, even what we are aroused by, will be a complex blend of our society's views and our own.

Pornography is an important shaper of attitudes to sex, which is partly why some feminists are concerned about its increasing normalisation. Feminists remain divided about pornography, about whether it negatively influences men's views of women, and whether most performers are willing participants. But most agree that the increasing availability of porn is troubling, especially if children use it to educate themselves about sex in the absence of a healthy and factual sex education. Many feminists worry that the majority of mainstream pornography is sexist, damaging and limiting – and also, on occasion, just plain boring, because the vast majority of pornography is aimed at heterosexual male viewers (often – literally – from their point of view). Amy C, 30, explains how she perceives the influence of pornography on her friends:

> The trickle-down of porn into mainstream culture has led to very definite ideas of what constitutes 'sexiness' for women – big boobs, a hairless, neat vulva, pouting lips, long hair – but this is merely a mirror of the desires of a narrow group of straight men, and has nothing to do with real female sexuality. I have female friends who are in their 30s; they regularly wax their pubic hair and buy lacy undies, but have never masturbated because they think it's dirty. I feel that the only way out of this clearly messed-up situation is

to educate teenagers and make a concerted effort in schools to counteract the damage done by porn. Girls should be asking, what do I want? What feels good for me? Rather than, is my vagina pretty enough?

Pornography's influence on children is particularly troubling; pornography performers like Jenna Jameson have stated that they wouldn't want their children to see it.[14] With the increase of mobile phone technology, the Internet, and general availability of soft porn in popular magazines and newspapers, children are exposed to pornographic imagery in a way previous generations never were. Today, boys are socialised by lad-mag culture and pornography to see themselves as sex-obsessed and the initiators of sex; girls learn through porn that they should be responsive to male needs rather than assert their own.

It has been suggested that the average age at which children first view Internet pornography is now 11.[15] When Channel 4's *The Sex Education Show vs Pornography* showed a group of schoolchildren pictures of women's breasts and asked them which were most attractive, they all picked the cosmetically enhanced pair. When asked why, they explained that this was what they were used to seeing in porn. 'We're going to want the plastic ones because that's what we're suggested to want', explained one boy. 'Because fake is what you think normal, you prefer fake boobs.' Likewise, when the boys were asked to pick out a photo of a flaccid penis they considered average-sized, they picked one that was two inches longer than the real average. Why? 'Because of porn', they said. This suggests that viewing porn at such a young age creates unrealistic expectations of women's and men's bodies and of sex itself.[16]

Feminist concerns about pornography go further than its impact on children. Many feminists complain that a lot of pornography (like all forms of media) is profoundly sexist, and sexualises gender inequalities by eroticising women's subordination and men's domination.[17] The sex portrayed is usually focused on penetration, which means that viewers don't learn about the other forms of sexual activity that women find pleasurable. In its more extreme forms, porn eroticises violence against women: films and images depict women being raped, physically hurt, tortured or penetrated by animals.

Not only is sexual inequity eroticised in mainstream pornography; racism and other inequalities are too. Patricia Hill Collins points out that pornographic representations allude to the historical oppression of black women under slavery. Black women are portrayed chained up, or as needing controlling by white men.[18] Asian women don't escape stereotypical portrayals either, since they are especially common victims in pornographic rape scenarios on the Internet.[19]

Feminists are also concerned about porn performers and their working conditions. Porn isn't 'free speech', as its advocates claim;[20] it's the depiction of *real* sex acts. It is impossible for viewers to know whether what is being shown is genuinely consensual, simple acting, or real pain and violence. Additionally, viewers cannot tell whether the circumstances that led the women and men into the industry were exploitative or not. For those reasons, many feminists have deep moral and ethical difficulties with most pornography, whether they are comfortable with the idea of pornography in principle or not.

Yet what mainstream magazines teach about sex is also problematic, as so many people get information about sex from the media. How about the sex advice offered by *Cosmopolitan* or *Glamour*: 'How to seduce a man in true Cosmo sex-kitten style'; 'Blow him away: rock his world with these blow job tips'; and 'Solo sex tips: get some "me" moves to try tonight!' Is this about a woman expressing her own sexuality or about pleasing a man?

Should we embrace *Cosmo*'s 'Good sex etiquette' tips (which, among other things, suggest pretending there's a problem with the plumbing so you can nip secretly into the shower to shave your legs before your boyfriend discovers – horror of horrors – a couple of days of hair growth)? Are the masturbation techniques a positive sign that women's sexuality belongs to them and no one else?[21] Should we be disturbed that all search results for 'bisexual' on *Cosmo*'s website are gossip pieces about celebrities?[22]

Similarly, education in schools leaves a lot to be desired. Sex education tends to focus on the practicalities of contraception, ignoring aspects such as consent, respect, mutual pleasure and emotional issues. Children need good sexual and relationship education in a variety of settings (at school, by parents, within youth work, in the media) which covers all types of relationships. This shouldn't just focus on the biology of heterosexual intercourse but should look more widely at sexual and romantic relationships, including gender and power dynamics. It should present LGBT sexualities, asexuality, singleness and celibacy as valid and normal sexual choices.

Homophobia

As we've seen, pornography, women's status as sex objects (self-imposed or not) and the sexual double standard are all examples of the way heterosexuality is prescribed (but unequally) for men and women. This is bad enough for those of a heterosexual orientation, but the pressures towards heterosexuality are felt especially hard by lesbian, gay, bisexual, transgender, queer and intersex people. Across the globe, LGBTQIs experience rejection by family members, discrimination in work and health-care settings, exclusion from religious organisations, mockery in the media and bullying at school. In many countries they can't challenge it

'Women are always watching our backs – in the dark, on a train full of football fans, in a club, wherever. But two girls together – what choice do we have? ...
It is so exhausting to be checking over your shoulder, the corner of your eye: maybe hold hands like we're not really, maybe put both hands into one coat pocket; if that guy sees us leant together on the train will he know? ... Should I wake her up and move her legs off my lap so we don't get into trouble?
I remember the unthinking ease of being with my boyfriends – no one in the street gave us a second glance; in shops and in restaurants, bars, we were greeted with sweet knowing smiles, we held hands glancing neither left nor right, we kissed in pubs, phoneboxes, glass elevators, in front of our parents...
Do you understand?'
ANON, *Cleaner Light* zine, n.d.

because the law treats them as second-class citizens. Homosexuality is illegal in eighty countries and punishable by death in five.[23] Four hundred years after Shakespeare penned *Romeo and Juliet*, the real tragedy is that human beings are still not free to love each other as they choose.

In contemporary media, lesbian sexuality – surely a sexuality which is *not* about men – appears as a kind of performance enacted only to titillate men. Think of Madonna and Britney's kiss at the MTV awards or Amber and Danielle's in *American Pie 2*.[24] In a typical spread from a British lads' magazine featuring photos of two (young, white) topless models in faux-lesbian poses cavorting on a bed, the accompanying interview includes the following:

Did things get a bit steamy on [the photo shoot] set?

R: It was pretty steamy but we both behaved. Her boobs are irresistible.

K: Rosie's gorgeous. I'm more into men but I could look at her all day...

Have you ever teamed up with another girl to do anything rude?

R: No, I haven't. I haven't even snogged another girl!

K: Nor me, but I imagine it would be quite rude. If Rosie and I got together with a boy, it would be the best night of his life. He'd have to take a week off to recover![25]

This contrived scenario – in which young women pretend to be lesbians for the male audience whilst going to lengths to emphasise that they're only interested in men – is as far away as you can get from most lesbians' lives.

A recent survey of over a thousand LGBT people in Hungary illustrates the sorts of discrimination LGBTs face. The people interviewed revealed the stories behind these statistics:

> They threw me out of the house with two bags of clothes because I am gay. (MALE, 19)

> I had to leave a secondary girls' boarding school because of my sexual orientation as the students ostracised me and publicly abased me. (FEMALE, 17)

> An acquaintance, who works at OMSZ [National Ambulance Service], encouraged a suicidal transgender girl to continue her attempt to end her life, and was not prepared to call her by another name than that on her identity card. (MALE, 26)[26]

LGBTs are still subjected to death threats, hate crimes and extreme social sanctions. Sexism and homophobia walk hand in hand; at the root of homophobia lie deeply entrenched sexist attitudes about what is acceptable behaviour for men and women. In South Africa (ironically the first country to include in a national constitution protection for gay people), lesbians are subjected to so-called 'corrective rape':

> We get insults every day, beatings if we walk alone, you are constantly reminded that … you deserve to be raped, they yell, if I rape you then you will go straight, that you will buy skirts and start to cook because you will have learnt how to be a real woman. (South African lesbian)[27]

In countries where being gay is illegal, the situation is especially acute. LGBT refugees and asylum-seekers escaping persecution find that their problems are not over in the countries they flee to. A report on LGBT asylum-seekers living in Turkey (predominantly Iranian, as since 1978 Iran is believed to have executed thousands of gay people) found most had been physically attacked, and most encountered discrimination accessing work, housing, education and welfare. Transsexual women refugees were told by police to dress 'like a man'. During one gay man's interview with a UN High Commission for Refugees officer,

> He told me on two occasions that I was lying. He asked me very detailed questions about the type of sexual intercourse I have, and how many partners I have had sexual intercourse with. I cried throughout the interview. These questions upset me a lot.[28]

The UK has not been very helpful to LGBT people seeking asylum. The Independent Asylum Commission has expressed concern that countries considered 'safe' by the UK are in some cases not safe for LGBT asylum-seekers and that the UK asylum system does not acknowledge their additional vulnerabilities.[29]

In Britain, the gay hate-crime survey 2008 found that 1 in 5 lesbians and gay people had experienced a hate crime or incident in the past three years (mostly insults and harassment, but also threats and physical and sexual assault); three-quarters did not report the incident to the police.[30] People are still being murdered for their sexuality, and ridicule of gay, lesbian and bisexual people is commonplace. Meanwhile, BBC Radio 1 DJ Chris Moyles receives little more than a slap on the wrist for homophobic 'jokes' at the expense of gay pop stars. Bisexual people are often ignored in these discussions, but as 18-year-old Sophie explains in her zine *Sinking Hearts* (2007), they face specific issues:

I feel like I don't belong with all the people who identify as gay and go to gay bars and gay pride and things like that. I feel 'not gay enough'. Like 'you must be this gay to enter.' I feel like I won't be taken seriously for who I am – guys think bisexual girls are hot just because they get it on with other girls, don't they? And other girls... well, they just think bisexual girls are doing it for attention.

Additionally, 'compulsory heterosexuality' (a term coined by the poet Adrienne Rich[31]) doesn't just affect gay people. Every time a boy is called 'gay' or 'fag' by his classmates or a single woman's made to feel inadequate because she doesn't have a man, we're witnessing the painful effects of compulsory hetero-sexuality (or 'heterosexism' as it's sometimes called). This is why discussing sexism without addressing *hetero*sexism is worse than short-sighted.

Our survey found a broad diversity in the sexuality of feminists: around 6 in 10 identified as heterosexual, 2 in 10 as bisexual, 1 in 10 as lesbian or gay, and 1 in 10 as something else, including queer, pansexual, asexual, celibate, bi-curious and 'prefer not to say'. As a 2008 Stonewall campaign in the UK put it: 'Some people are Gay [and, we'd like to add, bi, polyamorous, queer or asexual...]. Get over it!' Unfortunately, some people haven't got over it.

In our survey, a surprisingly high number of feminists said that one of the negative consequences of being a feminist was the ridicule they suffered. A key component of this ridicule was the use of 'lesbian' as a term of abuse.

To reject someone's arguments because of their – suspected or real

> 'Being accused of being a man-hater and lesbian (like being a lesbian was a bad thing).' FEMALE, 52

> 'Called names i.e. "radical dyke" – not proven, but missed out on promotion because of being seen as outspoken.' FEMALE, 40

– sexual orientation shows how stubbornly homophobia is in-grained, despite recent sexual equality legislation which now prohibits discrimination in employment and the provision of goods and services, and the legalisation of same-sex partnerships in a number of countries.

Most feminists are not put off by stereotypes describing femi-nists as 'hairy-legged dykes' – they're more likely to condemn the sexism and homophobia behind these stereotypes. Today, divisions that were evident between lesbian and heterosexual feminists in the 1970s and 1980s (Betty Friedan's National Or-ganisation for Women didn't want to include lesbians because she feared it would turn away 'mainstream' women',[32] and separatists angered heterosexual feminists by accusing them of 'sleeping with the enemy') are largely absent. Larissa, 25, says: 'although I identify as a heterosexual woman, as a feminist I am acutely aware of the hardships and issues at stake in the fight for recognition and equality of queer people.' She argues:

> Since heteronormativity is so ingrained in our collective (Christian) social consciousness, there are no quick-fixes for homophobia, just as sexism continues to be an ongoing problem in Western society a century on from the first-wave feminist suf-fragettes. Inroads have been made for Western women, however, and the same can be made for queer peoples if we persistently and continually voice our discontent and dissent.

Freedom to leave relationships

Later, we'll look at how feminists are fighting for the right to form intimate relationships outside of traditional heterosexual marriage. However, the relationships of most women in the world take place within a formal marriage system. So, an important goal of feminism is to ensure that women and men have equal freedom to divorce. Feminist campaigns have resulted in women gaining equal divorce rights in many countries; in Chile divorce was legalized in 2004, enabling separated women to take control of their own affairs (previously a husband's signature was required to buy a house or start a business).

But around the world many women still find divorce more difficult than men for legal or financial reasons. The Jewish Orthodox Feminist Alliance is concerned about 'Agunot' ('chained women'), Jewish women whose husbands are unwilling to grant them an official bill of divorce. Without this, a chained woman 'must remain in a dead marriage'.[33] In Nigeria, women's rights activists report that divorced women are often thrown out of their home, lose custody of their children, and end up destitute.[34]

Under such circumstances, who can say that a woman who has no option than to stay with her husband is consenting to sex with him? Only a person who is free to walk away can consent to sex.

Taking the sexism out of sex: the feminist response

Feminists are working hard to improve women's ability to make choices about their sexuality. They are writing and blogging about sexual issues, promoting women-produced erotic magazines and sex toys, reworking 'traditional' relationship models, challenging homophobia and developing sex education tools for young people. Let's look in more detail at some of these.

Representing men and women as equally desirable

Feminists are highlighting other ways to express our sexuality. For instance, they represent women as sexual subjects (who desire) instead of sexual objects (who are desired). Most feminists would argue that both aspects (subject and object) can be part of a healthy sexuality, but that for women the 'object' part has been given so much prominence that being looked at and desired are considered integral to female sexuality. For example, stripping is often described as an 'empowering' expression of female (but not male) sexuality. Feminists contend that the wish to be desired is not specific to women, and isn't wrong in itself; however, like yin and yang, both desiring and desired need to be brought back into balance for men as well as women, to enable them to play as 'objects' and 'subjects' as their own unique sexuality leads them. Many heterosexual and bisexual feminists are asserting that men are equally worthy of being desired. This is important, as it levels the playing field regarding a more open and accepting variety of sexual expression for women and men.

In 2009, New Zealander Suraya Sidhu Singh left her civil service job to set up *Filament*, a UK-based erotic magazine for women. *Filament* was the first UK women's magazine to include a photograph of an erect penis. Singh cites feminist ideas about the female gaze as her inspiration. Based on research among (mostly heterosexual) female readers, *Filament* is dedicated to challenging conventional notions that 'men are visual but women aren't', or that women are attracted to 'beefcakes' rather than 'narrow-hipped', sensitive men. Through including interview material with models, it presents men as whole people, not just sexual objects.

The *Erotica Cover Watch* blog, created by two British erotica authors, highlights how erotica aimed at heterosexual women almost always has a nude *woman* on the cover.

> As two erotica writers we're very interested in how our product is packaged. And sometimes pretty annoyed about it. This is BICEPS, our bid to Banish Inequality on Covers in Erotica, Porn & Smut... This is not about anyone's fondness for a particular peachy bottom. This is about ... challenging the deeply

entrenched gender bias in erotica-marketing which ignores women as consumers and prefers to serve them up as objects to be ogled.

Yet even a simple goal of 'getting men's bums onto covers' of erotic books isn't uncontroversial:

> Our biggest surprise when we kicked off this campaign was the strength of the backlash.... We were described as militant, ungrateful, sexist and desperate. We were called 'hard-headed feminists', 'do gooders' and, um, 'lesbians' (I still haven't figured that one out). We were taken to task for not reading the books whose covers we were analysing. We were accused of 'bathing in heated pools of hypocrisy', 'doing a hit job' on fellow writers, giving feminism a bad name, hurting people's feelings and wanting to do damage to erotica publishing.[35]

Pro-feminist men are also keen to stretch the boundaries of how male sexuality is viewed, by offering themselves up to the female gaze. Sexuality activist Meitar Moscovitz is a bisexual man who runs a blog called *Male Submission Art*. His blog is very popular with heterosexual and bisexual women, as this comment from reader Ireen shows:

> I've come across lots of people who claim that female bodies are inherently more beautiful [than] male ones, which is something I don't understand at all. The issue, I think, is rather that we don't learn to see beauty in men; that men are never even placed in that category.[36]

Moscovitz argues: 'sites like this one that acknowledge a female gaze are stepping stones to more than just access to quality erotica for women, but also to a healthier and happier sexual self-expression for men.'[37]

Feminist writer Abby Lee of *Girl With a One Track Mind* has made major strides in challenging assumptions about women's sexual desires by documenting her own voracious sexual appetites and adventures (although even she did not escape 'punishment', in the form of a forced 'outing' from a drooling press, and harassment over the Internet). She writes:

> Why can't women just like sex? Why can't we be seen to enjoy it, without being called 'sluts' or 'whores' or 'addicts'? Why must something be wrong with us, just because we openly express our needs, desires and wants?[38]

At the same time, feminist writers have tried to dismantle the idea, prevalent in porn and mainstream representations of sex, that enjoying penetration is the same thing as being submissive, subjugated and feminine (hence undesirable). Sex blogger Bitchy Jones argues:

> Having something pushed into your body that feels amazing is only submissive because someone decided that the female role in sex was a submissive one.... It is only seen as submissive because everything women do gets classed as submissive sooner or later (to buoy up idea that femininity and submissive are somehow interchangeable).[39]

Expanding women's access to sexual information

Feminists have expanded women's access to information about sex, and made it easier and more acceptable for women to access erotica and sex toys such as vibrators. Feminists are communicating alternative sources of information about a far wider variety of sexual practices than those pleasurable mainly for men. Without feminist activism around sex, we might still be stuck with the idea that the missionary position is 'correct' and everything else 'perverted'. All this is good for men too, as feminist-minded heterosexual men can enjoy a wider range of activities than would otherwise have been considered appropriate for them.

In the UK, *Scarlet* magazine has attempted to provide a forum for a female-focused angle on sexuality, with mixed reviews from feminists. Small-scale grassroots feminist zines on sex receive less attention, but have set out their visions for a radically different and hopeful sexual culture. *She's Got Labe*, in Canada, and *The Hand That Cradles the Rock*, in the UK, highlighted diverse sexualities, discussing emotional and practical topics that would later come to mainstream attention. Writers discuss topics such as sex after childbirth, female sex toys, women-only sex parties and the politics of pornography.

In the USA, concern about the commercialisation of sex education, the abstinence trend, sexism and the exclusion of different sexualities in mainstream discourse have led sexuality activists to organise a series of not-for-profit 'open source' 'un-conferences' called 'Kink for All'. The intention is to discuss all kinds of sexualities in a free, safe and non-commercial environment.

The growth in women-produced sex toys has paralleled the expansion of the mainstream sex toy market. Feminists have mixed opinions on whether women-run sex shops (like Sh! in London, Womynsware in Canada or Toys in Babeland in the USA) and producers of 'feminist pornography' succeed in breaking down stereotypes or are perpetuating them by expanding access to a mainstream sex industry.

Reworking or rejecting 'traditional' models

Some heterosexual feminists do get married, but many reject the symbolism of the traditional wedding, such as being 'given away' (like property) or the woman being expected to change her name (but never the other way round). Others reject marriage completely as an unnecessary and patriarchal institution that unfairly privileges heterosexual married couples (for instance, through tax allowances).

Likewise, legislation allowing same-sex partnerships is another way of reworking traditional models; it's increasingly common to hear gay women refer to their civil partner as their 'wife', even in countries where gay marriage per se is not allowed. LGBT people (and some heterosexual feminists) are divided on whether it's better to fight for access to traditional marriage, or simply reject state involvement in their personal lives. The group Queeruption, for example, is in part a backlash against the mainstream gay scene's commercialisation and its desire to push traditional heterosexual models such as marriage at the expense of alternative forms of relationship.

Not everyone feels monogamy is right for them. A few feminists (of all sexualities) are investigating polyamory. This isn't cheating, polygamy or 'wife swapping'; it's a form of honest and consensual non-monogamy in which individuals have relationships (which may be long-term, romantic and/or sexual) with more than one person. Influenced by books such as *The Ethical Slut*[40] polyamorous people feel that it is unfair to expect one individual to meet all their needs. In fact, in a world where people are increasingly isolated from a wider community network, one could argue that polyamorous folk are creating a new form of extended family network.

Many feminists disagree on these issues. But allowing people to follow their own path and make their own informed choices must be a good thing. And whatever their sexuality or form of relationship, feminists strive for relationships of equals. Although not always successful – we're only human, after all – feminist-minded couples try to ensure that decisions are taken together, that one partner's dreams and life goals are not prioritised over the other's, and often support each other to follow their individual ambitions as well as joint ones.[41]

Challenging homophobia

LGBT couples and allies aim to challenge fear and homophobia by the simple act of holding hands with their loved one in public, something heterosexual people take for granted. 2009 saw the first international same sex hand-holding day (otherwise known as Sshh!). The first day was held in memoriam of a shooting at an LGBT youth centre in Tel Aviv and murders and torture of gay men in Iraq.

Elsewhere, activists are challenging stereotypes through humour. Bryan Safi's Internet-based show *That's Gay* highlights gay stereotypes on television, such as the 'gay best friend obsession'. Safi sarcastically points out the double standards behind many faux-lesbian plotlines on television shows like *Friends*:

> Let's be clear. Gay experimenting only works as a storyline for female characters. Nobody wants to see Ross stick his tongue down Chandler's throat. But Rachel dyking out? Yeah! Let's make that happen! ... Homosexuality is totally cool when the dudes approve ... It's all for the bro' with the boner who's watching.[42]

Many organisations worldwide are fighting for LGBT rights. For example, Meem is a community of lesbian, bisexual, queer and questioning women and transgender people in Lebanon. In this extract from a talk at the LGBT Human Rights Conference in Copenhagen, Lynn describes Meem's goals and activism:

> The essence of sexual rights is our right to have great sex... When you can choose your partner, you can have better sex. When you have access to contraception, when you can change your body according to your gender identity, when you have sexual education in schools, you have better sex. We want to fight for all of these sexual rights, through a feminism that focuses on sexuality as the essence of gender inequality. The queers are fighting with their bodies, with their vaginas, with themselves. There *cannot* be a feminist movement without queers and without queerness.[43]

Conclusion

Feminists are at the forefront of the fight for good, consensual sexual relationships. Indeed, the sexual diversity among our questionnaire respondents illustrates this. Far more feminists than non-feminists choose to live their sexual lives in ways that are different from the norm. Even among heterosexual feminists, the rejection of much of traditional heterosexuality – the double standard, taking the husband's name, the virgin/whore stereotype, the white dress – is evident. In living their lives differently, they all face costs and attract ridicule and rejection. But they are pushing forward sexual changes that will benefit others.

Happily, there's evidence that being a feminist improves your own sex life too – researchers found that feminist women are generally more sexually assertive, better able to negotiate pleasurable and safe sex, and experience more equality in their personal relationships.[44] Conversely, women with more traditional attitudes, who associate sex with submission to a male partner, have more difficulty in reaching orgasm.[45]

But before we become too optimistic, the next chapter turns to the big issue of violence against women, of which sexual violence is a significant and disturbing aspect. The fight for good sex also involves putting a stop to the rape, harassment and sexual violation of women's bodies.

Take action!

1. When you hear people call a woman a 'slut' or claim men are uncontrollably ruled by their penis, point out the double standard.
2. Join a group campaigning against sexual objectification of women and girls in the media (such as Object! in the UK).
3. Support campaigns to reduce sexual bullying and peer pressure in schools, and empower young people to make informed decisions about their sexual relationships on their own terms.
4. Commit to ensuring that all your sexual relationships will be consensual.
5. Support organisations working for LGBTQI rights in your country or globally.

3

AN END TO VIOLENCE AGAINST WOMEN

OVER eight hundred feminists crowd into the hall. They've been stopping traffic in central London at November's annual Reclaim the Night march, in a crowd 2,000 strong. The atmosphere is jubilant and friendly. As the crowd settles down and women make space for each other on the floor, the speeches begin. One after another, women speak about violence: an activist from an Asian women's domestic violence project, a representative from a teacher's union. Finally, organizer Finn Mackay takes to the stage. Her rabble-rousing speeches are legendary and tonight's is no exception.

> We have marched together tonight as women because we have a struggle to win and each of you knows it. We live in a society where all of us, in all our diversity, know what it is to live with the fear, threat and reality of male violence ... It is a shame on our society that there an estimated 80,000 rapes every year, over 300,000 sexual assaults – and meanwhile, a rape conviction rate that stands at the lowest it has ever been, one of the lowest in Europe at only 5.3 per cent.

The crowd cries out, 'Shame, shame!' Mackay continues:

> You have marched for the two women every week murdered by a
> violent male partner. For the one in four women who are raped.
> For the five thousand young people prostituted on our streets
> tonight as every night. For our sisters around the world who
> represent the poorest of the poor, those most displaced by wars,
> those without education, those most affected by environmental
> destruction... You have sent a message to those who would silence
> us, to those who would keep us in the home where we are actually
> most at risk. You have said, we know. We know that it is always
> safer to resist.[1]

When we asked feminists what issues most concern or interest
them, one of the most frequently mentioned was violence against
women. Worldwide, at least one in three women will be beaten,
coerced into sex, or otherwise abused in her lifetime.[2] A survey
of young British women by *More* magazine in 2005 found that
95 per cent don't feel safe on the streets at night, and almost
three-quarters worry about being raped.[3]

When we say violence is a feminist issue, what do we mean?
Don't men suffer violence too, and don't women commit it? Are
feminists sexist for concentrating on violence against women? It's
true that men are victims of violence (they are more likely to suffer
violence than women, although this violence is mostly perpetrated
by other men), and women are violent too. *All* campaigns to stop
violence are important. But certain types of violence do affect
women (and people who transgress gender norms) more, and
we will make no apology for focusing on these issues. And, since
men's violence is such a huge global problem, stopping violence
against women will no doubt help reduce male victimisation
too.

Violence against women takes many forms: forced abortions,
female infanticide, female genital mutilation, acid throwing, child

sexual abuse, rape, forced prostitution, dowry and honour violence, domestic violence, elder abuse, and more. It is a huge topic, so this chapter will be limited to several major issues mentioned often in feminist circles: rape and sexual violence; domestic violence and abuse in intimate relationships; everyday harassment; and violence suffered by women in the sex industry.

Rape and sexual violence

In the UK, the Home Office estimates that around 21 per cent of girls and 11 per cent of boys experience some form of child sexual abuse; 23 per cent of women and 3 per cent of men experience sexual assault as an adult; and 5 per cent of women and 0.4 per cent of men suffer rape.[4] Only around 15 per cent of rapes are reported to the police, so it is estimated that, in total, around 80,000 women are raped every year in the UK.[5] Worldwide, the situation is just as shocking. In up to half the world's nations, marital rape is not a crime. In Sudan and Afghanistan, raped women can be prosecuted for adultery and even sentenced to death. Rape is a weapon of war, ethnic cleansing and genocide. The Democratic Republic of Congo, Darfur, Sierra Leone and Uganda have all been highlighted as particular areas of concern:

> Abduction, rape, and sexual slavery are ... systematic and widespread in the conflict in Sierra Leone. Rape victims often suffer extreme brutality. In one case, a 14-year-old girl was stabbed in the vagina with a knife because she refused to have sex with the rebel combatant who abducted her. In another, a 16-year-old girl was so badly injured that, after her escape, she required a hysterectomy.[6]

Yet even in countries at peace, justice for rape victims is often close to impossible. In England and Wales, the 2006 conviction rate for reported rapes was around 6 per cent, down from about 32 per cent in the 1970s, and one percentage point below Ireland. In Scotland, the conviction rate is less than 3 per cent. This has been described, rightly, as a national scandal; Britain has the lowest rape conviction rate in Europe (in France in 2006 the conviction rate was 25 per cent; Luxembourg's 85 per cent is the highest).[7] At the same time, Rape Crisis Centres are regularly under threat of closure. In 2008 69 per cent of centres said they were 'unsustainable' due to lack of funding.[8]

Public opinion on rape bears litle resemblance to the facts. A 2005 poll demonstrated that only 4 per cent of respondents knew how many rapes occur in the UK each year, with most guessing less than 5,000. People also overestimated the percentage of reported rapes that ended in a conviction. A third of respondents felt that the victim was totally or partially responsible for the rape if she had had many sexual partners or wore 'sexy or revealing clothing'. A third believed that if she had flirted beforehand, she was partially responsible.[9]

> 'Cry-rape girl, 20, dragged man into toilets for sex to claim £7,500 compensation.'
> *Daily Mail*, 14 August 2009

> 'Mother who cried rape after meeting man on dating website is jailed.'
> *Daily Mail*, 22 July 2009

> 'Calais migrant "cried rape as revenge against people smuggler who failed to get her into Britain".'
> *Daily Mail*, 29 July 2009

> 'The rape lies that ruined our lives: Taxi driver and his wife reveal the devastating cost of a drunk teenager who cried rape.'
> *Daily Mail*, 22 May 2009

> 'Jail for wife who falsely accused husband of rape because "she wanted him out of her life".'
> *Daily Mail*, 3 July 2009

> 'My cry-rape hell: Wrongly accused man tells of his 11-month nightmare.'
> *Daily Mail*,
> 17 September 2008

It's mind-boggling that despite this appalling state of affairs, whenever one hears about rape in the media, the tone is suspicious. As writers at the satirically named blog *Feminazery*[10] pointed out, a search on the *Daily Mail* website for the term 'rape' brings up page after page of 'cry rape' stories.[11] But false accusations are no more likely to be made in rape cases than in any other crime,[12] and our priority should be the fact that over 1,500 people are raped in the UK every week.

Contrary to popular belief, the cards are stacked against women when it comes to challenging rapists. Rape is more likely to be committed by someone the woman knows than a stranger. Maybe it was her husband or a friend. Making it public might be embarrassing; people might not believe her, and friends and family may ostracize her. If she decides to go to the police, the chance of her having proper evidence collected or being taken seriously is low. Ellie Blogs, a police constable who blogged about her experiences dealing with rape and domestic violence cases, reveals that 'there can be a definite "eye rolling" culture when certain types of rapes are reported. Male officers in particular often have doubts about women who report rapes.'[13]

If the victim is believed, agreement is made to prosecute and the case reaches court, she may have to face her rapist and suffer hostile personal questions. The 1999 Youth Justice and Criminal Evidence Act has improved things somewhat in that victims are supposed to be protected from questions about their sexual history or behaviour, and the statutory definition of consent now includes a test of 'reasonable belief' in consent. Even so, she'll face a jury who will come into the court having read 'cry rape' stories in the press. Location is crucial: in Cleveland she's eleven times more likely to see her rapist convicted than in Dorset.[14]

The system can fail so many times that a rapist can be left to commit dozens of crimes before finally being convicted. London taxi driver John Worboys was estimated to have assaulted at least eighty-five women over several years. The police fear the total number of victims could be much greater.[15]

Blaming the victim

Victims are told – or it is at least implied – that rape is, to some degree, their fault; that if only they hadn't drunk so much/walked down the street alone/flirted with that boy, or if they had worn flat shoes or trousers/carried a rape alarm, it wouldn't have happened. Well-meaning campaigns focus on warning women to protect themselves but neglect targeting potential perpetrators, as if rape was an inevitable consequence of being female.

Rape is regularly presented as the woman's responsibility, especially if she has drunk alcohol. Cara at *The Curvature* blog explains:

> When someone actually bothers to do a *responsible* study about how alcohol affects rape, they do indeed find that a large number of victims were intoxicated at the time of the assault. They also find that in most cases where alcohol was involved, both parties were drinking. And in cases where only the victim or the perpetrator was drinking, the rapist was more than twice as likely as the victim to be intoxicated.
>
> But I'll just keep on holding my breath for that article titled 'Alcohol tied to risk of being a rapist.' I'll wait for the simply *rational* advice that men shouldn't drink because there's a relatively small chance that drinking will cause them to rape someone. Can't you see it right around the corner? A time when a woman makes a rape allegation and people accusingly ask the man *well were you drinking?*[16]

In 2009, writer Ben Goldacre exposed a classic example of victim blaming in a *Daily Telegraph* article entitled 'Women who drink alcohol, wear short skirts and are outgoing are more likely to be raped, claim scientists at the University of Leicester.'

> It was based on the unpublished and unfinished dissertation of a Masters student and got the story entirely wrong. The title of the press release for the same research was 'Promiscuous men more

likely to rape', which gives you some small clue as to how weirdly this story was distorted by the newspaper.[17]

Goldacre telephoned the student and asked her about the article's claims. She responded:

> We found no evidence that women who are more outgoing are more likely to be raped, this is completely inaccurate, we found no difference whatsoever. The alcohol thing is also completely wrong: if anything, we found that men reported they were willing to go further with women who are completely sober ... When I saw the article my heart completely sank, and it made me really angry, given how sensitive this subject is. To be making claims like the *Telegraph* did, in my name, places all the blame on women, which is not what we were doing at all.[18]

Feminists are angry about rape and the harmful myths surrounding it. The fact is that women's drinking does not cause rape. Neither does what they wear. Rapists cause rape. Instead of putting all the responsibility on women, why don't we focus on teaching men – from a young age – that rape and sexual violence are always absolutely wrong?

Abuse and violence in intimate relationships

'Wife stabbed for bad cooking.'
'Wife stabbed in explosion of fury.'

These headlines introduced one story of domestic violence that appeared in a local paper when we were working on this chapter. It's one of many thousands that happen each day worldwide, and includes many features typical of domestic violence cases. The woman was stabbed in the stomach and chest with a knife she was using to peel onions; her husband had criticized her cooking and she responded by telling him (an out-of-work taxi driver) to get a job. He attacked her. He stopped when he saw how badly she was bleeding and called an ambulance; when paramedics arrived, they found the floor slippery with her blood. Her lawyer underlined his lack of care for his injured wife. His lawyer blamed the man's actions on an unhappy marriage with a large age difference. Episodes of violence had characterised the marriage; the woman had reported some to police, but withdrawn her complaints. His response to his wife's comment about his unemployment – challenging his traditional masculine role – is also fairly typical; domestic violence is perhaps most prevalent in situations where a man's perceived right to control his partner is called into question.

But in another way this story is different from most: it's one of the few where a prosecution was successful and where improved domestic violence services (owing to years of feminist activism) were instrumental to the prosecution and to safeguarding the woman against further violence. The presiding judge jailed the man for four years. The woman survived but needs ongoing physiotherapy. The police officer explained that this prosecution had been successful because of close working between the woman and officers specially trained to protect domestic violence victims.[19]

In the UK, about one in four women and one in six men experience abuse or violence from a partner at some time during their adult lives.[20] In 77 per cent of domestic violence incidents recorded by the British Crime Survey, the victim was female.[21] Globally, figures vary and are collected differently, so it's not always easy to compare directly, but Table 3.1 shows the proportion of women who have experienced abuse by a partner in a range of countries.

Other types of discrimination often combine with sexism to make certain women at increased risk of violence or reduce their access to support services. For example, a study of partner

TABLE 3.1   Percentage of adult women who say they have experienced physical abuse by a male partner or intimate

Pakistan	80
Bolivia	70
Ukraine	50
Egypt	47
South Korea	38
USA	31
South Africa	25
Japan	15

Source: Based on figures in Joni Seager, *The Atlas of Women in the World*, 4th edn, Earthscan, Brighton, 2009, pp. 28–9.

violence in Massachusetts found that 34.6 per cent of transgender people reported being threatened with physical violence by a partner, compared to 13.6 per cent of non-transgender persons.[22] Women with disabilities are up to twice as likely to be victims of sexual assault and violence.[23]

As with many crimes, it's difficult to get accurate figures, since people rarely report domestic abuse, and may be reluctant to tell researchers about it (perhaps for fear of reprisals). Researchers debate the extent to which women are the overwhelming majority of victims and men the overwhelming majority of perpetrators. Some point out that where women commit acts of violence, it is often in self-defence against an abusive partner, and most agree that it's normally women, not men, who are subjected to the most serious and ongoing physical assaults.[24] In 2007/8, 35 per cent of UK female homicide victims were killed by a current or former partner, compared to 6 per cent of male victims.[25] A reliable estimate suggests that the ratio of male-perpetrated to female-perpetrated violence is around 4 to 1.[26]

Another type of violence predominantly affecting women is so-called 'honour' violence. The United Nations Population Fund estimates that worldwide around 5,000 women die annually in honour killings, while the media quote an estimate of ten to twelve per year in the UK.[27] Some believe the true number is higher, and others point out that the label 'honour killings' obscures the similarity between gender-based violence within a whole range of ethnic groups. As Humera Khan from the An-Nisa Society in London explains:

> Just because honour issues are not associated with white people does not mean that it does not happen. It happens, but not in the way that people talk about it when it happens in a Muslim or Asian context. ... If an honour killing in these communities occurs it is usually referred to as a 'crime of passion'. But underneath this, the basic drivers such as pride and honour are still the same even if the motives are different.[28]

In honour-related violence, more than one perpetrator may be involved, including extended family members. For instance, for 'Sakina', a Pakistani woman interviewed in a British refuge:

> [My mother in-law] started hitting me and then pushed me down the stairs. I was semi-unconscious, but that didn't stop her with hitting me around the head with her shoes till I completely passed out. I can't remember the amount of times I have been abused; it was a daily thing with my husband, his mother and sister getting involved. Sometimes I had an iron thrown at me but not by my husband, he only used to punch and kick me.[29]

Forced marriage can be seen as a form of honour-based violence; families use physical or psychological coercion to make a young person agree to a marriage, sometimes to someone from the parents' country of origin. According to specialist South Asian women's project workers, women seeking help because of rape, financial abuse or psychological abuse are often in forced marriages.[30] The UK's Forced Marriage Unit deals with approximately 1,600 cases each year;[31] this, women's groups say, is a fraction of the real total. Rahni Binjie, project manager from Roshni Asian Women's Aid in Nottingham, explains:

> There are periods towards the end of the education process when women are taken out of school. The girls just stop coming to classes and the schools don't seem interested in following it up.... We've had women who have disappeared from the education system – and who then disappear from the system as a whole. We don't know if they've been taken abroad or killed or anything – we've got no idea.[32]

If they have been in the UK less than two years, migrant women find it hard to leave abusive husbands because unless they can provide 'evidence' of abuse they have 'no recourse to public funds', making benefits and housing inaccessible.

Feminists are also concerned about early marriage because, generally speaking, at younger ages women are less able to assert their rights and needs (especially if their husbands are significantly older). In some countries, the difference between girls' and boys' experiences is significant, with girls being forced to marry at a younger age to older men. In Niger, 70 per cent of girls are married by the age of 19, compared to only 4 per cent of boys. In Honduras, the figure is 30 per cent of girls compared to 7 per cent of boys.[33]

Patriarchal attitudes and domestic violence

> 'I was sometimes justified in hitting [her]. I never hurt her badly physically – I never cut her or beat her senseless.... She'd always [argue] until there was really no alternative.'
>
> *Why did you hit her?*
>
> 'I was wanting to show her who was the boss.'

Is there something she could have done to stop you being abusive to her?

'Yes. Keep her mouth shut.'

Have you wanted to stop being violent to her?

'No. She's my wife.'[34]

As these excerpts demonstrate, sexist and patriarchal attitudes seem to be a major contributor to domestic violence. The victim's perceived infractions of her feminine role are used as justifications; violent men seek to regain control by subduing their partners.[35] Domestic abuse of women, whether physical, sexual, psychological or financial, is rarely a one-off incident but is often part of a pattern where one partner (usually male) tries to maintain power and control over the other (usually female, often his wife). Indeed, arguments over a woman's cooking, housework standards, money, sex, going out with friends and arguing back are regularly cited by offenders as provocations for their 'explosions of anger'.[36] Feminists commonly argue that domestic violence is prevalent where men believe they have a right to control 'their' women.[37] Researchers Rebecca and Russell Dobash say that 'the social positioning of marital partners supports men's control and domination of women through various means, including the use of force.'[38] Domestic abuse is therefore not just about an individual's anger problems or high standards in the kitchen but an issue of sexism, deeply rooted in the history and culture of many societies.

Just as domestic abusers justify their actions by evoking patriarchal notions of male ownership, perpetrators of honour violence rationalize it through the concept of honour. A family or community's honour is believed to reside in its women's adherence to patriarchal behavioural expectations. Women who defy their parents' authority (for instance by rejecting their parents' choice of marriage partner), become too 'Westernized' or have sex outside marriage are perceived to have brought shame on the family. The dishonoured family may be socially ostracized, damaged economically (if their businesses are boycotted) or simply lose social status. In extreme cases, dishonour is 'dealt with' through violence.

Some societies are more patriarchal than others and in very specific ways, with patriarchy interacting with a country's economic, legal, religious and cultural conditions. In an analysis of honour-related violence in Pakistan, Tahira Khan argues that the capitalist system of private property is fundamental to women's oppression. She concludes with a statement applicable to a whole range of types of male-against-female violence worldwide:

> Honour-related violence is all about the inseparable deep connection between economic interests and sexual conduct of men and women. Honour-related violence is a story of male anxieties about keeping women within their defined spaces and marked boundaries and male worries about female transgression and defiance.[39]

Hence more shelters for women, or harsh prison sentences for abusers, are not sufficient to eliminate domestic violence; many argue that only a fundamental structural change to the economic world order, coupled with a demolition of the sexist attitudes that justify the violence, can make this happen.

But whilst sexism and patriarchy have major roles to play in violence towards women, this does not account for male victims of domestic violence or explain violence within same-sex relationships. Any partner violence is serious and specialist support services for all victims are necessary. But what must not happen is for increased awareness of male victims (who themselves suffer due to sexist assumptions that men cannot be victims) to lead to funding cuts for female survivors – in particular, for women already disadvantaged by poverty or racism, who experience the most injurious and systematic abuses and are the most likely to be killed. Interventions must be targeted appropriately.

Everyday harassment

> Barely a day goes by when I am not harassed in the street. I probably first really noticed it when at fifteen, an older 'gentleman' started masturbating beside me on the bus....
>
> I have been groped in broad daylight, I have been forced to get on buses that are going nowhere near my destination to get away from men forcing themselves on me at bus stops, I've been groped and grabbed at in clubs, I had to quit a bar job due to a regular thinking he was allowed to grab my arse. I've been flashed at outside my house. And I've had all the filthy comments, leers and jeers you could ever wish for. It never stops....
>
> I try SO hard not to let it alter my behaviour, but sometimes it just gets too much.... I am so resentful of a society where one half of the population is so ... arrogant, they can force their way into the consciousness of the other half without endorsement or invitation.[40]

Many women and girls are incredibly angry and frustrated about everyday harassment. A number of our survey respondents mentioned this, and the impassioned stories of street harassment contributed by hundreds of women to a post on *The F Word* demonstrates that this is an issue affecting many women and girls.

As Martha Langelan points out in *Back Off! How to Confront and Stop Sexual Harassment*, so-called 'low-level' public harassment can have a powerful cumulative effect on women, creating an undercurrent of fear.[41] Blogger Noble Savage explains how this affects her desire to go jogging in the evenings:

> In the summer, we fear wearing a dress or a top that is too revealing, even if the weather is unbearably hot, lest we are catcalled and

groped by leering passers by whose aggressions seem to rise in conjunction with the temperature.

In the winter, as the elements make car breakdowns and accidents more likely, we freeze in fear at the thought of accepting help from a stranger and would rather sit in our icy, broken cars while we wait hours for the orange flashing lights of the accredited and vetted roadside cavalry, doors locked and fingers on the panic button of our mobile phones.

In the spring, as everyone comes pouring back onto sidewalk cafés and parks and out of the stupor of hibernation, smiles and comments about the lovely weather between strangers have to be monitored and reined in for fear that exchanging passing pleasantries will give a man the 'wrong impression' and invite him to pester us for a date or a number or a smile....

So I can't help but feel a bit like a caged hen... as I look out my window at the autumnal city streets and then forlornly at the running shoes gathering dust at the front door.

Post-feminist world, indeed.[42]

Whether it's changing the route home to avoid quiet streets or harassment hotspots like building sites, calling home to 'check in' before walking the ten-minute journey home from the train station, sitting near the doors on buses, crossing the street to avoid a lone man, or clutching keys in your hand *just in case* someone attacks you... we've all been there. But as Langelan points out, the street is *public space*. It is our human right to walk around freely, without fear.

There's nothing wrong with giving women practical advice to keep them safe. But as with rape, feminists often feel that far too much attention is paid to putting the problem in women's hands, telling women to cope by restricting their freedoms. We need to work for a world where women are not harassed by men, or made to feel afraid, and where this behaviour is not accepted as normal. After all, as Langelan says:

From men who do not harass women, we can also draw another
important conclusion about the nature of sexual harassment.
That so many men choose not to engage in harassment makes it
clear that this behaviour is neither biologically determined nor
inevitable.[43]

Violence against women in prostitution

The sex industry, of which prostitution forms a large part, has been
one of the world's major growth industries in the late twentieth
century. The growth and normalisation of pornography, military
prostitution, and the ease and affordability of 'sex tourism' have
made sex a significant part of the economy in countries including
Thailand (14 per cent of GDP), Indonesia (2 per cent) and the
Netherlands (5 per cent).[44]

Ask feminists what they think of prostitution and you'll encounter widely divergent views. Even the terminology is the
subject of intense debate: are women in the sex industry 'sex
workers' or 'prostituted women'? How can one generalize about
such a diverse range of people anyway? But whatever their
opinion, all are very concerned about violence against women
who work in the sex industry. This was an issue mentioned by
many feminists we surveyed (several of them sex workers or
ex-prostituted women).

Sex workers suffer high rates of physical violence. It is estimated that street workers are sixty to a hundred times more
likely to be murdered than women who are not prostitutes;[45]
the 2006 murders of five street-working women in Ipswich are a
reminder of this. Reactions to their murders ranged from shock
to voyeuristic fascination – and the sort of chilling indifference
voiced by journalist Richard Littlejohn:

We do not share in the responsibility for either their grubby little
existences or their murders. Society isn't to blame … in their

chosen field of 'work', death by strangulation is an occupational hazard. That doesn't make it justifiable homicide, but in the scheme of things the deaths of these five women is no great loss.... Frankly, I'm tired of the lame excuses about how they all fell victim to ruthless pimps who plied them with drugs. These women were on the streets because they wanted to be.[46]

Interviews with 138 women in Managua, Nicaragua, revealed that 44 per cent had been physically assaulted by a client.[47] A study of England and Scotland found that two-thirds of 240 prostitutes had experienced client violence.[48] Few report these incidents to police; in fact, in many countries, sex workers suffer violence from the police. A study in Botswana, Namibia and South Africa found 'extensive evidence of police abuse towards sex workers, including sexual violence and beatings.'[49] Women talk of having to develop a sixth sense to protect themselves, but with many in the English and Scottish sample dependent on drugs (63 per cent of the street-working women, but only 1 per cent of indoor workers, cited this as their main reason for prostitution), this 'sixth sense' is perhaps less functional.[50] Transsexual and transgender sex workers are in greater danger. In Suzanne Jenkins' study of 483 escorts, nearly half of transsexual women reported feeling physically threatened as a result of their work, as opposed to a quarter of the non-transsexual women and 19 per cent of the men.[51]

Alongside violence, sex workers often suffer other health risks. The world of commercial sex is marked by inequalities.[52] Often those with the best pay and conditions are native-born women with legal residency, working with others in a safe building where they can choose their clients, with access to condoms and health-care services. The worst conditions are experienced by immigrants, women forced into prostitution, and trafficked women who cannot speak the language and don't trust the authorities, whose earnings go mainly to their pimps or traffickers. In between those extremes women experience varying degrees of harm, sometimes including psychological distress, drug addiction, physical violence, difficulty in entering other employment and health risks (especially HIV/AIDS and hepatitis B and C).[53]

Even women working in superior conditions face risks absent from other avenues of work. Teela Sanders, an academic who advocates treating prostitution as a job rather than as exploitation, explains that it is a particularly hazardous occupation where client violence is an ever-present danger. Her book *Sex Work: A Risky Business* was based on interviews and participant observation in British massage parlours. She discusses the techniques women use to protect themselves, such as not answering the door to suspicious-looking men or large groups of young men.[54] Many prostituted women (trafficked or drug-addicted women) are less able to protect themselves from violence than Sanders's interviewees.

Emotional harm also constitutes a significant cost for many sex workers. On the basis of twenty years of interviews with prostituted women, Kathleen Barry explains that, to survive emotionally, women have to distance themselves from what they are doing, to disengage emotionally during the sex act, while simultaneously 'acting as if the experience is embodied', acting out the part of the happy and submissive sex worker that the client desires.[55]

It is important to recognise that there are a variety of reasons why women find themselves in prostitution. The deepening of global inequalities has increasingly made women in economically deprived or politically unstable regions turn – or be forced – into selling sex. Lack of educational qualifications, insecure family backgrounds (growing up in state care or having lost parents to AIDS, for instance), experiences of childhood sexual abuse, homelessness, drug addiction, famine, natural disasters, ethnic conflict and civil war are other factors.[56]

However, there are sex workers who claim not only to participate by free choice, but to enjoy it. Kari Kesler, self-identified 'third-wave lesbian sex radical feminist', admits that her choice of sex work doesn't mean it's a perfect industry to work in – but neither is any job:

> The question I wrestle with is whether agency within prostitution is by definition still a form of oppression for women.... I strongly feel that this agency is not mere delusion. Like heterosexuality in general, prostitution represents a 'hard bargain', a process of negotiation, like courtship rituals and marriage, for access to the female body between two socially and economically unequal parties. The ... patriarchal culture continues to produce this uneven playing field between men and women, but within that uneven field, women make affirmative and relatively liberatory choices.[57]

Advocates of sex work say that women choose it because it is a convenient and legitimate way to earn money. It's easy work to get, fits around other commitments (like study and childcare) and, if you operate independently, can provide more autonomy than working for a boss. In countries without a welfare state or other means of support, it can be a way out of poverty. Eva Rosen and Sudhir Venkatesh talked to sex workers in an inner-city area of Chicago, and concluded that sex work is 'a short-term solution that [in their term] "satisfices" the demands of persistent poverty and instability, and it provides a meaningful option in the quest for a job that provides autonomy and personal fulfillment'.[58] As writers like Belle de Jour reveal, it is possible for women at the top end to make quite large sums.[59] In contrast, at the bottom end of the market in the streets of France and Italy, prices have not changed in twenty years, and penetrative sex with a condom costs only twenty to thirty euros.[60]

Different socio-economic, political and national circumstances shape women's experiences of sex work and its relative desirability. Men don't 'need' to buy sex any more than women do – doing so is a cultural, not a biological, desire. There is evidence that demand can be reduced,[61] and in fact demand varies from country to country. In affluent post-industrial nations, only a minority of men (around 10–15 per cent) buy sex,[62] but in rapidly industrialising countries figures are far higher (in Thailand 80–87 per cent of men have paid for sex, with 10–40 per cent admitting to doing it in the past year[63]).

For prostitutes' clients, buying sex is part of their male gender role. The phenomenon of sex tourism (popular destinations are Eastern Europe, Thailand and the Dominican Republic) fuels and justifies male demand, since buying sex on holiday or a stag weekend is considered by many men as a leisure activity, perhaps akin to buying a beer. As researchers who interviewed men who buy sex in London found, buying sex reflects an underlying sense of male entitlement. For those men, paying for sex is framed as an acceptable part of being a man and justified as a consumer choice (it is, they explained, 'the world's oldest profession'[64]). The response from this man was, the researchers say, 'not uncommon':

> There's no questions asked, there's no crap, I could, go out with a girl, take her to a bar, spend a lot of money, but now I could just give her the £40 and you have a half hour with her, and you get anything you want! ... you know, straight in and there's no questions asked and that's basically it ... I've taken girls out, and ok, I take her for a meal, that cost me bloody £40 ... you don't get bugger all after that.[65]

Prostitution, for most women, is at best a choice in confined circumstances. If better alternatives (state welfare, support by charities and alternative employment) were available, many would not choose it. And for unwilling sex workers, prostitution *itself* is surely a form of violence.

Sex trafficking is an obvious example of forced prostitution. It involves recruiting by deception and then transporting women and children across national boundaries by force, then selling them for sex. Sometimes moved frequently within and across destination countries, women are controlled and made to have sex with (or endure rape by) many men for a pittance, since traffickers often demand that they work for years to 'repay' the cost of their transportation.

At the end of 2006, an estimated 1.2 million people worldwide were working as sex slaves, having been trafficked. Annually, an estimated 500,000 to 600,000 are trafficked for sexual exploitation across national borders, with more trafficked within their own countries.[66] Factors such as poverty, withdrawal of state welfare services (following the rapid transition from communism to capitalism in the former Soviet Union and Eastern Europe, for example) or an unhappy family life make women vulnerable to exploitation and willing to take a chance when answering a (bogus) advertisement for a 'dancer' or 'waitress' overseas.

Some argue that trafficking figures are exaggerated, and most so-called 'victims' are in fact enterprising women choosing to travel abroad to find work. Laura Agustín believes that the 'rescue industry', which often forcibly returns women to the country they desired to leave, harms women more than it helps them, serving only to curtail immigration.[67] Research by Nick Mai into one hundred UK-based migrant sex workers suggested that the majority were not trafficked, but rather entered sex work mainly for economic reasons, and knew that this was what they were coming to the UK to do.[68]

However, whatever the prevalence of sex trafficking is, victims undoubtedly suffer greatly. Within a sample of 287 girls and women trafficked from Nepal to India from 1997 to 2005 and later repatriated, 38 per cent tested positive for HIV, with 61 per cent of those trafficked below the age of 15 infected.[69] And of 207 women released from trafficking situations in Europe, over half showed symptoms of post-traumatic stress disorder and twelve or more physical health symptoms (such as fatigue, stomach pain or dizzy spells) within the first two weeks of their release (these figures declined to 6 per cent for both when they had received care for at least three months).[70]

Challenging violence: the feminist response

Sometimes it seems that day after day the news headlines report women being murdered or raped; indeed, the United Nations' Trust Fund to End Violence Against Women has described this as a global emergency. It's easy to listen to all of this and feel helpless, but the good news is that feminists are resisting.

Organising public awareness campaigns

It's midday on a normal Tuesday at Mitre Square in London. Whilst city workers eat their lunches in the sunshine, a group of strangers slowly approach a bench and flowerbed. Seemingly unconnected, each lays down a token – ribbons, candles, flowers, poems. After observing a minute's silence, they walk away, leaving an explanatory note behind them for the curious onlookers. This is a feminist flashmob organized by London's Female Art Collective to pay respect to women who have been victims of violence and demand that it stops. According to the press release,

> The action will be recorded and shown as part of a mix-media art piece which addresses issues to do with violence against

women. These include the lack of respect with which the victims
and these events are treated, the glamorization of violence by
the media, and the invisibility and the denial of the fear and the
taboo.[71]

As with many of the issues in this book, it's not just laws that
we need to change but attitudes. Feminists are trying to raise
awareness of violence against women among the general public
through actions like this, and then to change attitudes.

In 2003, a California-based collective called the South Asian
Sisters produced *Yoni Ki Baat* ('Vagina Monologues' in Hindi),
a play inspired by Eve Ensler's very successful *The Vagina
Monologues*. The play showcased a collection of submissions
from Desi women throughout the country, exploring South Asian
women's unique experiences of violence, sexuality and love for
their vaginas. It has been performed at several colleges and community spaces and grows in popularity each year.

In several countries, feminists have organised 'Hollaback'
projects, where harassed women snap photos of their harassers
and upload them on a website along with an account of what
happened. In the UK, Anti-Street Harassment documented
hundreds of women's experiences of street harassment. This
became a powerful testament of women's anger and frustration,
a twenty-first-century example of the 1970s' feminist concepts of
consciousness-raising and 'the personal is political'. The organizers also ran training sessions and workshops.

In India, the Blank Noise project aimed to challenge street
harassment, known there as 'eve teasing', through art projects
(such as showing the clothing women were wearing when they
were targeted, with the words 'I Never Ask For It'), awareness-
raising, and direct action. One project challenged women to walk
'unapologetically', refusing to do any of the things that women do
to avoid being a target. Organiser Jasmeen comments:

Our street actions over the last few years have been based on emphasizing small simple scenarios – which can be challenging even though they appear 'normal' and everyday. For instance – should it be hard to just 'stand' on the street as an 'idle' woman? Would you 'dare' try it?[72]

In the UK, a campaign called The Truth Isn't Sexy worked over three years to raise men's awareness of sex trafficking by distributing 200,000 beer mats and 10,000 posters in pubs, clubs and student bars nationwide. They gained media coverage of the issue and spoke at smaller-scale events.

Similar campaigns have been run to change attitudes about rape. In the UK Truth About Rape published and distributed postcards with the aim of countering widely held victim-blaming beliefs and inaccurate information about the conviction rate and the extent of false accusations.

Feminists whose priority is to support and improve conditions for sex workers have organised a variety of public awareness projects. These have included the New York-based magazine *$pread*, launched in 2004 to 'illuminate the sex industry', 'build community' and 'destigmatize sex work by providing a forum for the diverse voice of individuals working in the sex industry'.[73] Projects also include writings by sex workers and their allies[74] and collaborative websites such as 'Sex Work Awareness' and 'Sex Work 101'. A key priority has been destigmatising sex work. In Canada, sex-worker project Stella provides advice on how to respond to a sex worker's request for help:

- Be careful about overgeneralizations and avoid merging this woman with the stereotypes surrounding her.
- Adopt an open-minded attitude. Watch, listen and ask questions to understand her world of references and her experiences.
- Validate and focus on her needs and expectations: reassure her and consider her, above all, a person like any other.[75]

Fund-raising and lobbying for specialist services and specialist crime teams

Adequate provision and care for victims of violence are crucial; this includes funding for Rape Crisis Centres and helplines, which are frequently under threat. Specialist care is required for groups with particular needs, such as sex workers, some minority ethnic women, disabled women, lesbians and transgender people. UK examples include Imkaan, Southall Black Sisters and Broken Rainbow (for LGBT people).

A misapplication of equal opportunities legislation has resulted in some local councils requesting that services expand their remit to include *all* victims, not just specific sectors of the community, or lose funding. However, specialist services are vital. It would be unacceptable to expect male rape victims to use a service aimed at and staffed by women, just as it would be unacceptable to expect a South Asian woman threatened with honour violence, or a lesbian asylum-seeker abused by her partner, to use a generic service that may not be able to help with the complexities of her specific situation.

In some cases, feminists have taken it upon themselves to fill gaps in specialist services. The anti-capitalist group Feminist Fightback organised a 'Sex Worker Open University' event in London in 2009, providing workshops and training. In Guatemala, which in 2005 had the second-highest illiteracy rate in Latin America and an estimated 17,000 women in (legal) prostitution, sex workers formed a football team, which raised awareness about discrimination they suffer and funds to help them exit prostitution.[76]

The UK Network of Sex Work Projects (UKNSWP) has produced a *Good Practice* booklet on exiting the sex industry, which explains the issues and considerations involved in exit programmes.[77] In London, Trust and the Poppy Project specialise in helping vulnerable women escape prostitution; the latter provides specialist help for trafficking victims. Globally, the Global Alliance Against Trafficking in Women and the Coalition Against Trafficking of Women work to counter trafficking into sex work.

Finally, feminists are arguing for more specialist approaches by the justice system and police to handle crimes like rape – specialist rape prosecutors, for instance. For example, the Metropolitan Police's Project Sapphire has specially trained officers to deal with rape investigations. Nevertheless, a recent review of 677 allegations reported to the Metropolitan Police found only a 5.3 per cent conviction rate, indicating that there remains significant work to do.[78]

Organising for improved legislation and international cooperation

Each government needs an adequate legal framework for violence against women and a national plan against which progress will be measured, to ensure it is implemented effectively. The United Nations Division for the Advancement of Women held expert groups on good practice in legislation on violence against women (2008) and good practices in legislation to address harmful practices against women (2009). One recommendation from these groups was for thorough and accurate statistical data (such as records of rape conviction rates). 'There remains', they state, 'an urgent need to strengthen the knowledge base on all forms of violence against women to inform legal development.'[79] The European Policy Action Centre on Violence Against Women, a division of the European Women's Lobby, advocates using a common framework across countries to monitor progress in combating violence against women. In the UK, feminists will be keeping a close eye on the government's 2009 Strategy on Ending Violence Against Women and Girls to ensure delivery of its promises.

When it comes to prostitution, the feminist community is deeply divided on what the legal approach should be. One group of feminists, the advocates of regulation and legalisation, consider the selling and buying of sex to be neutral acts that men and women should be free to engage in, for a fair market price and in safe, non-coercive and de-stigmatised conditions. Where it is not free and fair, steps need to be taken to make it so, such as legalising it and providing safe zones for it to take place and contraceptive and other health-care services. They argue that the Swedish model advocated by abolitionists – in which men are prosecuted for buying sex and women are offered help in exiting the industry – forces prostitution underground, making it riskier for women. For example, Laura GW, 24, believes that

> The criminalisation of prostitution and other forms of sex work leaves women and men who work in this trade unprotected by law and stripped of their human rights. This leaves them susceptible to violence and sexual abuse, with nowhere to turn because in the eyes of society they are criminals ... decriminalisation of sex work would also make it easier for safer sex regulations to be put in place and adhered to, as well as allowing prostitutes to work for a set rate to prevent them being exploited. Although many sex workers are forced to work as prostitutes, there are those who choose sex work as a profession. If we remove the stigma associated with sex work through legislation that legitimizes it, it will encourage openness and thoughtful debate rather than treating it as taboo.

For another group, the abolitionists, prostitution is a fundamental part of women's oppression by men; while a minority of sex workers are independent and successful, prostitution is almost always exploitative for women, almost never the result of free choice. Legalising prostitution is not, they believe, the right solution, since wherever it has been legalised (e.g. in the Netherlands, Germany or Australia) prostitution has increased and the illegal sector has flourished, allowing the sufferings of the majority of sex workers (who work illegally) to continue. Furthermore, legalisation stimulates demand, making buying sex an acceptable part of what it is to be a man and encouraging traffickers to continue exploiting young women.[80] UK campaigns such as 'Demand Change!' achieved legal changes in 2009 to criminalise buying sex from a person who has been exploited. Abolitionists argue that if prostitution was curtailed, the money that customers pay sex workers and their pimps and controllers would be spent elsewhere, creating alternative employment for women who would otherwise have worked in the sex industry. Many of these feminists believe that buying sex can never be ethical. The Coalition Against Trafficking of Women argues for

> decriminalisation of women in prostitution; criminalisation of those who buy women and children, and pimps, procurers and traffickers; rejection of State policies and practices that channel women into conditions of sexual exploitation; and education and employment opportunities that enhance women's worth and status, thereby diminishing the necessity for the women to turn to prostitution.[81]

Organising prevention and education programmes

Researchers suggest tackling demand for commercial sex by exploring, in schools and media campaigns, some of the ambivalences expressed by male buyers, for example about the impact of buying sex on their long-term relationships. They also suggest, based on the case of one London borough, that markets might shrink if local newspapers, where most clients discover brothel locations, ceased accepting advertisements for commercial sex.[82]

White Ribbon Campaign, a worldwide campaign that began in 1991 in Canada, is a male-run group that encourages men and boys to wear a white ribbon symbolising their commitment to resisting and challenging violence against women.

In Ethiopia, girls' clubs have been set up to educate girls about the importance of education and the harmful effects of early marriage. Girls in trouble frequently report plans of an early marriage to friends or the head of the club or women's association. Also in Ethiopia, local organisations form 'early marriage cancellation committees' involving people from all sectors of society. When the committee is informed of an early marriage arrangement, they alert law enforcement or assist with legal representation.[83]

Conclusion

In this chapter we have seen how violence affects women. But, as the chapter has suggested, global poverty and economic inequality can put women at greater risk of violence. Poverty can contribute to war, putting women at risk of rape or death; poverty can restrict women's ability to escape domestic violence or leave prostitution. So, it's understandable that many feminists concentrate on wider economic issues, criticising capitalism, or calling for an expanded welfare safety net for women. As the next chapter investigates, equality at work and in the home is therefore a major focus of feminist organising.

Take action!

1. Support violence prevention campaigns such as White Ribbon; organise a speaker or session at your school, university or organisation. Ensure that the seminar addresses men as well as women.

2. Support your local Rape Crisis Centre, refuge or specialist service. Donate, fund-raise or volunteer.

3. Challenge messages you hear that imply that violence against sex workers is acceptable, inevitable or less important than other kinds of violence.

4. Give constructive feedback on government and police campaigns on violence. Respond to consultations, and keep a close watch on government strategies on violence.

5. Challenge myths about rape or prostitution: put up posters, write to newspapers, distribute postcards or start an Internet awareness campaign.

4

EQUALITY AT WORK AND HOME

FOR 1970s' feminists, equality in the workplace was fundamental. 'Equal pay now' was the first of the seven demands, with 'equal education and job opportunities' and 'financial and legal independence' following close after. The financial situation of women in comparison to men was a grave concern. It still is, as we'll explain.

Feminists still want equality and fairness for men and women at work. Financial independence is crucial for women. Depending on where in the world she lives, lacking an independent income can restrict a woman's access to health care, make it difficult to leave an abusive partner, or reduce the quality and length of her life. For many women, work is simply about survival.

But there is a flipside. For many of the feminists we surveyed who grew up in increasingly consumerist and work-obsessed Western societies, a good work/life balance is equally important. We do not want to be defined solely by our jobs, rewarding as they can be; our lives are more complex than that. In our updated demands, we are making this explicit. We don't want to be house-slaves, but neither do we want to be wage-slaves. We want to share work *and* home equally with men. Women want the joys and rewards of work as much as we want men to share the joys and rewards of childcare or home-making (as well as the burden and the chores!).

In this chapter we'll consider the role education plays in determining future employment. We consider 'work' in its widest context, including what people – predominantly women – do within the home, without pay. We argue that the domestic burden needs to be rebalanced, with men taking a greater share and state support given through gender-equal parental leave policies.

In regions like Western Europe, North America and Australasia, women have much to celebrate – and take for granted. Equal pay laws enable those treated unfairly to claim redress, girls are achieving unprecedented educational success, maternity leave policies give new mothers financial support, and men are somewhat more involved in caring and domestic work. But there are still significant issues to resolve.

Moreover, the successes of privileged countries exist alongside – and have exacerbated – the disadvantages suffered by countries outside the West. In the past few decades global economic divisions have increased, and political conflicts have brought some countries to their knees. Things are better than previously for rich women and worse for many poor ones.

Education

In affluent nations girls are outperforming boys and entering higher education in higher numbers. Some 81 per cent of European women aged 20 to 24 have at least an upper secondary school education, in comparison with 75 per cent of young men. A total of 59 per cent of university graduates are female.[1] Indeed,

TABLE 4.1   Gender-related development index,
selected countries (2006)

	Rank	Adult literacy rate (% aged 15 and over)		Gross enrolment rate in education (%)		Estimated earned income (PPP $)	
		F	M	F	M	F	M
Iceland	1	–	–	100.0	88.2	29,283	40,000
New Zealand	20	–	–	100.0	90.0	21,181	29,391
United Kingdom	21	–	–	92.8	85.9	26,863	38,596
Estonia	40	99.0	99.0	98.2	84.6	15,122	23,859
Belarus	60	98.8	99.0	92.3	86.8	7,722	12,028
Jordan	80	88.8	96.3	79.1	77.5	2,174	6,989
Uzbekistan	100	95.8	98.0	71.7	74.7	1,646	2,727
Mauritania	120	47.5	62.9	50.5	50.7	1,290	2,474
Zambia	140	59.8	76.3	60.7	66.0	897	1,650
Sierra Leone	157	25.7	49.0	37.6	51.7	396	872

Source: Adapted from United Nations Development Programme, *Human Development Indices 2008*, pp. 37–40, http://hdr.undp.org/en/media/HDI_2008_EN_Tables.pdf.

girls' success is judged so significant that educationalists and policymakers have shifted their focus to the 'boy crisis', bringing in measures to 'correct' girls' success.

However, young women's educational advantages are wiped out on entering paid employment, as Table 4.1 shows. What does it matter if a young woman has a first-class honours degree in English if she finds it harder to get a job than her lower-scoring male contemporary, and the job she ends up with commands a lower salary? Purcell and Elias surveyed 4,500 people who graduated in 1995, and found that as graduates got older, the gender gap increased: women's annual earnings were 10.5 per cent less than their male peers in their first main job, 15 per cent less in 1997/8 and 18.5 per cent less in 2002/3.[2]

If girls' better qualifications do not bring equal remuneration at work, what's going wrong?

The gendered curriculum

The answer lies partly in the subjects girls and boys study. Thanks to equality legislation in democratic nations, the compulsory curriculum has become more egalitarian. But when school students are given the chance to select what they study, gendered subject choices emerge. As Table 4.2 shows, whilst there is some crossover,[3] males predominate in science subjects; females in the arts. These gendered choices continue in higher education.[4]

But gendered subject selections are not always freely made choices. Physicist Rachael Hawkins recalls her experiences growing up in the 1990s:

> The careers teacher who advised me on my choice of work experience placement in Year 10 told me to put primary school assistant top of my list and research assistant at the local government research establishment last as 'lots of boys will apply for that'. I learned several things from this incident, that women are better suited to caring work, that I don't stand a chance in competition with males, ... and that obviously (by the tone of the man's voice) I am unsuited to a career as a scientist.... When I told people ... that I studied physics at university they asked me 'is that because you want to be a teacher?' ... I told my father when I was 11 that I wanted to be an astrophysicist, he laughed.[5]

This kind of socialisation reflects traditional views of women's place in society and perpetuates gender inequalities in pay, job

TABLE 4.2   Ten most popular A-levels by gender (in rank order), England 2006

MALES	FEMALES
Maths	English
General Studies	Psychology
English	General Studies
History	Biological Sciences
Biological Sciences	Art and Design
Physics	History
Business Studies	Maths
Chemistry	Sociology
Geography	Chemistry
Physical Education	Media/Film/Television Studies

Source: Adapted from Department for Education and Skills, *Gender and Education: The Evidence on Pupils in England,* DfES Publications, Nottingham, 2007, p. 36.

'choice' and working hours. In short, it sets young women up for disadvantage and compounds differences of class or ethnicity.[6] According to the Equality and Human Rights Commission, gender has more of an impact than social class on career aspirations of boys and girls.[7] And this starts early, as engineer Wisrutta Atthakor observes:

> If building and construction toys … and science toys like chemistry sets and microscopes are packaged to include the words 'for boys', in a way that is implied that girls 'shouldn't touch', then the toy companies are deliberately excluding half of the child population: girls. And if girls are only encouraged to, and are expected to only play with Barbie dolls, life-like baby dolls and kitchen sets, then what kind of messages are these kids being sent?[8]

Becky Francis's study confirms Atthakor's observations. Francis found that 'toys aimed at girls seem to lack the educational and skills development qualities found in many of the toys that target boys.' Toys for boys involved action, construction and machinery, while girls' toys were mainly dolls or catered for 'feminine' interests such as hairdressing, suggesting girls should be caring and creative. What's concerning is that play with the different toys developed skills and knowledge in these particular areas.[9] It's not the case that girls and boys 'naturally' have contrasting interests or aptitudes. Mark Brosnan's research concluded: 'It is wrong to think that they [the boys] are all more "scientific" than girls... In fact there is an overlapping range of interest in and aptitude for science in both groups.'[10] Similarly, research into mathematics in sixty-nine countries found that 'girls will perform at the same level as the boys when they are given the right educational tools and have visible female role models.'[11]

In schools, men's dominance in the academic hierarchy, teachers' stereotypical attitudes and peer pressure subtly connect femininity with interpersonal skills and caring roles, and masculinity with scientific, leadership roles. Girls are seen as bright and academic but are channelled into arts, humanities and languages, and away from science and computing.

From education to employment

There is no inevitable correlation between an arts degree and a lower-paid career. Nevertheless, it's clear that the professions women enter bring them lower financial rewards.

This is particularly the case for young people who take the vocational training route. The UK government introduced the apprenticeship scheme in 1993 for post-16s, and over 200,000 people embark on one each year.[12] Apprentices gain skills and experience in a workplace and study for a qualification at a local college. But there are near-rigid patterns of gender disparity in their take-up (girls select childcare and hairdressing, boys the more lucrative construction and engineering), and with male apprentices earning an average of £39 per week more than female apprentices in 2007, the gap gender gap in apprentices' wages was 21 per cent.[13]

Researchers investigated why young people rarely select apprenticeships that cross gender boundaries. Students and employers were open to non-traditional paths, they found, but they were obstructed by parents (who tended to be in gender-traditional roles and who students thought might not approve), peers (who might laugh at them) and schools (teachers and careers advisers who rarely challenged gender stereotypes or gender-traditional work experience placements).[14] Education and careers advisers had, it seemed, done almost nothing to promote non-traditional apprenticeships.

Differences in the kinds of apprenticeships men and women do should concern the government because UK skills shortages exist precisely in those areas where women are barely represented. Encouraging women into plumbing, construction and sciences would both improve gender equality and solve skills deficits.[15]

Gender and education in the global context

In 2000, the United Nations committed to achieving eight Millennium Development Goals by 2015. The second goal, 'Achieve universal primary education' will be especially good for girls, who are most likely to be poor and undereducated with limited reproductive and health knowledge or rights. With 2015 not far off, despite some progress and major initiatives like the United Nations Girls' Education Initiative (UNGEI), which partners with various agencies to narrow the gender gap and achieve free primary schooling for all, these have not yet been achieved.

Globally, educational institutions replicate gender inequalities in wider society. Yet, as Jyotsna Jha, adviser in the Education Section at the Commonwealth Secretariat in London, explains, schools 'have the potential of playing a transformative role in changing the prevalent notions and unequal relations.'[16]

Work

The issues that concern us about employment are wide-ranging, but can be boiled down to two key problems: global poverty and working conditions, and workplace inequality and discrimination.

Global poverty and working conditions

In our global society, we are more tightly connected than before with the rest of the world, politically, economically and culturally. In the last three decades of the twentieth century, industrial production began moving out of developed regions such as Europe, Australia and North America, and into so-called 'developing' countries. Affluent nations have become post-industrial, outsourcing industrial and agricultural production to poorer countries.

The 1980s saw divisions increase between rich and poor nations. Indebted nations accepted loans from wealthier nations via the World Bank and the International Monetary Fund, on condition that they facilitated export-oriented industrialisation. Free-market principles enabled richer countries to trade with poorer ones, and privatisation saw land, infrastructure and utilities removed from family, community or state ownership and allocated to transnational corporations that produce products such as clothing, toys and electronic goods. This brings trade and investment, but at considerable cost, especially to women.[17]

Certain countries (including China, India, Malaysia and Indonesia) have experienced rapid development due to industrialisation, with manufacturing plants set up in areas known as export processing zones (EPZs). In need of foreign investment, governments allow transnational corporations to set up EPZs on underused land. The corporations can find cheap labour and, crucially, are allowed exemption from national employment laws; they do not have to provide employees with the same level of rights as in the rest of the country.

Women are around 80 per cent of workers in these factories.[18] Mostly migrants from rural areas aged between 15 and 22, women in garment factories are favoured over men because their smaller fingers are believed to make them better sewers, and they are considered more subservient.[19] They take jobs to enable them to send money to their families, but their low pay (often 5–10 per cent of the US minimum wage) is barely enough to sustain themselves. They commonly work shifts of at least twelve hours, often with compulsory overtime, six days a week, without sick pay or pension benefits. Often they live in crowded dormitories. Their health suffers: lacking protective clothing and ventilation, working with harmful chemicals in high temperatures, pregnant women often miscarry or are forced to abort.

Factory work isn't the only area where exploited women predominate. In developing countries, women make up 67 per cent of the agricultural workforce. In sub-Saharan Africa women produce up to 80 per cent of food for household consumption and for sale.[20] The poor wages and marginalisation of agricultural workers, the commercialisation of agriculture, not to mention the devastating impact of climate change on crop production, all make this a feminist issue.

Globally, women are 70 per cent of the world's poor and the majority of the poorest of the poor.[21] This is reflected in the

UK, too, although the gap is smaller: 22 per cent of women have a persistently low income, compared to 14 per cent of men.[22] These stark global disparities under capitalism – indicated by the income figures in Table 4.1 – explain why many feminists are also involved in socialist or anti-capitalist politics. Feminism cannot be successful without considering fundamental economic inequalities throughout the world. As *F Word* reader Polly put it, 'I can't see the point in women being equal to men if men are not equal to each other.'[23]

Workplace inequality and discrimination

The pay gap between men and women is an enduring problem. Women's mean disposable weekly income (including earnings, benefits, savings and pensions) in the UK is less than 60 per cent of men's.[24] For earnings alone, the gap is still significant; the mean full-time hourly pay of men in 2009 was £16.07, compared to £13.43 for women. The pay gap is greater when we include part-time workers, who are predominantly female; when all workers' hourly earnings (including part-time and full-time) are compared, the pay gap is 20 per cent.[25]

The pay gap also varies by ethnicity, ability, sexuality, religion and age. Generally speaking, within every group women's pay is lower than men's. But there are sectors of the male population whose pay is lower than some women's: for example, Bangladeshi and Pakistani men's average pay is lower than black Caribbean or white women's. Jewish men earn the most of any gender and religious group and Jewish women's pay average is higher than both men and women's of all other faith groups.[26] The pay gap peaks in the 40 to 49 age group and is smallest among younger people.[27]

Why do women, on average, earn less than men? Two factors are women's under-representation in well-paid, senior positions (vertical segregation or the 'glass ceiling', so called because the top jobs are visible but somehow women are unable to reach them), and women's over-representation in lower-status jobs, including part-time work (horizontal segregation or the 'glass wall').

The glass ceiling

Women are only 9 per cent of directors of the UK's top companies, 7 per cent of top police officers, 23 per cent of civil service top management, and 9 per cent of editors of national newspapers.[28] In Europe in 2006, women constituted only 33 per cent of managers.[29] The jobs that attract the highest salaries are those where there are the fewest women.

But this isn't simply about women 'choosing' not to enter these positions; it's also about women in areas like engineering, construction, the police, car sales, fire-fighting and computer programming finding it harder to reach the top. By entering these 'men's jobs', women have much to gain in terms of reward, prestige and skill enhancement. But they face obstacles in reaching the top, for which gender is the only explanation. Historically, for more than two centuries, femininity has been associated not with paid work but with the wife and mother role. Even though women's lives have moved away from this stereotype, women are still treated as if they are out of place when working in jobs that have historically been done mostly by men.

Indeed, some men have perceived women's entry into the workforce as a threat to their status. Journalist Michael Buerk, whose controversial television documentary maintained that the world of work was being taken over by women, commented:

> Female employment has risen by a fifth since the early Seventies; male employment has fallen by the same amount.
>
> The result has been a decline in the social status of men, particularly in what used to be known as the working class (signi-

ficantly, a description now rarely used), as traditional blue-collar jobs disappear and men lose their role as sole financial provider.

This is a disaster for men...

Women now set the agenda, in the media and elsewhere...

Manliness is out. Androgyny is in.[30]

But women haven't come as far as Buerk asserts. Neither should they be blamed for economic changes (the decline of mining, shipbuilding or manufacturing) that were decisions taken largely by rich men. Women in male-dominated jobs often tell of the difficulty they face being taken seriously as professionals. Organisations assume the ideal worker is male – able to work away from their home when necessary, without homes or families impinging upon their work, with time to network and socialise during evenings and weekends.[31] Women often find that their face doesn't fit, that they have to work harder to be accepted, while also guarding against being criticised for becoming 'like a man' or undermined or sexualised for being 'too feminine'.

There have been steps forward: policies enabling flexible hours, some homeworking, parental leave, and legislation prohibiting sexual harassment have alleviated some of these problems. Nevertheless, to take the example of sexual harassment, prohibitive legislation and policies do not mean that sexual harassment stops, or that women feel able to report it without facing negative consequences. In Uggen and Blackstone's survey of 1,000 people, women reported experiencing 1.5 to 3 times more sexual harassment than men did.[32] Surveys across different countries indicate that around half of the working female population have experienced sexual harassment at work.[33]

Betty Eisenberg studied American tradeswomen's experiences of harassment. She found a high level of incidents of men sabotaging the women's work, causing accidents to happen which injured the women, making sexual comments and using pornographic material to intimidate them. Women were rarely protected by their unions, whose members also engaged in harassing behaviour, and when they tried to report it often nothing was done or the woman was encouraged not to make an issue of it. Yvonne, an apprentice painter, was harassed by her foreman:

> I was hanging some wallpaper and he came to me…. He goes, 'Hey, you want to see some pictures of my girlfriend?' And I said, 'No.' He said, 'Oh, come on, I'm training her to be an apprentice, too. Don't you want to see some pictures of how I train my apprentices?' I said, 'No, why don't you just leave me alone?' …
>
> All of a sudden he stuck a Polaroid picture in front of my face and he goes, 'Look.' And I looked. And he starts laughing.
>
> It was a picture of a young woman laying down with her legs open … and she had what they call in wallpapering a seam roller. She had the handle inside her vagina. And he starts, 'Yeah, that's how I train my apprentices.' …
>
> I was really upset. I went home that day and I called the apprenticeship school and I told the head of the apprenticeship school, 'I got a problem on the job. I'm being harassed and I just want you to know what's going on.' …
>
> But nothing ever happened. He had told me too, 'You know, Yvonne, I can report this but it might not be good for you.'
>
> I said, 'Well, there's only one thing I'm afraid of. I've heard that women that file lawsuits against their companies, they end up getting blackballed. I wouldn't want to have that mark against me.' He said, 'That's true, that could happen.'[34]

Men, especially younger and financially vulnerable men, also experience harassment, predominantly from male colleagues; this demonstrates that harassment is a way of asserting a dominant, macho masculinity, and occurs at some men's expense as well as women's.[35] Additionally, being in a racial or sexual minority compounds harassment, with lesbian women told 'you just need a good fuck'[36] and Asian women targeted with racist stereotypes of sexual docility.[37]

In the UK, the 2007 Gender Equality Duty requires public-sector organisations to consider the impact of their policies and activities on gender equality. This has enabled women and men to challenge discrimination when they encounter it. But this only applies to the public sector. In the private sector women still suffer from a great deal of discrimination. Women working in city firms have reported that meetings are regularly held in lap-dancing clubs, and visits to prostitutes are arranged for clients.[38]

The glass wall

Women's pay deficit also exists because women and men generally do different sorts of jobs. The majority of women work in female-dominated jobs, and these sectors have lower pay than sectors employing mostly men. Women tend to work in the public sector, in administrative positions, retail and personal service. British women's top five occupations in 2007 were: (1) sales assistants and retail cashiers, (2) teaching professionals, (3) health care and related personal services, (4) secretarial and related occupations and (5) childcare and related personal services.[39]

Why do jobs in female-dominated sectors attract lower pay? The chief answer lies in the gendered nature of 'skill'. Skills that are traditionally associated with women are undervalued and men's are overvalued in comparison. The jobs considered most skilled, especially those involving the honing of a single specialist skill through education and qualifications (such as barrister or doctor), attract the highest wages. Traditionally, administrative or communication skills were not prioritised, so did not attract high remuneration.

But differences in pay between occupations aren't fully explicable in terms of skill or training; a nurse (generally female) has probably had more training than a police officer (generally male),

FIGURE 4.1 All in employment: by sex and occupation, 2008 (UK)[40]

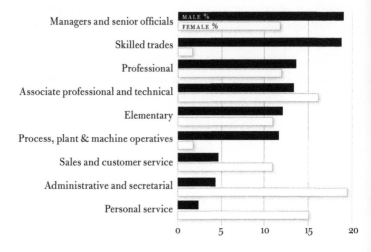

yet is paid less. As Phillips and Taylor argue, women's work is deemed inferior simply because women do it.[41]

Clerical work provides an example. The expansion and reduction in status of temporary clerical jobs over the last century or so paralleled clerical work's transformation from a predominantly male job to a predominantly female one.[42] Rogers argues that now women do it, clerical work is no longer considered skilled, but simply a reflection of women's 'natural' ability at typing, organisation and getting on well with people. And if it isn't skilled, then it merits little reward. Skill is, therefore, not an objective economic fact but an ideological category attached to certain kinds of work because of the sex and power of the workers who do it. Even though stay-at-home mothers exercise skills that would be considered high level in the workplace (teaching or managing the family's accounts), the housewife is not considered a skilled worker.[43] Moreover, women in so-called unskilled jobs may actually be highly skilled. Hochschild discusses the 'emotional labour' required of flight attendants who have to deal with upset or fearful passengers in a highly skilful way yet whose skill is not recognized.[44]

Part-time and 'flexible' work

Part-time work is another factor in the lower status of women's work. In Europe just below a third of employed women work part-time, compared with one in thirteen men.[45] Part-time work is less secure, and in some countries less protected through employment legislation and union activity. Women often engage in part-time work to help them balance paid work and caring responsibilities. But part-time work is no panacea, since it tends to be low-waged, insufficient to build up a good savings or pensions fund, and does not provide enough to spend on leisure.[46]

Flexible work is a growing form of part-time work. Flexible work comes in two forms. One, involving entitlement to work from home or electronically and advantageous leave policies, favours full-time workers on permanent contracts in high-status employment. But the other, probably more prevalent, is more precarious, involving a growing number of people employed on temporary, fixed-term, zero-hours contracts, in hourly paid, seasonal work or homeworking or by agencies providing staffing for lower-level administrative jobs; students, young people, migrants and mothers often do flexible work.

Temporary workers are popular because they're cheap: they enable organisations to break tasks into higher paid 'specialist' tasks done by full-timers, and the low-priced work, like photocopying and envelope-stuffing, given to temps. Thus what happens to temps is a form of deskilling. Even where temps are employed for specific skills such as computer programming, they rarely receive pay anywhere near that of a full-time employee. In these cases, temp work is not deskilled but devalued.

Even in professional careers, going part-time involves a loss of status and career prospects. Lawyers who go part-time are stigmatised and seen as uncommitted. One woman who had to remove herself from the partnership track upon having a child, explained:

> [A colleague] was told gratuitously in an elevator that she couldn't be serious about her work because she worked part-time. I am serious about my work. But not in the way he meant, which is totally single-minded with nothing else mattering.[47]

In order to avoid the stigma, many part-time lawyers avoided telling clients and colleagues they were part-time, even getting secretaries to transfer calls to their home numbers on their days off.

Sociologist Catherine Hakim argues that women with caring responsibilities choose lower-skilled, shorter-hours, part-time work because it fits with their family commitments. Many women make a rational choice to prioritise their family, and see employment as a supplementary activity to their 'real' work within the home. These women don't want higher level work, Hakim argues, and express high levels of satisfaction with their part-time jobs.[48] Indeed many women do place high value on parenting and caring roles.

But the argument that women choose low-paid work is a difficult one to make. It might be better to say that women settle for low-paid work in the absence of viable alternatives. Sally Walters interviewed fifty women from north-west England working part-time in retail. She found that women are more diverse than in Hakim's portrayal and less satisfied. They said they were 'making the best of a bad job', appreciating the opportunity to earn money, socialise with colleagues and fit their job around childcare. If given the choice, they would prefer a better job or the opportunity to retrain:

> At the moment I'm quite happy with the job, because it fits in round me. You know, I'm not really putting myself out for the job, the job's doing it for me ... I suppose really if the jobs were better, and I could fit the hours round the children, I would have probably gone somewhere else. I would never have dreamed of going to a shop.[49]

As has probably become obvious by now, one of the key issues affecting women at work is home and family responsibilities. In fact, the two are inextricably linked.

The home

During the last feminist wave, one of the problems pinpointed was women's unpaid labour. Feminists believed the housewife role many women occupied was oppressive. Not only were working women exploited within the market by businesses that paid them poorly in order to reap profits, but women at home were exploited as labourers by their spouses. Women worked long hours, without payment, for husbands who provided for their financial upkeep, gave them children, but extracted from them domestic work, sex, emotional support and childcare. Being a wife was rather like prostitution, some even concluded; in both, women serviced men for economic support. Their economic vulnerability made women vulnerable to domestic violence, since without independent financial means it was difficult for them to leave abusive partners.[50] Also, being a housewife was isolating and not intellectually stimulating. Observing her college friends led Betty Friedan to call housewives' unhappiness 'the problem that has no name';[51] the housewife's oppression thus began the second wave of feminist activism.

These were very negative analyses. They ignored the joy that many women experience nurturing children and caring for a home. And they reflected the woes of privileged women potentially able to find pleasurable employment, not those of working-class women who had to take unrewarding jobs. But it was an analysis that – though stark and pessimistic – reflected many women's circumstances. Indeed, some women's liberation groups sprang from mother and toddler groups.

Today a lot has changed: a sharp rise in women's paid employment (due partly to property prices necessitating two incomes) means that only a minority of women are housewives, even if they are mothers. In the United States, for instance, professional women born during the twentieth century took less and less time out of work. Today, fewer than 8 per cent of women born since the mid 1950s take a year or more out of paid work whilst in their prime childbearing years.[52]

Who's doing the housework?

As women have taken on paid work, has their unpaid domestic contribution correspondingly reduced? The short answer is no; research has shown the burden for domestic work is still shouldered mainly by women, even if they work similar hours to their male partners. For instance, in 2003 American men did, on average, 88 minutes of unpaid work per day whilst women did 176 minutes. Women are doing nearly double the amount of unpaid work as men, while men are undertaking two and a quarter hours more paid work than women.[53] Housework is most likely to be shared in post-industrial democratic nations, households with egalitarian attitudes and where women work full-time and earn a similar salary to their partners.[54] Elsewhere, traditional gender ideology creates extreme pressures for women, who work a 'second shift'[55] and are employed in low-paid work that fits around their housework.

Some researchers go further, asserting not only that women do more unpaid work, but that women do more work than men full stop. Indeed, surveys that track people's time indicate this is happening in some countries. One study found that on an average day in economically deprived countries women do one to two hours more work than men.[56] For example, women and girls in developing countries are largely responsible for carrying water, on average walking 6 kilometres a day, which reduces the time available for education or other activities. Data are not available for every country, but for the data we have the Netherlands is the only country where men do more work in total than women.[57]

In affluent households where women now do less housework, men aren't necessarily picking up the dirty socks; the solution to women's reduced domestic availability has instead been a (low-paid) cleaner or nanny, who is almost always female. What's more, women working in others' homes as domestic workers are often migrants and women of colour, reproducing a global, gendered and racialised division of labour.

For the first time in history, women are migrating in larger numbers than men. More than half the world's estimated 120 million migrants each year are women. This 'feminisation of migration' has only recently been noticed, probably because the work female migrants do is often in the private sphere, invisible.[58]

Rhacel Parreñas provides a (perhaps typical) case study of one woman she encountered in her research on female migrants from the Philippines. With 5.5 million Filipinos working in 193 overseas countries in 2002, the Philippines is a country with particularly high female migration; its government has encouraged it as a key source of national income and set up support and facilitation organisations for migrating women.[59] Hochschild explains:

> Vicky Diaz (a pseudonym) is a 34-year-old mother-of-five. A college-educated former schoolteacher and travel agent in the Philippines, she migrated to the United States to work as a housekeeper and as nanny to the two-year-old son of a wealthy family in Beverly Hills, Los Angeles. She explained …:
>
>> Even until now my children are trying to convince me to go home. The children were not angry when I left because they were still very young when I left them. My husband could not get angry either because he knew that was the only way I could seriously help him raise our children, so that our children could be sent to school. I send them money every month …
>
> The Beverly Hills family pays Vicky $400 a week and Vicky, in turn, pays her own family's live-in domestic worker back in the Philippines $40 per week. But living in this 'global care chain' is not easy on Vicky and her family. As she told Parreñas:
>
>> Even though it's paid well, you are sinking in the amount of your work. Even while you are ironing the clothes, they can still call you to the kitchen to wash the plates. It was also very depressing.[60]

Vicky is caught up in a 'global care chain', so-called by Hochschild because it involves a series of links between people based on caring work, paid or unpaid. Most global care chains consist only or mainly of women, beginning in poor countries and ending in rich ones. A typical care chain involves: (1) an older daughter from a poor family cares for her siblings, while (2) her mother works as a nanny caring for the children of a migrating nanny, who (3) cares for the child of a family in a rich country. Those cared for are mostly children, but sometimes elderly people. Although their mothers' jobs pay for their schooling, the impact on migrant women's children at home is considerable. As Ellen

Seneriches, whose mother moved to New York as a domestic worker when Ellen was 10, explained to Parreñas:

> Especially after my mother left, I became more motivated to study harder. I did because my mother was sacrificing a lot and I had to compensate for how hard it is to be away from your children and then crying a lot at night, not knowing what we are doing. She would tell us in voice tapes. She would send us voice tapes every month, twice a month, and we would hear her cry in these tapes.[61]

As Hochschild puts it, 'love is the new gold'. By encouraging women to migrate to do care work, rich countries extract care, even love, away from poor countries. Looking beyond care work to the global expansion of migration for sex work, what's occurring is the 'global transfer of the services associated with a wife's traditional role – child care, homemaking, and sex – from poor countries to rich ones.'[62]

Today in post-industrial countries, it's the birth of children which produces the most significant gender inequalities at work and home. Women's employment rates drop when they have children, the reverse of what happens for men. Maternity leave helps women keep their jobs, but if they take longer out of the labour force, it can be difficult to later return to an equivalent-level job. In part, this originates in traditional gender ideals, as Ginn and Sandall explain:

> Because of gender ideology which allocates family caring work primarily to women, employed women with dependent children are under more pressure than similar men to work reduced hours and in relatively undemanding jobs which may be beneath their capabilities.[63]

In many countries, maternity- and/or paternity-leave policies are built around the assumption that the mother cares for the child, rather than offering the parents the option of sharing the

TABLE 4.3   Employment rates (%) for men and women aged 20–49 in Europe (2006)

	MEN	WOMEN
With children under 12	91.4	62.4
Without children under 12	80.8	76.1

Source: Commission of the European Communities, *Equality Between Women and Men – 2008,* Brussels, 2008, pp. 19–20.

task. These not only embed gender inequalities for the months when the mother is away from paid work, but also set up inequalities that persist for future years. To add insult to injury, no matter what compromise the parents make, or whether or not the mother works, the mother is made to feel guilty and told (by tabloid newspapers and other people) that she is failing her children or herself, and often both. Even women who never want children are affected by sexist judgements such as this one, uttered by entrepreneur Alan Sugar:

> If they [women] are applying for a position which is very important, then I should imagine that some employers might think 'this is a bit risky'. They would like to ask the question 'Are you planning to get married and to have any children?' That's the bottom line, you're not allowed to ask so it's easy – just don't employ them.[64]

As Gatrell comments, 'In many workplace situations women are regarded primarily as potential mothers ... and secondarily as productive individuals, even if they have achieved "success" in a professional or economic context.'[65]

Achieving equality: the feminist response

Feminists are working to offer people more genuine choices, stop discrimination at work and make life fairer at home.

Expanding women's career choices

The UK branch of non-profit organisation Robogals are 'a bunch of Imperial College students who are teaching schoolgirls LEGO Robotics and getting them excited about Science, Engineering & Technology!' With branches in Australia and London, they organise fun activities like attempting to break the world record for robot dancing.[66] At a more advanced level, MentorSET is a Women's Engineering Society project providing mentoring and support to women in science, technology, engineering and mathematics. Projects like these expand girls' and women's career options by supporting them in male-dominated areas; they are classic examples of practical feminist activism and can have huge impacts on individuals' lives.

Sometimes it is policy that needs to be amended. Delegates at a seminar run by Oxfam and the Institute of Education in London made the following suggestions for global improvements to developing educational curricula in gender equitable ways:

- Ensure adequate resources are allocated to involve learners, teachers, parents, NGOs, community-based organisations and employers in the process of curriculum review and development as a matter of course and make sure the processes are gender equitable with regard to who can attend and speak at meetings or write submissions.
- Work within teacher education programmes to develop an understanding of the dynamics of gender equality in learning and teaching and in the hidden curriculum. Avoid a 'one off'

session on 'gender'. But if this is the only way to include a focus on gender such an approach is better than nothing.

- Review learning materials to consider what particular sections of text and pictures mean to learners from particular contexts and how these might develop understanding of gender equality.[67]

The Female Stipend Programme in Bangladesh, a country with the second highest rate of child marriage, illustrates the difference improving educational access makes to girls. Stipends (around US$1 a month) have been paid since 1994 to girls and their secondary schools in rural areas, conditional on their attending and achieving at certain levels. In 1970 only about 18 per cent of school students were girls; by 2000 numbers had equalized. One mother explains:

> It's changing social status in the family. She's going to get a better job and because of that a better life, and better living conditions will follow. In the past it was only boys, but now it's also girls, and girls are a huge proportion of the population and girls and boys add up, and that's going to develop economic and social status much more. Girls are already much more free because of this programme and they have new aspirations and hopes and they can probably discern a brighter future.[68]

Worldwide, the challenge to improve gender equality in education is not just about equal access to schooling, but about creating educational institutions that promote gender equality in wider society, educating girls to expect and demand their human rights.[69]

Challenging global poverty and working conditions

Vandana Shiva is an international expert and activist in the fight to alleviate female poverty in India. Responsible for setting up Navdanya (a network promoting biodiversity and sustainable agriculture) and its women's division Diverse Women for Diversity in the mid-1990s, Shiva is an ecofeminist pioneer. Women are going hungry because agricultural land has been given over to corporations for export to affluent countries. Food prices are rising out of the reach of ordinary people and seed 'has moved from women's hands to the hands of giant corporations', where it is genetically modified (bringing health risks) and scores of varieties destroyed. Diverse Women's national arm, the National Alliance for Women's Food Rights, is calling on the government for policy intervention to protect access to food; locally, Mahila Anna Swaraj (Food Sovereignty in Women's Hands) projects teach women skills in biodiversity conservation.[70]

In EPZ factories, some union action occurs, and small victories are being won; for instance, after a year-long battle supported by the Clean Clothes Campaign, a Turkish leather factory agreed to reinstate workers sacked for union organising.[71] But female factory workers are tired and overworked, so it's not easy to find time for it; indeed, they are attractive to employers precisely because they are less likely to be in a union.

Fighting for pay equality and challenging discrimination at work

In the UK, the Fawcett Society has petitioned the government to extend the right to work flexibly to all, end the opt-out of the EU Working Time Directive and make pay audits compulsory. In addition, Fawcett says that businesses should pay all employees a living wage, stop funding the sex industry, and challenge working cultures that discriminate against and stereotype women.[72] The Society encourages employers to sign up to a charter setting out their commitment to making workplaces fairer.

On an individual level, women who challenge discrimination at work make important strides for other women – but often at great personal cost. Lubna, 43, pursued a gender discrimination grievance case. She knows several other women who also did:

> We all felt forced to settle in the end for a variety of reasons – including personal details such as a history of domestic violence being raised in the grievance which would have been made public had the case gone on to Tribunal hearing. The result has been unemployment for us all. Stand up for your rights and see your career destroyed. I wonder how many women are in this position?

Valuing parenting and promoting equality in the home

Oliver T, 31, believes that 'equality in the home is one of the most direct feminist issues that affects men as much as women.' He argues:

> The issues surrounding parental leave especially have knock-on effects in terms of the gender pay gap, stress levels, the ways in which boys and young men come to see their role in life in gendered terms, and the ways in which different skills are valued differently (e.g. caring roles are seen as less important, and de-valued as well as being 'women's work'). While obviously it's not the only factor, inequality of parental leave is a strong economic means by which all these patriarchal constraints on men as well as women are upheld. Probably the best way to address these issues is through legislation creating generous paid leave time for both parents.

Feminists in the 1970s demanded free 24-hour nurseries. We still support the demand for better, more affordable childcare. However, reliance on nurseries may reduce parents' time with their children, and combined with the use of migrant women as replacement carers can have unwelcome consequences. Where care is marketised, as in the USA, the demand for care firms' profit drives down wages for the (almost always female) care providers. Childcare provision should go hand in hand with more equal parental leave policies and working time regulation, as in

Scandinavia, France and Belgium, so that parents can choose to spend time with their children as they grow, and enjoy their parenting role.

These countries operate a 'dual-earner/ dual-caregiver' model, in which gender equality is inbuilt. In this model, both parents are enabled to take equal responsibility for work and care for dependants, should they wish to. *Family leave* policies give both parents the right to equal and non-transferable amounts of paid parental leave (six months each, say) after a child is born or adopted, as well as a small amount of paid leave for family emergencies. *Working time regulation* limits the number of hours individuals can spend in paid work (for example, to 35–39 hours per week) and enforce a certain number of annual holiday days (for example, four weeks), making workers spend more time at home; this especially benefits men. Finally, *early childhood education and care* is financed publicly (perhaps with a means-tested element), available in different forms (from family childminders to large nurseries) for the duration of people's working hours, staffed by trained and regulated professionals who are paid at higher levels than in many countries. Policies must be able to accommodate the needs of lone parents (nine out of ten are female), LGBT parents, people who care for adults as well as children, and families which don't match the traditional two-parent model.

The move to a model like this needs cooperation from individuals and workplaces as well as the state – men need to be willing to drop some hours of paid work to take up care for their families, and workplaces need to adapt to flexible working hours. But, nevertheless, given that it partially exists in several countries, it isn't a pie-in-the-sky idea but, as Gornick and Meyers explain, 'has the qualities of a Real Utopia…, because it is possible to imagine the social, institutional, and structural transformations through which it could be realized.'[73] To give an example, in

2005 Spain enacted a law obligating married couples to share household tasks and caring responsibilities (if the contract isn't followed, judges can take this into consideration when deciding on the terms of divorces).

But, as with many other issues, the key is changing attitudes as well as policies and laws. In particular, increased value must be given to men's role in parenting. Isaac D. Balbus declared that shared parenting 'holds the key to the liberation of the relations between the sexes'.[74] More recently, writer Amy Richards has argued,

> For parenting responsibilities to be shouldered and experienced equally by both men and women, fatherhood has to matter as much as motherhood. We must assume that for men, too, it's a given that multiple things – work *and* family – are elements crucial to one's life.
>
> Men being more nurturing fathers won't exclusively benefit mothers. They can become more complete human beings. Men can tap into a more nurturing role that might have otherwise been suppressed.[75]

Feminism contends that breadwinning is no longer the sole reason for men's existence. Feminist-minded men are working towards broadening men's identities and experiences. At the annual Feminism in London conference, men provide childcare, enabling mothers to attend the workshops. Feminist dads have been welcomed onto feminist parenting forums such as Mothers for Women's Lib, or have set up their own blogs (like Feminist Dad). Keen to stress that anti-feminist groups like Fathers 4 Justice (who, among other things, have campaigned against 'Lesbo Dads') do not represent them, feminist fathers are working for a more equal future, with mothers rather than against them. Writer Hugo Schwyzer explains:

Here's what I can say about being a feminist father at this point: men can parent small infants very well, thank you, if they're willing to overcome the programming that says women 'mother' while men 'babysit'. Men can feel an intense bond with a baby and a fierce sense of protectiveness; men can change diapers and wipe up endless amounts of spit-up. Men can find deep reservoirs of patience and endurance inside themselves, reservoirs that they hadn't known existed.... Above all, those of us who are partnered with the mothers of our children can make clear in words and actions that raising babies is not just a woman's responsibility. Testosterone is no barrier to tenderness.[76]

Conclusion

When it comes to work, home and education there has been some positive progress in Western countries. But women have not 'made it' in achieving equality at home and work, and lag behind in pay and job opportunities. Both genders lack the ability to balance work and home in a way that would bring maximum benefit for them and any children they might have. What's more, a growing global division of labour is placing burdens on women that are – literally – life-threatening. Feminist activists around the world are taking action. Nevertheless, as we'll see in the next chapter, women's marginalisation in politics is hampering their efforts.

Take action!

1. If you have a job, join a union and/or get involved in its work on gender.
2. Do something to make children and young people's experiences more equitable – sponsor a child, become a school governor or volunteer to mentor a young person.
3. If you experience or witness sexism at work, challenge it.
4. Join a feminist organisation which lobbies your government about equality at work and home.
5. Encourage men to expand their options beyond 'breadwinner', as fathers or home-makers, and take equal responsibility for housework.

5

POLITICS AND RELIGION TRANSFORMED

POLITICS AND RELIGION both have a major impact on our lives, for good or bad. Neither political nor religious institutions have, on the whole, had a particularly positive impact on gender equality. Feminists want to transform this situation. Some feminists want transformation through equal participation in existing institutions; others want to change the very nature of politics and religion. Some want to challenge their influence on our lives; and others focus on how politics and religion can contribute to transforming gender relations positively. We'll see in this chapter how feminists are fighting for change.

Politics

The long battle for suffrage has been one of feminism's major successes. It has run alongside the fight for suffrage for working-class men and for the prising of political power from the hands of the landed aristocracy. Gaining the vote (and access to education and paid work) enabled women to move from a dependent position, in which they were but chattels passing from father to husband, to independent citizens who could participate in society. Women today have figures like Mary Wollstonecraft, John Stuart Mill, Sojourner Truth, and the suffragists and suffragettes to thank for this. Rather than fighting for women's *right* to enter politics, today's feminist struggles are about challenging the (often invisible or unacknowledged) barriers that make equal participation difficult to attain, as well as transforming the political system itself. Politics, as a female minority ethnic interviewee pointed out in a recent government equality office report, is 'not about wanting personal achievement or personal power, it's about wanting to have access to resources, to make a difference to other people's lives.... It's not about power for the sake of power.'[1]

Women are half of the population, but worldwide form on average only around 18 per cent of members of parliaments.[2] Other factors such as race and class further disadvantage some people. Ethnic minority women make up about 5.2 per cent of the UK population, but there are only two ethnic minority women MPs; out of approximately 20,000 local councillors in England fewer than 1 per cent are ethnic minority women.[3]

Why should we care about women's involvement in politics? Obviously, voting for someone purely based on their sex isn't what we're advocating. But equal representation should be a fundamental aspect of democracy, a basic human right. The International Institute for Democracy and Electoral Assistance (IDEA) has argued:

> women comprise half the world's population. Their perspective on all issues – and thus their active and equitable involvement in politics – are an integral aspect of any process of civic engagement. And, since politics is ultimately about ruling people's lives, it is not possible to believe that it can be done without representative and just inclusion of those who are affected.[4]

This point of view is supported by over 180 governments, who in Beijing in 1995 agreed that 'Achieving the goal of equal participation of women and men in decision-making will provide a balance that ... is needed ... to strengthen democracy and promote its proper functioning.'[5]

As we have outlined throughout this book, there are some issues which predominantly affect women or affect women in different ways from men; without women in political power, these issues are less likely to be addressed. Take climate change. Due to their relative poverty, their role in food production, and restricted ability to travel in some societies, women will bear a disproportionate burden of the consequences of climate change (in floods in Bangladesh, for example, the death rate for women was five times that of men[6]). US feminist magazine *Ms* estimated that the money that President Bush spent on *one day* of the Iraq War could buy health care for 423,529 US children.[7] In the UK, campaigners challenged the London mayor's decision to spend £600,000 on a new logo for the city, whilst simultaneously failing to deliver his election manifesto promise to fund Rape Crisis Centres properly.[8]

So, whilst men and women are concerned about the same basic issues, women tend to prioritise them differently. Clark, Mortimore and Rake explain:

> There have been historically significant and consistent differences between men and women in their answers to questions that ask about the most important issues facing the country or the issues which will most influence their votes. Women are more likely than men to choose 'caring' issues ... notably health care... and education.[9]

Whether you believe that the sex of the person representing you in Parliament is irrelevant or not, evidence shows that unless a large number of women gain access to political power, issues that matter to women are not prioritised, and are considered – ridiculously – 'minority' issues. There is evidence to suggest that the more women there are in government, the more likely it is that women's priorities are addressed.[10] Some argue that having a more representative government would improve things for everyone. Commenting on reports about the positive impact of gender equality on the private sector, Lee Chalmers (director of the Downing Street Project) pondered: 'If having more women on company boards makes them more effective, what would happen to the country if the same were true of the government?'[11]

Finally, most people *want* more women in government. A 2002 Ipsos MORI poll found that 70 per cent of respondents believed there are too few women at Westminster.[12]

What should we be aiming for, and how are we doing?

First, we have to be aware that participation in the political process is not just about members of Parliament but also about access to voting itself. Even in countries which in principle have universal suffrage, vigilance is still necessary to ensure that certain groups of voters are not discriminated against. The 2000 election in the USA demonstrated this: evidence was found of voters in poor, predominantly black districts being prevented from casting their vote. Marleine Bastien, campaigner for the rights of Haitians living in Miami, found that Creole-speaking volunteers were prevented from providing language assistance to Haitian American voters, and legally required ballots in Creole were not provided.[13] As women form two-thirds of the world's illiterate, many are excluded from accessing election material and unable to read the voting paper.

The Convention on the Elimination of All Forms of Discrimination Against Women was ratified by the majority of UN member states. The committee that monitors its implementation

TABLE 5.1 Women in national parliaments, selected countries

Rank	Country	Women in lower or single house (%)
1	Rwanda	56.3
20	Belarus	31.8
40	Lesotho	25.0
60	El Salvador	19.0
80	Greece	14.7
100	India	10.7
120	Montenegro	6.2
136	Oman	0.0

Source: Inter-Parliamentary Union, www.ipu.org/wmn-e/classif.htm (accessed 27 October 2009).

recommends that women should form at least 30 per cent of members of political institutions – a modest goal when women are at least half of the world's population. How countries decide to achieve that goal is up to them.

The Inter-Parliamentary Union monitors the progress of various nations, creating a league table showing how well countries are doing. Whilst the rankings change from year to year, Table 5.1 is a good reflection of the overall situation.

The UK's position varies from year to year, but at the time of writing, with 19.5 per cent women MPs, it is ranked 58th out of 187,[14] languishing behind countries such as Tanzania, Argentina, Spain, Belarus, Cuba, Pakistan and Switzerland (which, incidentally, only gave women full suffrage in 1971). The United States is in joint 70th position at the time of writing, with only

16.8 per cent. Twenty-four countries have reached the 30 per cent benchmark.

Barriers to participation

So what is hampering women's participation? The factors vary and depend on each country and its political system. There are some commonalities worth highlighting.

Poverty, illiteracy and lack of education

In some areas of the world, women are less educated than men, lack access to finances to start their campaign, and, as discussed in the previous chapter, are more likely to live in poverty. Razia Faiz, a former MP from Bangladesh, explains:

> The two most overwhelming obstacles for women in entering parliament are lack of constituents and lack of financial resources. Women move from their father's home to their husband's home... They have no base from which to develop contacts with the people or to build knowledge and experience about the issues. Furthermore, they have no money of their own; the money belongs to their fathers, their husbands or their in-laws. Given the rising cost of running an effective campaign, this poses another serious hurdle for women in the developing world.[15]

Socialisation and stereotyping

One argument marshalled to account for the reduced number of female politicians is that women aren't interested in being in politics. Often, women's assumed 'biological' suitability to domestic life, rather than the cut and thrust of politics, is invoked. As we can see from the league tables, there are countries where women are well represented in politics, so we can discount that theory; women are not innately uninterested in the public realm.

But socialisation does, subtly or overtly, discourage women from contemplating a political career. As we discussed in Chapter 4,

POLITICS AND RELIGION TRANSFORMED 143

the careers girls are encouraged to go into at school and by parents and peers are still gendered. Class and ethnic background also have a major impact on this; how willing would a careers adviser or local political party be to support a working-class, ethnic minority woman in entering politics, compared to a middle-class, white male? Men come forward for selection at about 2.5 times the rate of women in the UK.[16] The middle-class white male remains what Nirmal Puwar calls the 'somatic norm' within politics, so people whose bodies look different face an uphill battle to be seen as legitimate occupants of political positions.[17]

> 'It is very difficult for a woman to make up her mind to enter politics. Once she [does], then she has to prepare her husband, and her children, and her family. Once she has overcome all these obstacles and applies ..., then the male aspirants against whom she is applying make up all sorts of stories about her. And after all this, when her name goes to the party bosses, they do not select her name because they fear losing that seat.'
> SUSHMA SWARAJ, MP, India[18]

Discrimination when women try to get into politics

Another problem that has been identified is political parties not encouraging their female members. Parties act as 'gatekeepers', deciding who the public will be able to vote on. Women have generally not been selected by local parties, preventing them from putting themselves forward to the public vote. The Fawcett Society has uncovered stories of female candidates being asked sexist questions in the interview process:

You are told things like 'your children are better off with you at home' ... 'you are the best candidate but we are not ready for a woman'.

They are absolutely adamant they will not consider a woman ... it was said to me ... 'we do enjoy watching you speak, we always imagine what your knickers are like'. It is that basic. We picture you in your underwear when you are speaking. That is what you are dealing with.[19]

Local parties tend to put forward candidates who resemble previous MPs. Even where there is a mixed list of women and men available, local parties more frequently select men.

Discrimination after women enter politics

Women in politics are subjected to sexist comments and abuse. Take this journalist's comments on British cabinet minister Harriet Harman:

> So – Harriet Harman, then. Would you? I mean after a few beers obviously, not while you were sober. The alcohol is sloshing around inside your brain, you've enjoyed a post-pub doner kebab together and maybe some grilled halloumi (a woman's right to cheese) and she suggests, as you stand inside the frowsy minicab office: fancy going south, big boy? … I think you wouldn't … I think you'd do the same with most of the babes who were once, or are now, on the government front bench … what other reason could there be for the presence in high office of Jacqui and Harriet, other than some form of gender discrimination – i.e. for their looks – or for discrimination of the better, 'positive' kind, i.e. they are the only women around.[20]

Powerful women become hate figures – as do many powerful men – but in a particularly misogynist way. A female politician fails because she is a woman and shouldn't be in politics anyway. Female politicians are heavily sexualised in satirical media; a crass cartoon of cabinet minister Jacqui Smith after her husband was discovered to have claimed for pornography on expenses showed *her* naked. Another time, Smith was ridiculed for (gasp!) having *breasts*! And on the Conservative benches, the media's focus on Theresa May was generally not her policies but her high heels. During Hillary Clinton's campaign for the

Democratic nomination for the presidency, she was described as a 'stereotypical bitch',[21] a 'mad bitch',[22] a doll was made of her that cracked nuts between its thighs, and other instances too horrible to list. Sarah Palin, Republican vice-presidential candidate, was portrayed in highly sexualised ways; images were circulated of her dressed as Britney Spears, a sex doll, a schoolgirl, and crude mock-up images were made of her in sexual positions. As bloggers at *Feministing* said:

> The real sexism against Palin … has been the flip-side of the sexism against Hillary Clinton. A sadly perfect illustration of the Catch-22 women face. You're either a scary, ugly, old, mannish harpy. Or a ditzy, perky, fuckable bimbo.[23]

Ethnic minority women are subject to racialised sexist stereotypes: Condoleezza Rice was often depicted as a 'mammy' figure, while an interviewee in a Fawcett Society report revealed: 'I've suffered racism here in Parliament. I have been asked what I was doing in the Members' lift because somebody assumed I was a cleaner.'[24]

It doesn't have to be this way. In contrast, let's examine the response to the election in Iceland of the world's first openly lesbian prime minister, Johanna Sigurdardottir, in 2009:

> I don't think her sexual orientation matters. Our voters are pretty liberal, they don't care about any of that. (SKULI HELGESON, general secretary, Social Democratic Alliance)[25]

Unwelcoming national political structures

As many have identified, the UK's House of Commons is not very welcoming to women. Female MPs have reported receiving sexual taunts or gestures intended to intimidate and humiliate them when rising to speak in the House. The confrontational 'alpha male' culture that pervades national politics, the booing and the jeering, does not sit easily with women who have rarely been schooled in this form of so-called 'debate'.[26]

It's no coincidence that women who have progressed far in UK politics have been described as having 'masculine' characteristics (Margaret Thatcher is the obvious example). This should not be necessary. Anna Tibajuka, a professor from Tanzania, explains: 'Women have tried to enter politics trying to look like men. This will not work. We have to bring our differences, our emotions, our way of seeing things, even our tears to the process.'[27] Many women feel that by entering politics they would be forced to 'play act' at being tough and macho. Moreover, this excludes men who are also put off by the macho style. Do we really want politics run by the side that can make farmyard noises the loudest?

Westminster has traditionally not been a female-friendly space. Notoriously, ladies' toilets were scarce until recently, as many new female MPs found when they entered Parliament in 1997. And like many places of work (but worse, since Parliament sits in the afternoon and evening), there is little ability for women and men to balance family life and work reasonable hours. And in our culture, as women are assumed to be the primary carer, men tend to have wives to look after the home, while female MPs have struggled on, juggling work and family life.

The electoral system

Finally, some have argued that the political system itself works against women MPs. In countries with comparable political systems and culture (for example, in Europe), more women get elected under proportional representation (PR) systems.[28] The argument is that in a 'winner takes all' system (where the person with the most votes gets all the power), such as in the UK currently, people are more likely to play safe and vote for candidates who look like previous winners. In PR, where power is distributed according to the percentage of votes cast, there is more incentive for parties to put forward candidates who they think will appeal to a range of people.

The Electoral Reform Society certainly believes PR would be a big factor in getting more women into the British Parliament. This is proven by the Scottish and Welsh Parliaments and the London Assembly, which operate a form of PR, and in which women have around 33 per cent, 47 per cent and 33 per cent of seats respectively.[29]

Transforming politics: the feminist response

Women's activism and pressure are fundamental to making political change happen. The International IDEA states that 'women's activism and mobilisation at the country, regional and international level have been pivotal to keeping gender equality firmly rooted on the international agenda.'[30] We should not sit back and assume everything will naturally become more equal over time. Improvements to the system are not the only things required; cultural attitudes to women in politics must change too.

Encouraging participation in the voting process

Encouraging women to take an interest in politics and vote is an important priority for some feminists. In some countries, where women have lower education and literacy rates and have been excluded from leadership positions, women may need extra help to take full advantage of their rights. For instance, voter registration drives can be very successful in increasing participation. Activists in Liberia, where women have an average of six children and the female literacy rate is around 40 per cent, mobilised voters for the 2005 elections and raised the percentage of female registered voters from 30 to 50 per cent.[31]

The Fawcett Society's campaign *femocracy* targeted ethnic minority women, one of the most under-represented groups in UK politics. The campaign involved events around the UK, and direct contact with ethnic minority women.

> With so few ethnic minority women represented in politics, the dejecting message that is being given to ethnic minority women up and down the country is 'politics has little to do with your lives'. *femocracy* aims to put a stop to this message by increasing the number of ethnic minority women registered to vote and engaged in politics.[32]

Campaigning to reform the system

Improving the political system has proved to be more effective in the short term than changing an entire sexist culture (a very long-term project!).

In the USA, Doris Haddock, otherwise known as Granny D, is a fantastic example of how a single person can highlight important issues. At the age of 90 she embarked upon a fourteen-month, 3,200-mile walk across America to bring attention to the need to get 'legalized bribery' out of US politics (for example, donations made by the tobacco, alcohol and oil industries to parties in order to get preferential treatment for their industry when the candidate got into power). Despite suffering hospitalisation and arrest for causing civil disobedience, she was indefatigable. Her campaign led to a national debate, draft reform bills, and she went on to front other campaigns.

Feminist activism to reform politics has often tended to focus on the idea of quotas, often as a temporary measure, to 'kick start' the process of making politics more equal. Often considered the 'lesser evil', in many countries quotas (whether for candidates or reserved seats in parliament) are the only thing that has made a big difference.

Quotas take different forms. First, there can be quotas for candidates put forward by political parties (removing the ability of local parties to nominate only men). Second, quotas can set aside a certain number of seats for MPs. Quotas can be gender-neutral, specifying simply that one gender should hold no more than 60 per cent or less than 40 per cent of seats. In practice, because of women's widespread lack of access and historical and current oppression, quotas have tended to be specific to increasing their numbers.

In countries which have never applied quotas to national politics, the very concept can be controversial. But in others it is accepted as normal and right. Indeed, in some Arab countries reserving seats for certain religious or ethnic groups is a long-standing practice. India reserves seats for the dalit (lowest) caste. The Iraqi constitution states that 25 per cent of the parliament should be female. Rwanda surpassed its 30 per cent constitutional minimum, getting women in over half the seats. Afghanistan and Pakistan both have reserved seats for women, as does Spain, which increased from 6 per cent women MPs in 1977 to around 36 per cent now.[33] This is not just the case in party politics; trade unions have a long tradition of reserved seats for women, and other under-represented groups.

The idea of quotas is a move away from the idea of equality of opportunity in a competitive, winner-takes-all environment to equality of result or outcome, in which equality is guaranteed. This concept is controversial, and not all feminists agree, but quotas raise important questions about how democracy works. As Drude Dahlerup points out, in the Swedish Social Democratic Party's principle of 'every second on the list a woman', women are no more 'quota women' than men are 'quota men'.[34]

In Italy, feminists at Unione Donne developed a manifesto (50e50) which aimed to ensure that women made up 50 per cent of political structures; this would involve an amendment to the Italian constitution. Aiming for 50,000 signatures, they ended up with 120,740.[35] In the UK, similarly, the charity One World Action is campaigning for governments to achieve 50 per cent representation for women. They argue:

> Positive action aims to rectify systemic inequalities in a bold and comprehensive manner. Slow, incremental changes are no longer sufficient.... It took a long time for women to get the vote. Without positive action, it will take centuries more to gain gender balance in political institutions.[36]

Finally, women in parliaments continue to argue for better childcare and working hours. In 2009 the UK's House of Commons announced its first nursery for MPs, peers and staff (to be housed in a former bar!). Feminists also tend to favour a revamp of the way that the House of Commons works, with less jeering and posturing, and more constructive debate.

Pressing for change within political parties

As feminists have different views on how to solve this problem, they are working within their own parties to deal with the issue in different ways.

In the UK, the Conservative Party has used priority lists, in which women and men are present equally at each stage of the local party's selection process. Party members have been active in Women2Win, which offers mentoring, training and support to prospective female candidates. Selection committees have been given training in interview techniques. More recently David Cameron announced a plan to implement all-women shortlists for certain constituency seats, but this remains controversial within the party.

The Labour Party began with enforcing 50:50 final shortlists but found that the local parties still predominantly voted for men and progress was too slow. They began implementing all-women shortlists for certain constituencies (before a legal challenge). This resulted in a substantial increase in women in Parliament at the 1997 election.

Within the Liberal Democrats, a women's pressure group encourages and trains prospective female candidates, providing resources and supporting women through the process. They have so far shied away from targets or quotas.

For all parties, progress is achingly slow. It has been estimated that at current rates, it would take the Conservative party 400 years to reach equality, the Liberal Democrats 40 years and Labour 20. Feminists must keep the pressure on their parties.

Supporting, encouraging and mentoring female candidates

In Northern Ireland, the Women into Politics campaign runs training courses for young women and organises mentoring and shadowing schemes, with the aim of increasing 'the number of women in decision making roles at all levels in our society'.[37]

In the USA, the Emily's List project helps raise funds to support pro-choice female candidates. And in the UK, the Downing Street Project provides training programmes for 'women interested in running for political office but who don't know where to start'. It aims to 'bring together women and supportive men from all political parties, business and the arts, to support women, in order for women to bring about a better world for all of us.'[38]

Analysing and critiquing parties for pro-feminist policies

A woman in power is not necessarily going to be feminist purely because she is female. So, feminists are keeping a close eye on party policies and evaluating them against feminist principles. Feminist bloggers and journalists routinely report and discuss proposed policies affecting women, encouraging debate and enabling voters to make appropriate choices. Commentary can be found on collaborative blogs such as *The F Word* and *Feministing*, and on those of individuals such as *Penny Red*.

Envisioning a new world

A substantial minority of feminists we surveyed identified as anarcha- (anarchist), socialist or Marxist feminists. Indeed, many feminists, whatever their politics, feel that simple equality for women in existing political systems – governments built on centuries of oppression of various peoples around the world – is not good enough. A blogger from *Edinburgh Feministing* mused:

> I am not about equality, because – well what does it really mean? I have no desire to see women as equal oppressors, or equally oppressed as men often are…. Equality in politics is only a good thing if politics is not oppressive but rather exists to facilitate the happiness of all those involved…. So sure maybe feminism means equality – but more than that for me it has to mean liberation.
>
> Equality for me seems to signify that somewhere in our tangle of oppressive structures there is one group that we are all aspiring to be like. I don't want to live the life of a rich, white man…. I do want to be liberated however from gender which threatens and restrains me, and from the connotations of my white skin and British passport that link me to some histories which make me ashamed even whilst they still make me materially richer.[39]

The anarcha-feminist approach to politics is summarised in a 1971 Chicago 'Anarcho-Feminist Manifesto', copies of which still circulate in anti-capitalist circles:

> We believe that a Woman's Revolutionary Movement must not mimic, but destroy, all vestiges of the male-dominated power structure, the State itself…. The world … cannot survive many more decades of rule by gangs of armed males calling themselves governments…. Whatever its forms of justifications, the armed State is what is threatening all of our lives at present. The State,

by its inherent nature, is really incapable of reform. True social-
ism, peace and plenty for all, can be achieved only by people
themselves, not by representatives ready and able to turn guns on
all who do not comply with State directives.[40]

Just as feminists in mainstream politics lobby their party
to make changes, anarcha-feminists challenge the often male-
dominated anarchist scene. At an anarchist conference in 2009
feminists rushed the stage, showed a short film and handed out
a statement comparing sexism in capitalism and anarchism:

> If the anarchist movement doesn't recognize the power structures
> it reproduces, its resistance will be futile. For as well as fighting
> sexism 'out there' we must fight sexism 'in here' and stop pretend-
> ing that oppressive systems disappear at the door of the squat or
> the social centre. Only a movement that understands and fights its
> own contradictions can provide fertile ground for real and effec-
> tive resistance...
>
> The state's incursion into our private lives and the relationship
> between sexuality and productivity from which it profits affects
> people of all genders. The gender binary system violently allocates
> us roles on the basis of our anatomy. A refusal to accept even these
> basic precepts will be a great hindrance to the movement.[41]

Religion

In popular feminist texts religion is often absent or attacked.
Indeed, in some feminist quarters conventional wisdom decrees
that religion should be shelved; as one journalist put it:

> Whether it's one of the world's major faiths or an off-the-wall-cult,
> religion means one thing and one thing only for those women
> unfortunate enough to get caught up in it: oppression. It's the
> patriarchy made manifest, male-dominated, set up by men to
> protect and perpetuate their power.[42]

Unlike their first-wave foremothers, for whom feminism was a natural expression of their religious faith, many second-wave feminists took a secular stance. Religious women were often ignored by feminists, considered difficult to engage with since they had apparently chosen patriarchy over liberation. Religion was not specifically mentioned in the 1970s' feminists' demands. There's some evidence that women with feminist attitudes are less likely to be religious.[43]

Just as black women felt excluded by a feminism in which white women's experiences were taken as the norm, so religious feminists (many of them of Asian, black and mixed ethnicities) feel that secular feminism denigrates an integral part of their identity, requiring them to justify why they are religious *and* feminist. One young feminist calls her blog *Christian Feminist: this is not an oxymoron*; another, who runs a blog entitled *A Christian Feminist Journey*, says she is 'bridging the gap between two worlds'. Likewise, the chair of a Muslim women's LBT project writes about the 'Muslim bashing' she experiences from a gay media that she considers 'anti-faith' and that 'reproduce' 'white, patriarchal power structures' in their depiction of Muslim women.[44]

We believe questions of spirituality and religion should be included within any discussions of contemporary feminism. Nearly 3 in 10 of the feminists we surveyed described themselves as religious or spiritual. And even those who have no religious or spiritual beliefs may be concerned about how religion impacts on gender equality. To create a world where men and women are liberated, religion and spirituality are as much in need of feminist work as, say, popular culture or politics. As one of the feminists we interviewed put it, 'How can there be true equality without spiritual equality?'[45]

Religion and second-wave feminism

Feminists of the second wave who worked on religion fell into four groups: religious reformists, religious revisionists, spiritual revolutionaries and secular feminists. These approaches continue today.

Religious reformists are liberals; they seek equal opportunities for women and men within religious traditions. They don't want to revolutionise styles of worship, reject sacred texts or change the gender of deities. But they believe religious texts and doctrines have been misinterpreted in a way that disadvantages women, hindering their participation in religion and its leadership structures.

For instance, the late Benazir Bhutto, former prime minister of Pakistan, wrote in her autobiography: 'it was men's interpretation of our religion that restricted women's opportunities, not our religion itself. Islam in fact had been quite progressive toward women from its inception.'[46] Reformist feminists think scriptures about women's and men's spiritual equality are neglected. They question the idea that men should be the head of the household or interpret his role as non-authoritarian. When Qur'an 4:34 states that men should be *qawwamuna 'ala* (responsible for, or guardians of, women), Muslim feminist reformists explain that the context of this has been neglected, leading to its misinterpretation. As Islamic scholar Amina Wadud explains, the verse does *not* say that men are preferred by Allah over women or that men are authority figures in the family, responsible for subjugating their wives in the home. Rather, the verse indicates that some men are given the responsibility of providing materially for their wives if their wives are undertaking the important role of bearing and nurturing children.[47] Reforming marriage is a priority for reformists, but so is promoting women's decision-making and leadership. Reformists contend that scriptures and traditions advocate women's leadership; in fact, evangelical Christian feminist arguments are believed to be significantly responsible for persuading the Church of England to vote to ordain women in 1992.

Religious revisionists believe that expanding women's roles within the existing structures isn't enough. They look for a liberating core within their religion, reject the rest, and believe a deeper transformation is required, of religious structures and society. They believe religious texts shouldn't be imbibed unquestioningly but should be examined through the lens of women's experiences: '"women's experience" becomes the norm or one of the norms by which the adequacy of theology is to be judged'.[48]

Revisionists use women's experiences to reinterpret traditional religious symbols. Feminist theologian Sally McFague has challenged the 'patriarchal' model of Father, Son and Holy Spirit and created a model of God as 'mother, lover and friend'.[49] Instead of religion being about preparing for an afterlife, revisionists want liberation from oppression on earth now. Rita Gross reworks the Buddhist concept of community or *sangha*. She challenges conventional interpretations of the *sangha* as the place where adherents develop self-reliance. Gross sees that as a masculine ideal and reinterprets it in terms of what she sees as feminine values of nurturance, communication, relationship and friendship.[50] Revisionist feminists believe that traditional religious doctrines reflect patriarchal assumptions, so redefine them. They have redefined sin not as selfishness or pride (since women are often too self*less*), but as women's oppression and self-neglect, making standing for gender justice and thinking for yourself integral to what it means to resist sin.[51] Womanist theologians (a term coined by Alice Walker to describe black feminists struggling against the interlocking systems of racism and sexism) have interrogated the doctrine of sin from black women's perspective; for Delores Williams, defilement of women's bodies through sexual violence (common during slavery) constitutes sin, and standing against it is vital. The Old Testament figure Hagar, forced to be a surrogate mother by Abraham when Sarah could not conceive and then cast into the wilderness where a divine messenger visits her, becomes a picture of black women's experience of oppression and endurance through struggle.[52]

Spiritual revolutionaries are highly critical of institutional religion, and reject religion in its conventional forms. Often distinguishing religion (which they dislike) from spirituality, they create woman-centred experiences that re-establish femininity's sanctity. Some join women-only spirituality groups, or embrace Goddess spirituality, viewing the Goddess as a symbol of women's creative power. One prominent example is Carol Christ, whose essay 'Why Women Need the Goddess' galvanized the Goddess feminist movement. Christ critiques the absence of feminine images in Christian and Jewish theologies and draws on ancient forms of Goddess worship reconstructed from prehistoric societies to create a spirituality that affirms life now. She uses the figure of the Goddess to challenge male domination and legitimise women's claims for equality. Like her contemporary Starhawk (influential in the Wiccan or pagan community), Christ emphasises women's connections with the earth, the material and the sexual, because these have been downgraded in masculine religion.[53]

Secular feminists include those who want to separate religion from the state, and those who have abandoned religion and spirituality completely. For the latter group, religious texts and practices are not relevant and will harm women who continue with them.

The Bangladeshi novelist Taslima Nasreen, who has had several fatwas pronounced against her, is an example. She emerged as a champion of Bangladeshi women's rights in the late 1980s, writing newspaper columns and poems highlighting Bangladeshi women's plight at the hands of men. In a letter to *The Times* in 1994 she wrote about Islam: 'Our religion doesn't give women any human dignity. Women are considered slaves ... I write against the religion because if women want to live like human beings, they will have to live outside the religion and Islamic law.' Elsewhere, she describes all religious texts as 'out of place and out of time'. 'We have to move beyond these ancient texts if we want to progress,' she says. She now describes herself as a secular humanist.[54] The Somalia-born feminist writer Ayaan Hirsi Ali is similarly critical of Islam. She converted from Islam to atheism in 2002 and has lived in hiding in the Netherlands since her screenplay for Theo Van Gogh's film *Submission* resulted in death threats from Muslim extremists. Philosopher Mary Daly caused a storm in 1971 when she used a sermon at Harvard University to lead women in an exodus from church; 'if God is male, then the male is God. The divine patriarch castrates women as long as he is allowed to live on in the human imagination', she declared.[55]

Women and religion today

Some decades on, what are feminists thinking and doing with and about religion and spirituality? Before we turn to this, it's important to acknowledge how the religious cultural context has shifted. The progress in women's access to positions of religious authority in the twentieth century has come about in large part because of the achievements of religious feminists. The Church of England voted to ordain women as priests in 1992 and bishops in 2008. Women have been ordained as rabbis in Reform and Reconstructionist branches of Judaism since 1972. In Hinduism, female gurus (teachers) are now more common, especially in India and the United States.[56] In 2005 in New York Amina Wadud became the first Sunni Muslim woman in recent history to lead a mixed-gender group in Friday prayers.

Feminist work has also ushered in new forms of worship, the veneration of divinity as female and inclusive language in holy scriptures. They have worked for – and achieved – change both within and without. Indeed, while secular or revolutionary spiritual feminists disagreed with those who remained in traditional religions (and vice versa), change would probably not have been achieved without the combination of their different strategies.

But the battle is not over: Roman Catholicism, Orthodox Judaism and Islam don't allow female priests, rabbis or imams. Many Protestant denominations will not permit women to lead congregations. Religious arguments are still being used to justify the oppression of women across the globe. And spiritualities popular with women have yet to gain widespread institutional recognition, often being denigrated as 'fluffy' since they don't fit established ideas of what constitutes 'proper' religion. Meanwhile, secular, atheist and agnostic feminists are worried about the growth of fundamentalism and the influence of religion on women's lives.

Interest in these faith-related issues is unsurprising, given the new prominence of religion in public life. In the twenty-first century, the numerical decline in Christian and Jewish affiliation has been matched by a corresponding renewed public interest in religion and mounting allegiance to Islam and alternative kinds of spirituality. Concerns about Islamic fundamentalism post-9/11 and political awareness of the needs of the growing Muslim population are additional factors in the return of religion. Faith groups are playing an increasing role in welfare and education (for instance, homelessness services and faith schools).

In the British context, the dominant religious tradition, Christianity, is in decline, particularly among women, although there are still more women in church than men. In Britain, most religions attract broadly similar numbers of men and women, with a clear female majority in Christianity (53 per cent female), paganism (54 per cent), spiritualism (68 per cent) and Wicca (67 per cent), and a male majority in 'no religion' (56 per cent) and the smaller Rastafarian (71 per cent) and Zoroastrian (54 per cent) groups.[57]

Transforming religion: the feminist response

When we asked feminists to describe their spiritual or religious views, two-thirds said they were agnostic, atheist or had no particular spirituality. About a tenth of feminists remain in traditional religions, the largest being Christianity. A similar proportion identify as spiritual, seeing themselves as 'spiritual but not religious'; being involved in various alternative, earth-based forms of spirituality, including paganism, Goddess spirituality or Wicca; or combining more than one kind of religion or spiritual expression. The remaining few didn't respond, considered themselves 'lapsed' (mostly lapsed Roman Catholics), or identified as humanist.

We will now explore what the different feminists are doing, starting with the largest of these groups, atheism/agnosticism/no religion, then moving on to consider feminists in major world religions, and finally 'spiritual' feminists.

Atheist, agnostic and non-religious feminists

Most young people today – including those who identify as feminists – grew up in non-religious families; for them it's less a case of rejecting religion and more a case of never having considered it

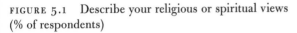

FIGURE 5.1   Describe your religious or spiritual views
(% of respondents)

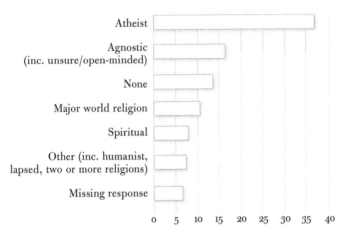

in the first place. Families are increasingly diverse, and religious organisations' emphasis on 'family values' has turned off those outside traditional nuclear families – divorced people, single people, cohabitees, single parents and lesbian and gay people. The family forms which are growing in society are the forms that are under-represented in religious communities. Sexuality, too, is a sticking point. With sex before and outside marriage a feature of the vast majority of people's lives, religious messages about abstaining until heterosexual marriage have not gone down well.

Many feminists who don't describe themselves as religious or spiritual in a defined way nevertheless reflect on questions of faith, especially as they apply to women. For instance, Sonja White, 26, explains, 'religion is a huge issue now in the area of women's rights as human rights.' White points out that 'Throughout history and up to the present day women have been oppressed by the beliefs and practices of the world's major religious traditions, by their scriptures, authorities and leaders.' She believes that religion is often 'abused by those in power and with authority, usually men, in order to fulfil an agenda usually not religious in nature but political – and the importance of women within society is downplayed to serve this cause.'[58]

Rebecca Watson, 29, is the founder of *Skepchick*, a blog dedicated to 'promoting skepticism and critical thinking among women around the world'. Founded in reaction to the male domination of the growing Skeptic movement (which is very closely aligned to atheism and agnosticism), the blog critically analyses pseudoscience, myths, conspiracy theories and superstitions as well as religion. Watson sees scepticism and feminism as natural allies, citing frequent attacks on women's rights from the religious right in the USA and around the world.

She promotes 'skeptical-feminism', using scientific research evidence to counteract common arguments used by the religious right to justify restricted access to sex education, birth control, emergency contraception, and abortion. Sceptical feminists have shown, for instance, that religious arguments for female genital mutilation and persecution of 'witches' in some parts of the world do not hold water.[59]

'Feminism and religion, is there a way to reconciliation?' wonders agnostic Anna Mavrogianni, 27. She is concerned with the way religion is used to control both men and women, and to justify violence against women who don't conform to restrictive sexual codes. 'Is religion bound to lead to gender discrimination?' she asks, concluding:

> Only if we closely examine religious beliefs within the context of the societies that produced them and re-translate religious texts by taking away the relative influences of patriarchy away will we

be able to produce religious lifestyles that are compatible with humanitarianism/feminism.[60]

Women Against Fundamentalism (WAF) formed in 1989, bringing together women of all faiths and none, to challenge the political movements that constitute fundamentalist religions. WAF is concerned that the UK government's increased partnership with faith organisations means that money and influence are falling into the hands of religious fundamentalists who are restricting women's rights. WAF contends that 'only secular institutions – which have no religious agenda – can begin to bring about equality for people of all religions or none.'[61]

Concerned about issues such as the quality of sex education in faith schools, feminists are also active in the National Secular Society, which promotes the separation of church and state in the UK and the EU. Supporter Johann Hari, for example, has challenged the tendency for worldwide outrages against women such as stonings or child marriages to be considered a 'religious issue' and hence beyond all criticism.[62]

Feminists in major world religions

Blogs like *feminism.com*, *Feministing* and *The F Word* have all featured debates about spirituality and religion, with many contributors agreeing that it's possible to be religious and feminist. In a discussion on *Feministing* about whether Christianity and feminism are compatible, almost all contributors agreed that they could be:

> I have come to the point where my faith enhances my belief in equality and women's rights. How? I left church and 'organized religion' and I now rely on my own understanding of God without interference. The 'church' has become something apart from the Christian faith, and most people in churches believe in gender roles and traditional family structure because of their cultural

traditions, not their faith. People put culture and faith together until they cannot tell the difference. I tell people that Jesus was a feminist, who had women disciples (Yes, there are 15 disciples named in the Bible, but people in the church have ignored the women)! Focus on Jesus ... and you will find plenty to affirm feminism in his words and actions.[63]

For these feminists, it's not about choosing religion *or* feminism. An either/or choice isn't one most are capable of making; religion is integral to their personal and cultural identity, not an optional extra. Kate Dugan and Jennifer Owens run a blog on young women and Catholicism and have edited a book on this topic. They write in their introduction:

being Catholic is having a powerful impact on our lives. Catholic social teaching is the reason many women decide to commit themselves to lives of service. A lifelong appreciation of the depth of the Catholic tradition inspires a new generation ... to work for change from within the institution.... Despite the church's position on gay marriage, the pull of Catholic identity keeps lesbians attending Mass. And a realisation that Catholicism can be written into our DNA, ingrained in our bones, is part of why Catholic women called to priesthood have not become Episcopalians.[64]

Reformism and revisionism remain important ways for feminists in major world faiths to negotiate spaces for themselves, spaces where spiritual equality can be lived out. Rooted in Catholicism, the Women–Church movement is a coalition of feminist revisionist groups, predominantly in North America. Women–Church has provided women with a spiritual feminist space for worship, community and social justice for nearly thirty years.

Christian reformism is still around: in Britain the evangelical feminist group Men, Women and God, now twenty-five years old and less prominent, is joined by the younger Return network and the Sophia Network for women in church youth work. 'Our ultimate aim is to encourage women and men to *work together* more closely in a way that reflects the heart of God, but we recognize that sometimes issues need to be addressed before women can contribute on a level playing field', explains founder Jenny Baker.[65]

Reformists often avoid the term 'feminism', probably because of its negative connotations in conservative religious communities, and this seems as much the case for the Sophia Network as for Muslim feminists. Nevertheless, Islamic feminism in the UK is in the ascendancy: since the year 2000 the Muslim Women Talk campaign and the Muslim Women's Network have been set up to promote Muslim women's voices in the public realm, enabling them more effectively to communicate their insights to government and to share their skills. The Muslim Women's Network's desire to interpret religion in an egalitarian way is visible in their strapline: 'Islam means the surrender of humankind to the will of God, not the submission of women to the will of men.'[66] With up to 60 per cent of Britain's mosques not allowing women to enter to worship, and very few allowing women a say over how mosques are run, a group of women from the Muslim Public Affairs Committee set up the Women and Mosques campaign to lobby for change, visiting local mosques to debate with their leaders.[67]

The Safra Project, a network of Muslim LBT women, uses the work of reformist and feminist Islamic scholars to develop frameworks for a 'progressive Islam'. Progressive Islam believes true authority lies in the Qur'an, rather than the more restrictive sharia (Islamic law) and Hadith (sayings, many of which scholars deem unreliable), which reflect and encourage oppressive ideas about women derived from men's experiences in a patriarchal society. Qur'anic verses used to condemn homosexuality, transgender and intersex identity may have been mistranslated, they believe. Progressive Islam also offers a framework where sharia is understood as an evolving entity, offering the possibility that same-sex sexuality can move from the category *haram* (forbidden) to *mubah* (permissible).[68] Muslim feminist and journalist Yasmin Alibhi-Brown is chair of British Muslims for Secular Democracy, which, like the Secular Society, promotes separation of faith and state, but also religious understanding and harmony.

Today, the Internet facilitates global religious feminism in each of the major religions. For the global Sikh community, *Sikhnet.com*, Gurumustuk Singh Khalsa's blog on Sikh life, promotes gender equality by running regular features like 'Why Sikhs need more female granthis' (granthis are ceremonial scripture readers).[69] The site also features videos about the rise of turban-wearing among female (as well as male) Sikhs in the West, a practice which is seen as the gift of the Guru Gobind Singh and an expression of religious commitment and dedication to the service of others.[70]

Spiritual

For feminists who opt for the 'Spiritual but not religious' designation, spirituality is about recognising another dimension to life, but resisting its institutionalisation. Increasingly, spirituality is advocated as furthering feminist activism; indeed, some have even described the new feminist spirituality as a 'fourth wave' of feminism in which activism is motivated by joy, not anger.[71] When women of a broad swathe of spiritual and religious affiliations come together to worship and practise their faith, they feel it ignites a collective energy capable of achieving global social change. Leela Fernandes argues that spirituality gives us strength to imagine a better world and break out of the 'cycles of retribution' in which social movements become implicated as they struggle against oppression.[72] At the Omega Institute's annual Women and Power conference in the USA, activists including Gloria Steinem and Eve Ensler took part in spiritual rituals that embraced the need for women to lead the democratic world to embrace *service of* instead of *power over*, others.[73] Gather the Women is good example of this. Started by a group of women after 9/11, Gather the Women is now a global network with twice-yearly gatherings and 'circles' in the USA, Australia, Costa Rica, Italy, the Canary Islands and elsewhere. The network describe themselves as 'part of an exciting, fast-growing movement – a new wave of energy – to joyfully reclaim feminine principles for creating a world of peace, balance, and well-being for all.'[74]

Laurel Zwissler's research with Canadian anti-globalisation and anti-capitalist activists shows how at international trade conferences, activists use spiritual rituals like prayer, web-weaving and spiral dance (common in pagan ritual) 'to help combat political and economic systems that oppress and dehumanize people around the world'. Their rituals promote peace, diffuse tension, create community and 'express alternative visions' of how the world could be. As pagan peace activist Sue said, 'Religion is really grounding. [It's about] shifting the energy, instead of the agenda being set by the police.' Zwissler concludes that this ritualisation 'calls into question popular assumptions that mixing religion and politics yields necessarily conservative results', since 'Engaging new movements in their religions, feminist activists incorporate their spiritual traditions into progressive political protest, hoping to literally change the world.'[75]

Some of feminists we surveyed were spiritual in a more defined way, committed to various earth-based, pagan or holistic spiritualities (popular in the West since the 1960s). These draw on nineteenth-century occult and esoteric movements and older polytheistic or pantheistic traditions which venerate nature. They believe that disregarding female divinity has caused the oppression of women and nature. As Caroline Ophis, 44, who defines herself as 'spiritual, Taoist/wiccan', explains, 'as long as women are not seen in the image of God, our bodies are thus not considered sacred, but dirty, messy and sinful, and likewise, the earth is not seen as sacred and this belief justifies all means of control and power over both women and the earth and its inhabitants.' For spiritual revolutionaries, restoring the female divine will recognise the sacredness of women's bodies. But aware that gender is not dichotomous, Ophis believes in reclaiming the 'Divine Androgyne'. 'If men and women and those people whose gender is other were all to imagine God in their own image, we would have a composite creation in our collective consciousness of a human God composed of many genders, sexualities and races', she explains. Ophis is in the process of setting up Barbie Shakti, the Barbara Shakti Foundation for Divine Equality. Barbie Shakti is loosely inspired by the ethos of one of the mansions (branches) within the Rastafari movement, which believes every man is a priest. Caroline explains that Barbie Shakti will 'invite women and those whose gender is self defined to re-imagine a numinous Divine Creatrix, to be their own self appointed Priestesses, of their bodies and of the earth.'[76]

Today's spiritual and Goddess feminists contrast with their foremothers in a few ways, as researcher Giselle Vincett explains. The younger Goddess feminists she interviewed are more polytheistic. In a context where Christianity is less influential, 'the necessity for a "big Goddess" to differentiate from the Christian God, is likely to become less important.' Younger feminists are more likely to have a DIY approach to spirituality. They connect with like-minded others online and are nomadic, trying to connect with local goddesses during their travels to different countries rather than 'importing' goddesses from other cultures. That, they feel, is 'cultural colonialism'. With less emphasis in today's increasingly postmodern world on 'woman' as a stable or coherent identity, younger feminists aren't so focused on celebrating distinctively female bodily experiences. As Jasmine explained, '[I like] doing kind of special women stuff like honouring menstruation, ... [but] I don't agree with excluding ... transgender people ... I don't think there's a problem if they want to be involved.'[77] Instead, they're more interested in playing with or performing different identities or versions of femininity, for example dressing up as a goddess at the Glastonbury Goddess Conferences. Queer feminists are more at home at the Reclaiming Witchcraft and Radical Faerie events, where participants change into brightly-coloured 'gender-bending' 'witchy-wear' clothing. This enables them to make a political statement about the cultural construction of gender, as well as to challenge contemporary media representations of witches as sexually attractive young women (Buffy or Sabrina). Catherine Telford-Keogh, who has studied these movements, explains:

> When these Reclaiming Witches 'put on' their Witch identity, they reveal identity as an ever changing performance or a prosthetic that can be put on and taken off. This performance of 'Witch' and gender variant identity also makes evident that one's gender performance does not always follow from one's sex.[78]

Conclusion

In many ways parallel issues, religion and politics are being challenged by feminists who are concerned about the marginalisation of women in each as well as the impact of both on gender relations.

The next chapter turns to an area absent entirely from the seven demands of the Women's Liberation Movement. Like religion, popular culture has often been seen as a lesser issue when compared with things like work and violence against women, but it is a key battleground for feminists today.

Take action!

1. Support organisations fighting for women's participation in politics, whether by getting more women in parliaments or by changing the political system itself.
2. Take female candidates seriously; challenge those who focus on their appearance rather than their politics. Put pressure on MPs to take women's issues seriously: lobby your MP, analyse their policy proposals and monitor their progress.
3. Press for more women speakers in political and religious debates.
4. Challenge religious groups and institutions to do better on gender equality. Point out that gender equality can be justified theologically.
5. Support groups which apply feminist perspectives to religion.

6

POPULAR CULTURE FREE FROM SEXISM

POPULAR CULTURE surrounds us. It's in the images we see every day on billboards and television, the music videos we watch, the way people talk about men and women in school playgrounds, pubs and public transport. It tells us what it means to be a woman or a man, and it has real, practical consequences in our lives.

Sometimes feminists point their finger at 'the media', as if they are a static body of white men sitting in a Hollywood mansion who lock the doors when they see women coming down the path. In reality, things are much more complicated. Looking at popular culture from a feminist perspective requires us to look at media *representations* of women and men, at how people *engage with* pop culture, and at feminists' work *critiquing* and *producing* new forms of culture.

Making culture less sexist is one of the biggest challenges for feminism today. Sexist attitudes can't be tackled simply through legislation. This is about changing how people think: making people more accepting and less judgemental.

So, when contemporary feminists concentrate on popular culture, it's not because they are unconcerned about 'real' material inequalities like poverty or violence. Popular culture is not trivial. It is an unavoidable part of people's lives today and is inextricably linked to material forms of social injustice. Engaging with it is an essential survival mechanism and a valid way to change society. Cultural attitudes, for example myths and jokes about rape, have knock-on effects on how women are treated in society. Feminists also feel that attitudes promoted in the media may in fact exacerbate economic or power inequalities: being required to spend money on enhancing their appearance may lead women into debt, for example, and the mainstreaming of pornography may prompt men to demand porn-inspired sexual activities from their girlfriends. As the second-wave feminist slogan asserted, 'the personal is political'. The 'personal' troubles of individuals are actually public issues; they're connected to wider social patterns.[1]

> 'One incident that sticks in my mind happened to my girlfriend Emm... Just before the soundcheck at one of their gigs they were sitting round a table, while staff from the venue kicked non-band members out, so they wouldn't get in for free. Anyway, one guy came up to the band's table and said to Emm "Oh you're one of the band's girlfriends aren't you? Better get out cos it's just bands now." Luckily Emm isn't the kind to take any shit and was in a bad mood that day anyway so he got a "what the fuck?! I'm the fucking drummer you bastard!!!" ... If even a small issue like music contains extreme sexism, then how bad must everything else be?' SOPHIE SCARLET, 'My feminism and sexism in rock', *Riot Grrrl London zine* 1 (*c*. 2002)

In this chapter, we'll look at gender inequalities in popular culture and their impact on people's lives. We'll begin with sexism in music, then turn to advertising, 'Mars/Venus' gender stereotyping and celebrity culture, before showcasing some of the work feminists are doing in response to cultural sexism.

Music

Women are achieving success in the music industry. But the successes of Beyoncé, Lily Allen or Lady Gaga do not mean sexism's been solved. As Sophie's story illustrates, feminists believe women should have equal opportunities to create music, especially in male dominated genres like rock, indie/alternative, metal and classical. At Ladyfest Manchester in 2008, Amelia Fletcher reported that of the sixty-four band members in the Indie Chart Top 30, only four were women, and of the seventy-seven band members on the Xfm playlist, only one was female. Here's rock music fan Collette talking about *Kerrang* magazine:

> I've been buying the magazine for the last few years and am confounded by the total absence of any real coverage of women's music within its pages... women in fact only feature only a handful of times, and primarily for male titillation.... Flicking through the 5th August issue, imagine my dismay when I only counted seven real instances of women within seventy two pages of material[2]

Feminists also want to ensure that music gigs and festivals are safe spaces for females. Here, a teenager describes crowdsurfing for the first time at a festival:

> As I got nearer the front I was handed over to some guys WHO, FUCK KNOWS WHY, DECIDED IT WAS FUNNY TO PULL MY CLOTHES OFF... I felt violated.... My jeans were pulled down, revealing my small panties to all, making matters worse I was on my period and feeling totally humiliated.... Whilst this was happening I had this hugely fake smile on my face contradicted only by the tears that started to roll [down] my face when I was passed over to the security guards who put me back on the ground and I got myself dressed again. When I was down I ran back to my best friend who was so nice and hugged me till I stopped shaking.... This hasn't happened to any guys I know.... I was trying to enjoy some great bands and some dick has tainted my memory of that

and replaced it with the feeling of helpless, powerless humiliation and emphasises that girls are not as safe at gigs. (MISS MICHELLE, *PaperDollCuts zine* 1, *c.* 2000)

The highly sexist content of song lyrics and music videos increasingly concerns feminists. Rap and hip-hop music are often singled out as an extreme example of misogyny and sexualisation. When 50 Cent, Dr Dre, Snoop Dogg, or Lil Wayne call women 'hos' and 'bitches', many condemn them. A female interviewee in Byron Hurt's documentary *Hip Hop: Beyond Beats and Rhymes* explains, 'I jokingly say that I'm recovering from hip hop. It's like being in a domestic violence situation – you know, your home is hip hop and your man's beating you.' Hurt's documentary shows how mainstream rap music promotes a one-dimensional masculinity that's about violence, homophobia and dominating women. As Hurt explains, citing black men's higher likelihood of becoming homicide victims, 'we live in a society where manhood is all about conquering and violence. And what we don't realise is that kind of definition of manhood ultimately destroys you.' These aspects of hip-hop culture, and its distinctive kind of black masculinity, are bad for women and men. Performance artist Sarah Jones comments:

The image of scantily clad women is supposed to affirm some image of masculinity … this sexually powerful virile example of manhood. But in actuality what they show themselves to be is incredibly insecure. And the idea is that this man is so important and so powerful and these women are so dime a dozen… they don't matter, they're just eye candy, they're worthless.[3]

But it's wrong to place the blame just with rappers. As third-wave hip-hop feminist Eisa Davis remarks, hip-hop 'is the whipping boy for a misogyny that is fundamental to western culture.'[4] Hip-hop culture emerged in New York City's South Bronx in the

1970s as a kind of poetic resistance to white capitalism and spread through the inner cities. Record companies have profited from – cynics would say co-opted – hip-hop, buying up independent rap labels and selling a misogynistic range of 'gangsta rap' to its (now mostly white) audience. They award contracts to rappers who present a 'hyper-masculine', aggressive image rather than more thoughtful rappers whose rhymes touch on issues of fatherhood, community or political resistance.

And it's not just gangsta rap that contains misogyny. Electro rap outfit 3Oh!3's song 'Don't Trust Me' caused controversy; its lyrics proclaimed 'Don't trust a ho' and, in a derogatory reference to deaf–blind author and political activist Helen Keller, continued: 'Shush girl, shut your lips/ Do the Helen Keller and talk with your hips.' Justin Timberlake has been criticised for his behaviour towards black female co-stars; in the video for 'Love Sex Magic' he pulls on a chain around singer Ciara's neck (in the USA this has connotations of slavery), and the incident in which he removed part of Janet Jackson's clothing, revealing a breast, at a Superbowl performance is infamous. In the video for nu-metal band Limp Bizkit's 2003 song Eat You Alive, a kidnapped woman (actress Thora Birch) is tied to a chair whilst singer Durst screams aggressively: 'I want you, ain't nothing wrong with wanting you cause I'm a man and I can think what the hell I want, you got that straight?' In a world where men's violence against women is a huge issue, the messages these musicians send are disturbing.

Advertising

The average American is reportedly exposed to more than three thousand advertisements every day.[5] We can't escape ads or their (alternately insidious and blatant) gender stereotyping. Advertising takes the gender stereotypes we're familiar with and sells them back to us as glamorous, life-changing, yet also achievable – if only we buy the advertised product. Studies of television commercials in eleven countries over a twenty-five-year period found:

- voiceovers are usually done by males, and women are more likely to be presented visually;
- women are usually portrayed as users of products, and men as the authoritative figures;
- men are more likely to appear in professional or interviewer roles and women in dependent roles (e.g. as parent or homemaker);
- women are often depicted in domestic settings, whereas men appear in a wide range of different locations;
- the central female figures are young, while their male counterparts are middle-aged;
- females are frequently shown advertising products for the home (e.g. food, toiletries).[6]

In short, women in advertising are younger, more silent, and occupy domestic roles. But although there are considerable global commonalities, there are some interesting differences between countries. Danish advertising uses fewer gender stereotypes than advertising in Kenya or Japan, for instance. In some countries, advertising is beginning to reflect changes in women's lives better, such as the growth in female paid employment; in Spain, where women's employment rates are increasing, men are only slightly more likely to be depicted in professional roles. Most product categories in Spanish ads weren't significantly skewed to one gender; stereotyping was only present in transport, telecommunications (male-dominated) and toiletries, perfumes and cleaning products (female-dominated).[7]

But sexism isn't dying out, and, as the case of Bulgaria shows, the transition to megabucks spending on advertising hasn't been good for women. Bulgaria's economy has recently undergone the transition from communism to capitalism. This has meant an end to full female employment and a return to a traditional maternal role. Sexualised images of women have proliferated and the new sexist advertisements depict females as responsible for the home, generally silent, and on the whole scantily clad.[8]

Liberation for sale

In many Western countries, feminism has been co-opted by advertisers to sell women empowerment through buying products. The Spice Girls – who provided a marketable form of 'girl power' – exemplified this. The Spice Girls sang about female empowerment, but this empowerment wasn't connected to any kind of collective gains for women, or a critique of the structure of society; it was about buying products.

Like the Spice Girls' girl power, advertising frequently uses terms like 'empowerment' and 'liberation' to sell products. A 2001 advertisement for Thorntons confectioners declared '1918 Votes for Women. 1975 Equality for Women. 2001 Women finally get what they want.' Immediately below was a picture of Thorntons' new range of continental chocolates. Here, feminist achievements are acknowledged as a positive stage in women's evolution. But only the arrival of this chocolate can produce full female satisfaction. This is an example of what Angela McRobbie calls post-feminism; this ad 'positively draws on and invokes feminism as that which can be taken into account, to suggest that equality is achieved, in order to install a whole repertoire of new meanings which emphasise that it is no longer needed.'[9] Feminism is simultaneously taken for granted and dismissed.

The Dove Campaign for Real Beauty is a third example of what Robert Goldman calls 'commodity feminism'. Complete with an educational website about young women and self-image,

Dove's campaign featured women of different sizes, ages and ethnicities, with slogans like 'Because every girl deserves to feel good about herself and see how beautiful she really is' and 'New Dove firming. As tested on real curves'. Feminists were divided: happy to see a more representative group of women adorn the billboards, but unhappy that feminist critiques of stereotypical images of women were being harnessed to sell toiletries. As Rosalind Gill comments, 'the irony of selling creams to slim and firm the body on the back of a campaign for real beauty was not missed by everyone'.[10]

'Ironic' sexual objectification

Sexualisation of women and girls is a major issue in British advertising – in fact, the UK's independent regulatory body for advertising, the Advertising Standards Authority (ASA), say that complaints about sexist ads are that 'men are stupid and women are sex objects'[11] (we'll talk about the first part of that later). Women may be increasingly depicted in professional roles, but this progress is hampered by the new, sexualized stereotyping of women (and increasingly, girls) as objects of men's sexual pleasure.

It's not just in advertising that humour and irony provide an excuse to present women as sexual objects. In a mere decade, lads' mags' soft-porn images have become so acceptable that they are sold at children's-eye level in supermarkets and newsagents. *Nuts* magazine's website features the 'Assess my breasts' feature, where girls send in pictures of their breasts and readers rate them out of ten. The sexualisation of female students has occurred as more and more young women are entering universities, with increasing debt, paralleling the rise of lap-dancing clubs in major student cities, which seek to employ students to create 'upmarket' 'gentlemen's' establishments. 'Sexy student' pictures

Virgin Atlantic celebrated 25 years in the airline industry with an ad showing a group of female flight attendants in short red skirts, blazers and stilettos walking through the airport in front of a male pilot, as crowds ogle them. The ad ends with the line 'Still red hot'. The Advertising Standards Authority received 48 complaints accusing the campaign of sexism. The ASA dismissed the complaints, saying that although sorry people 'may find the representation of the women and men in the ad distasteful, most viewers would understand that the ad presented exaggerated stereotypical views of the early 1980s and played upon perceived attitudes of that time in a humorous way'. Virgin, meanwhile, conjectured that the complaint 'probably come from competitors jealous of our fantastic cabin and flight crew'.[12]

are now ubiquitous in lads' mags, and beauty pageants for female students are making a comeback. In 2009 a British university vice-chancellor appeared to sanction this sexualisation, suggesting that male lecturers should consider lusting after students a perk of their job:

> Enjoy her! She's a perk ... she will flaunt you her curves. Which you should admire daily to spice up your sex, nightly, with the wife.... As in Stringfellows, you should look but not touch.[13]

If we object to women's portrayal as sexual objects by lads' mags (or sexist vice-chancellors), we're called humourless and told it's 'ironic'. But as *Jezebel* blogger Anna N put it, 'a joke is not a magic form of speech that is above all criticism'.[14] Adding humour doesn't negate the message that women exist to be ogled, it just makes ogling more palatable, helping readers feel less guilty about it and making it harder for women to voice their disapproval.

And even if magazine editors and advertisers don't *really* see women as sexual objects, the 'irony' will be lost on most readers. Annabelle Mooney comments: 'The obvious reading of [lads' magazines] is that it is permissible to look at naked women and to enjoy doing so. An ironic reading would be the exact opposite';[15] how many people looking at a lads' mag would interpret its message as 'women are diverse individuals and are not sex objects'?

'So easy, a man can do it': Gender stereotyping

The stereotype of a bumbling, inept man is now commonplace in advertising, comedy, television and film. As Holly Combe puts it, if women suffer from the beauty myth, men are subject to 'the stupidity myth'. Many people blame feminists for the way men are portrayed, forgetting that these portrayals originate in our sexist society, just like every stereotype about women.

But ads are not harmless. Advertising scholar Katharina Lindner explains: 'Research suggests that exposure to gender role stereotypes in advertising often influences gender-stereotypical

---

The ASA received a record number of complaints (673) for an ad for OvenPride oven cleaner. The advertisement features a pink-rubber-gloved man using the product to clean an oven shelf, presided over by his bossy-looking pregnant partner. 'Let OvenPride do its thing, so he can do more', the female voiceover explains, before ending with: 'OvenPride, so easy a man can do it' and female laughter. Objectors considered the ad disparaging towards men and said it upheld gender stereotypes that suggested that cleaning was women's domain. The ASA again dismissed the complaint as unlikely to cause widespread offence, defending the ad as slapstick comedy; the makers explained that the ad used tongue-in-cheek humour to play on gender stereotypes but didn't intend any offence.[16]

attitudes' and 'gender stereotypes in advertisements also have an effect on people's psychological well-being'[17] (see Chapter 1, where we discussed how restrictive cultural beauty ideals contribute to negative body image). Sceptics should bear in mind the so-called 'third person effect': asked 'are you influenced by advertising?' most people say no, liking to think of themselves as autonomous agents who make choices for themselves. But ask 'are people you know influenced by advertising?' and they will say yes, giving examples of people they know who buy things because they saw them on television.

The problem isn't simply that ads get us to laugh at genuine differences between men and women; rather, they actually encourage viewers to see these differences as 'real' and essential in nature. When growing up, advertising is one of the ways we learn about gender.

The use of humour to make people feel alright about gender stereotyping is a major issue for the ASA, which time and again defends the use of 'sexist' humour. When the ASA say it is 'not a social engineer or a social commentator. It is responsible for ensuring the content of ads do not go against prevailing standards in society', it becomes clear that they're not on the side of gender equality; in fact, they're part of the problem.[18] Lindner explains:

> [Advertisements] act as socializing agents that influence our attitudes, values, beliefs, and behaviors. Advertisements contain messages about gender roles in terms of appropriate behaviour for both men and women. They shape our ideas of what it means to be male or female in society.[19]

Let's look a bit more closely at what those ideas are.

Women in the media

In 2007 and 2008 members of Bristol Fawcett Society and Bristol Feminist Network observed the media's representation of women and men on a single day.[20]

TELEVISION

- Of 366 instances of turning on the television, the screen showed 'only men' on 196 occasions, men and women together on 94 occasions, and 'only women' on 70. Women were portrayed as active on 36 occasions, as opposed to 87 for men.

CHILDREN'S TELEVISION

- All story narrators were male.
- Only 30 per cent of main characters were female.
- A clear majority of anchors and presenters were male.

NEWSPAPERS

- 61 per cent of images of people in newspapers were of men only, 26 per cent were of women only, and 13 per cent featured men and women together.
- Women were most frequently shown 'without much on' (as the 10-year-old daughter of a Fawcett member put it).

MAGAZINE COVERS IN SHOPS

521 covers picturing people were analysed according to whether the person was featured because of their looks (idealised) or their work and achievements.

- 84 per cent of the 'idealised' (to be looked at) images were of women.
- 85 per cent of people shown for their work and achievements were men.

FILMS

- Out of 27 films showing in Bristol, *not one* was directed by a woman.

Why men aren't from Mars

When feminist research in the 1970s demonstrated that gender roles were mostly a social construction, not a biological inevitability, and there was no real connection between possessing a penis and successfully erecting a set of shelves, many breathed a sigh of relief. Feminist research in sociology, psychology, anthropology and related fields came to a number of newsworthy conclusions. Men and women are much more similar than different, and gender roles are very heavily dependent on our culture, rather than on biology. The average man is 7 per cent taller and 30 per cent stronger than the average woman, but many women are stronger and taller than many men, so it's foolish to think of men as strong and tall and women as being weak and short. Chromosomally, women and men are about 5 per cent different. 'Men and women are very similar' would have been a good headline, but didn't grab editors' attention, so the research never left the pages of the sociology textbooks.

But when John Gray came along with *Men are from Mars, Women are from Venus*, his books became bestsellers. Others followed, such as Anne and Bill Moir's *Why Men Don't Iron*[21] and Allan and Barbara Pease's series with increasingly improbable titles, *Why Men Don't Listen and Women Can't Read Maps*, *Why Men Lie and Women Cry*, *Why Men Don't Have a Clue and Women Always Need More Shoes*, and... well, you get the idea.[22] Based mainly on anecdotes about clients or friends (normally middle-class white people), these self-help books were touted as the answer to society's gender problems. Drawing on 'evolutionary psychology' and sociobiology, a branch of biology that claimed to 'monitor the genetic basis of social behavior',[23] these books maintain that gender differences are hard-wired into us as a product of evolution.

These ideas were picked up across the media. Amy Hasinoff reports that sociobiological arguments featured in *every single* issue of US *Cosmopolitan* magazine from 1995 to 2005. *Cosmo* writers use sociobiology to justify why men prefer blondes with pale skin (apparently, they signify youthfulness and fertility – a clear example of sociobiology's racism) and don't clean up after themselves ('Leaving a trail is a primitive way for guys to mark their territory'). Meanwhile, women are instructed to excuse their boyfriends ogling other women's breasts ('Hon, it's caveman biology') and stop complaining that men don't do enough house-work ('Women have more rods in their eyes, which allows them to spot particles like dust and crumbs more easily').[24]

Gender-difference literature tries to help men and women communicate better by understanding and tolerating each other's differences, John Gray argues:

> We have forgotten that men and women are supposed to be different. As a result our relationships are filled with unnecessary friction and conflict.
>
> Clearly recognizing and respecting these differences dramatically reduce confusion when dealing with the opposite sex. When you remember that men are from Mars and women are from Venus, everything can be explained.[25]

Why not just accept this as a theory that might work for some people? Unfortunately it's not that simple. The gender-difference industry is not only misguided but potentially harmful.

First, men are clearly not from Mars but Earth (an obvious point, you'd think). Second, most of the gender differences the pop-psychology writers identify are not substantiated by research. For instance, as Deborah Cameron documents in *The Myth of Mars and Venus*, the idea that women talk more than men turns out to be false: most research finds that men talk more. Men's and women's communication styles are remarkably similar, with only moderate differences in frequency of smiling and accuracy of spelling (both are greater among women), and any other differences (for instance, men interrupt very slightly more often) small or close to zero. Variations among groups of women (or men) are greater than any differences between the genders: so age, culture, social class and the context of the interaction come into play.

It's easy to think that when a scientist says gender differences are 'hard-wired', he (and it usually is a he) must be right. But as neuroscientist Lesley Rogers has shown, these are not things that science has proven without reasonable doubt; brains, genes and (sex) hormones are malleable, changing as they interact with each other, our social environments and our individual actions. We shouldn't say that testosterone 'causes' men to be aggressive. She writes: 'It is all too common for biologists and psychologists to focus on genes or sex hormones (often only a single hormone) and to make only passing reference to the potential effects of experience.' The 'science' of gender difference is full of decidedly unscientific presuppositions, Rogers explains, and we need to listen to those who take a more rounded view: 'Speculations about causes are shaped by the practices and views of society, and should not be seen as objective facts simply because they are stated by scientists. Scientists have always both reflected and reinforced the attitudes of society.'[26] In evolutionary psychology, as feminist blogger Aerik sarcastically observed, 'the gender dynamics of our savannah ancestors [look] curiously like those of 1950s America'.[27]

Third, the self-help industry's gender myths are not harmless but have practical consequences: being a 'touchy-feely' woman means doing the emotional labour in a relationship as well the housework and childcare, while your 'cave-dwelling' man works in the day but escapes to the pub by night. Cameron shows how false ideas about gender differences adversely affect rape trials, where the idea that men 'misunderstand' women's refusal of consent and therefore shouldn't be found guilty of rape has been one of the – admittedly unintended – effects of the gender difference industry. In Gray's logic, women must communicate non-consent with a direct 'no', as anything else will be understood by men as a 'yes'. This insultingly assumes that men are stupid, and blames women for the sensible 'softening' tactics they adopt to refuse sex (e.g. saying they can't because they have their period) because they fear the consequences of an outright 'no'.[28]

Cameron also explains how myths about women being better communicators mean men are disadvantaged when applying for jobs requiring communication with the public; service-sector employers may prefer female applicants if they think women are 'naturally' good at customer service (she quotes a call centre manager who admits that 'I suppose we do ... select women some-times because they are women rather than because of something they've particularly shown in the interview'[29]). These are good examples of why 'frivolous' ideas in pop culture are important to challenge, since they influence our 'real' experiences in work and relationships.

Celebrity culture

Reality television, talent shows and celebrity magazines have enjoyed unprecedented global success in the last few years. A record 200,000 people auditioned for *The X Factor* in the UK in 2009. Many who audition admit that their motive is fame. Yet for every 200,000 auditionees, there is only one winner, only a few who will make a living out of their fame, and 199,990 or so will have put their energy into chasing a dream that remains elusive.

The lure of fame is attractive to young people from all walks of life and may be seen as a way out of financial hardship for those from less privileged backgrounds who haven't done well in education. In the UK, reality television has taken hold at precisely the time when young people's lives have become more risky. Jobs for life are virtually non-existent; many of the manufacturing jobs that school-leavers once took on have been outsourced to developing countries; and work-based training or university is often available only to those with higher qualifications and financial support. The number of young people classified by the government as NEET (Not in Education, Employment or Training) has risen in the last decade to around 1 in 10.[30]

Some researchers believe celebrity culture is actually discouraging young people from sticking with formal education. 'The evidence', they say, 'suggests that young people can develop unrealistic aspirations fuelled by a focus on the lifestyle of celebrities, such as those portrayed in magazines and TV shows. The belief that becoming a celebrity is a realisable ambition can prevent young people from engaging in learning because they neglect to focus upon academic goals or developing life skills.'[31]

For many young people, becoming famous seems a magical way out of a difficult life. Liz Atkins interviewed young people retaking English in further-education colleges. She found more evidence of the hold celebrity has over young working-class people. '*All of the young people…*, irrespective of gender or ethnicity, demonstrated a fascination with celebrity culture, and a conviction that one day they would experience a sudden transformation which would lead to a celebrity lifestyle', she writes (our stress).[32] When asked to pick pseudonyms, almost all chose celebrity names like 'Paris' and 'Leonardo'. She found that young people know very little about possible careers or how to get into them. Their role models are celebrities like the Beckhams or Katie Price, who achieved financial success despite (mostly) coming from working-class backgrounds.[33]

'I am working increasingly in voiceovers and new media, such as computer games, where many of the same problems exist. In the games industry, there are still too few women's roles, and the ones that are there tend to fulfil male fantasies (my favourite joke is that I can voice any cup size).'

'Why is a woman always "a woman" when a man is "a human being", a person to tell your story through? We need to get beyond that to truly be equal.'

'We often only see one Black or ethnic minority family in a soap – and rarely families of mixed races living together ... if we go onto our streets this is the reality ... but this is never seen or reflected in the arts.'

'It's very disheartening that men in their 40s often get juicy supporting roles and women become almost invisible except as mums and occasionally doctors and teachers ... women are doing a wider variety of jobs and at higher levels than ever before. Why isn't this represented on the big and small screen?'[36]

Inequalities of social class are at the heart of celebrity culture. Many of the poorest of us are lining the pockets of the celebrity elite and the industry profiting from them, whilst those who achieve fame often come from the ranks of the most privileged. How easy would it be for a young woman with embryonic vocal or television presenting talents from, say, a Manchester council estate to achieve the success of a Peaches Geldof, Miley Cyrus or Paris Hilton?

While these are primarily class issues, they have a gender dimension. Women's and men's likelihood of achieving success are not the same. An analysis of 15,000 speaking characters in American films showed that male characters outnumber female ones by nearly 3 to 1.[34] Male drama and dance-school graduates are more likely to gain employment in the professions than females.[35] A study sponsored by the International Federation of Actors (FIA) found that, among European performers, men were more likely to work for longer and regularly, to have increased choice about the roles they took on and to earn more. Women were considerably less likely to think that their age and gender were represented realistically.

Men are, therefore, more likely to achieve acclaim through talent than women, and not just in the arts. Most of the money, media attention and fame in the sporting world go on sports*men*. And it's not a case of 'men are better at sport so that's why they're the focus', because the high status sports (football, basketball or cricket) are simply the ones that we've decided are high status. Why don't we throw money and airtime at gymnastics or skating? Perhaps because they're perceived as 'feminine'. Additionally, when a women's team does well (such as the England Women's Cricket Team winning the World Cup in 2009), barely a peep is heard in the media.

Women in sport

- In England, just 1 in 8 women regularly play sport, compared to 1 in 5 men.[37]
- 4 per cent of sports coverage in the national and local press focuses on women's sport. The Women's Sport and Fitness Foundation says this matters because 'the media play a central role in informing our knowledge, opinions and attitudes about women and sport, which in turn, influence participation levels.'[38]
- Only 3 per cent of the journalists writing for the sports pages of the newspapers are women. Often, even when women are mentioned, the focus of the article is their personal appearance.[39]
- The WSFF states that, along with practical barriers like lack of money and time, cultural attitudes can be a barrier to female participation. The male-dominated culture of sport is offputting to many girls. Sport is rife with homophobia too; the WSFF say that 'many boys are called gay for playing "un-manly" sports and girls are often labelled lesbians if they play almost any sport.' Attitudes to people based on disability, age or ethnicity have also been highlighted as problems (for example, assuming that people with disabilities or Asian women won't want to play sport).[40]

Many great actresses, like Halle Berry, Kate Winslet or Meryl Streep, have gained success through great talent and hard work. There are also those represented by the media as 'trainwreck celebrities', people like Amy Winehouse, Britney Spears and Lindsay Lohan, who are depicted as unhinged by drugs and alcohol and unable to sustain stable relationships. The public love to hate these women, and they're treated more cruelly than their male counterparts (think Pete Doherty, Robbie Williams or Owen Wilson).[41] A 2008 survey by *Marketing* magazine found that the five most loved celebrities were men (Paul McCartney, Lewis Hamilton, Gary Lineker, Simon Cowell and David Beckham). Of the five most hated celebrities, women made up the top four (Heather Mills, Amy Winehouse, Victoria Beckham and Kerry Katona).[42] There's also a long list of female celebrities who are famous less for their talents and more for their relationships with a male celebrity (think of the WAGS – wives and girlfriends of footballers), their sexual exploits (Abi Titmuss or Rebecca Loos) or for soft-porn modelling (Jordan or Jodie Marsh). Many people begrudge these women fame or accuse them of lacking 'real' talent; but it's more important that we criticise a society where women find it so difficult to succeed that they need to show their breasts or marry an influential man to carve out a media career for themselves.

Girls know that in a society that devalues women's talents and likes to watch them embarrassing themselves and showing off their bodies, this is what they'll need in order to be a success. In one study, 14–15 year olds were asked to think of three words to describe 'a star, celebrity or famous person who you would like to be ... or ... who you think is good or cool ... and which also describe how you would like people to think of you?' Responses showed a clear gender difference (Table 6.1).[43] The girls in this research value attractiveness and money as the most desirable

TABLE 6.1   What does success mean to you? (% respondents)

	FEMALES	MALES
'Pretty'/'attractive'	57	0
Other looks/style	11	14
Talent (range of words)	39	55
'Confident'/'strong-willed'	18	0
'Funny'/'good laugh'	7	32
'Cool'	4	23
'Popular'/friends/loved	21	5
'Rich'/money	54	5

qualities for themselves, whereas for boys talent was at the top of the list. They perceived that their appearance, rather than talent, was the most important determinant in their success.

Changing culture for the better: the feminist response

Just as popular culture is often dismissed as unimportant for feminist concern, so is activism that engages with it. What use is a girl making cut-and-paste zines in her bedroom compared to an organisation agitating for legal changes? But one form of activism does not necessarily exclude the other; the woman who organises a feminist arts festival or writes a feminist blog may also volunteer at her local Rape Crisis Centre. Also, cultural activism is important and valid activism in and of itself. As Melanie Maddison explains in *I'm not waiting* zine (2004):

> Activism can be viewed as broad actions with political conse-
> quences for individuals, even the everyday, personal revolution

that occurs upon hearing music or reading a 'zine.... Messages in lyrics & in linear notes to LPs and CDs read by girls in their bedrooms can form revolutions from within, leading to confidence & a belief in personal action. These messages are activism, as are the direct personal actions that girls take in their own lives.... As one individual 'feels differently' about her abilities, she 'does something', thus creating ripples of multiple ends within her localised community.

And, after all, what we are fighting for in the realm of culture is not necessarily changes in the law (although that might be the goal of some campaigns), but rather changes in attitudes; this is a far greater challenge and a long – but worthwhile – process.

Speaking out against sexism

Over three-quarters of the feminists we surveyed said that they challenge anti-feminist views they hear expressed in daily life. This was the most common form of activism they took part in; it's probably the most basic form of activism anyone can do. This can range from a friendly debate with friends in the pub about whether women should change their name after marriage, to more difficult situations, like this example posted on feminist blog *Fugitivus*, which aimed to collect anecdotes of men helping the feminist cause:

My friend told me about a situation involving a male friend of hers who is a soldier. She said one day at the barracks (or whatever) he came upon a group of male soldiers watching porn. It was exploitive and they were laughing at it because the girl was crying. He confronted them and 'made a scene,' continuing to object even as they tried to rebuff him, asking them what if it was their daughter, or sister, or friend (not that it should matter, but I get why he was saying that).[44]

The Muffia are a performance art group who challenge media stereotyping of women through public performances. This might involve staging a fake death from starvation outside a Topshop window featuring a particularly emaciated model, or sticking fake hair onto advertisements for hair-removal products.

> We went out on the streets dressed in trench coats, with our 'muff' wigs. We stood outside Oxford Circus and began to talk to the public using megaphones, asking them if they wanted new hands or new hymens and pretended to inject each other using large needles labelled botox… We wrote on each others bodies a series of questions and comments in relation a woman's body as a literal construct.
>
> Why? … It was partly an instinctive and impulsive reaction to sexualized images that we have absorbed as young girls, now as adults we want to find a way to comment on the stereotypical images of women in the media. We feel that the extent to which this has accelerated since we were teenagers is astonishing. It is also frustrating that this has become so normalized within our culture.[45]

Refusing to conform

Feminists who are visibly different from mainstream gender stereotypes – who stand out and live their lives the way they want to in spite of everything – should be applauded by the rest of us who are too scared to be visibly different. The girl who chooses a career as a stand-up comic despite the disapproval of her traditional family, the boy who comes out as gay at his school, the woman who chooses not to shave her legs and doesn't care what people think, or the parents who struggle to raise their children in non-sexist ways in a sexist culture; all of these people are pioneers.

Reclaiming denigrated forms of 'feminine' culture

In a world where 'girl' or 'cunt' is the worst insult that you can hurl at a man, it's understandable that some feminists are reclaiming activities which have been denigrated purely because they are seen as 'feminine'. For instance, did you know that a feminist kick-started the knitting revival? Debbie Stoller, founder and editor of *BUST* magazine, wrote a book called *Stitch 'n Bitch Nation* back when knitting was seen as uncool (hard to imagine now). She writes:

> why, dammit, wasn't knitting receiving as much respect as any other hobby? Why was it still so looked down on? It seemed to me that the main difference between knitting and, say, fishing or woodworking or basketball, was that knitting had traditionally been done by women … why weren't boys learning to knit and sew?[46]

Knitting is not inherently feminist, and some criticise what they see as a return to female domesticity in its revival; but pointing out that many traditionally 'feminine' activities have value *is* feminist. In particular, if children learn that activities are gender-neutral, maybe they'll learn that men and women *aren't* from different planets, and that a wider range of hobbies are available to them. Feminist festivals often have workshops teaching women traditionally 'male' hobbies like drumming or DJing; nearby you might see a group of men learning to knit. Reclaiming traditional crafts also taps into the feminist trend of rejecting consumerist lifestyles and sweatshop fashion.

There are many examples of reclaiming denigrated 'feminine' activities. Several projects have documented the heyday of Riot Grrrl – another influential but underestimated element of women and girls' history. The Riot Grrrl Portraits Project, in which Jade French photographed portraits of people affected by the movement, and books such as *Riot Grrrl! Revolution Girl Style Now!* (2007), have given Riot Grrrl the emphasis it deserved.

Another example is Radical Cheerleading. Emily S in *Born in Flames* zine (2003) describes this phenomenon:

My first encounter with radical cheerleaders was at a large anti biotechnology protest in Minneapolis, Minnesota. I heard a group of grrrls' voices shouting cheers like you would imagine at a traditional American football game. Only these cheers were about animal rights, capitalism and globalization. I looked up to see a cheerleading squad that was anything but traditional. The grrrls were all sizes unlike usual cheerleading squads where there is a lot of pressure to be thin or muscular. They had pom poms made out of shredded garbage bags and comfortable looking outfits.

It's especially gratifying when men and boys are able unapologetically to enjoy something that has been traditionally considered 'feminine'. An example of this is the Peewee Boyz from Leeds, a troupe of boys aged between 9 and 11 who won third prize at an international cheerleading competition in 2009.

Producing alternative media and events

When the mainstream culture doesn't represent you, there's only one thing to do: represent yourself. This isn't about marginalising women further by separating them from the mainstream. By creating their own alternative culture, feminists show by their actions how culture could be different.

Publishing

Following in the footsteps of publishers like Kali for Women in India, Virago in the UK and Spinifex in Australia, feminists have also set up publishing companies. FEMrite in Uganda organises women's writing workshops. Founder member Goretti Kyomuhendo explains some of the problems women face as writers:

> As a literary association committed to women's freedom of expression, we have realised that women often refrain from telling the stories in their hearts. Many women think of themselves as wives, mothers or daughters, and when they write, they concentrate on

the feelings and reactions of others.... Very often, anxiety and fear about how a story will be perceived precedes the need to tell a good story. I remember an obvious example of this. One of our members had written an extremely evocative story using the first-person narrative mode. When her husband read it, he objected strongly to the use of the first person (in lines such as 'I was raped on my wedding night.'). 'People will think it is you, my wife,' he argued. She ended up rewriting it in another mode, and this weakened the impact of her story.[47]

In the last two decades the Internet has enabled feminist writing to grow exponentially. Blogs focus on specific issues such as women in science or politics, men as feminist allies, or feminist science-fiction. Blogging can be very powerful in influencing attitudes; indeed, many feminists we surveyed mentioned coming to feminism through reading them.

Some contemporary feminist magazines

Canada: *Good Girl*
Croatia: *Crow*
Belgium: *ScumGrrrls*
Germany: *Emma*
India (Telugu): *Bhumika*
Iran: *Zanan*
Ireland: *Women's News, The Rag, Lash Back*
Kashmir: *She*
UK: *Subtext, HerStoria, Eve's Back, Trouble & Strife, Gender Agenda, Race Revolt, Lippy, Wee Bissums*
USA: *Ms., Bust, Bitch, Off Our Backs, New Moon, Lilith, Make/Shift, HUES*

Organising feminist cultural events

Many events promote women's or non-sexist culture, such as the Birds Eye View's women's film festivals and the Independent Heroines Feminist Film Festival (Bristol). The most prominent of these are the Ladyfest festivals ('Lady' is tongue-in-cheek); not-for-profit, volunteer-run events celebrating women's art and music held in cities across the world for ten years. Most major UK cities have hosted a Ladyfest. As there is no central organising committee, Ladyfests have a local feel, reflecting the organisers' priorities and politics.

Ladyfest provides a supportive atmosphere for female-centred bands to perform. The band The Gossip famously played at Ladyfest Glasgow in 2001; Beth Ditto inspired many women that night and has since become famous in the mainstream.

Some see Ladyfest as superficial frippery. Journalist Clare Rudebeck, reviewing Ladyfest Bristol in 2003, was puzzled: 'I'm struggling to see what this has to do with feminism at all' she wrote, watching a performance by the Actionettes, a dance group.[48] But detractors should consider the impact a supportive, fun feminist space can have on those attending:

> There is definitely a strong sisterhood between all Ladyfests – you just have to show up at one in another country and feel instantly welcomed and at home! I think we all learned so much from doing the festival and met so many interesting intelligent women from all over the place. (SHELLEY, Ladyfest Cork, *The Rag* 3, n.d.)

Often inspired by Ladyfest, feminists have organised club or social nights promoting feminist culture along with political activism. In the UK these include Frock On (Glasgow), Unskinny Bop (London), Wanc Cafe (London), Girl Germs (London), Manifesta (Leeds), Mass Teens on the Run (Manchester), Club Disaster (London), Local Kid (Bristol), Homocrime (London) and Come on let's go (Cardiff).

Promoting women's art, music and sport

In 2007, anarcha-feminist Siobhan and a group of friends put the finishing touches to a hundred CDs of female, DIY, alternative bands they'd just burned and decorated. They hit the streets of Dublin's Temple Bar area and handed them out to teenage girls. Siobhan explains:

> I felt that it was important for more younger girls (future genera-tions!) to be exposed to female, alternative, diy music at a young

age so that early on in their years they would have some awareness that there was an alternative route to the mainstream for them to take if they wanted to do something with music, or anything else creative and self empowering as females.

An insert in the CD cases explained the reasons for the project:

Hey up. You have been given this cd because you're a girl. Cool wha?

Why? Well, loads of reasons but the main reason is to expose and maybe encourage you towards a more alternative, creative, independent appreciation of what being female is.

All the songs on this cd are by women in bands with other women, or with men, or just women on their own. The idea in giving you this cd is that you, as one of the many teenage girls kicking around the town of a Saturday will be so amazingly inspired by this cd that you'll stop kicking around the town watching the boys go off starting their bands and you'll either go and join them, or better still go and like all the girls on this cd did, start something of your own.[49]

Kate Graham organises Guerilla Cabaret, an event supporting emerging female playwrights, theatre directors, singers or songwriters. She explains:

Our intention is to provide a forum where women can experiment safe in the knowledge that their work will be performed. Work will only ever improve by practice and performance, but access to the structures that enable these is often fraught. Guerilla Cabaret aims to help women access these structures through annual showcases across the globe.[50]

Alongside events, feminists are using other methods to promote women in the arts, including radio shows such as FEISTY (Bradford) or a club night to promote female hip-hop artists (Dutty Girl, Bristol). Like artists Queen Latifah, Sister Souljah and slam poet Aya De León, who have used their music to challenge the misogyny of hip-hop, women-centred hip-hop magazine *Verbalisms* supports Gwendolyn Pough's argument that the future of rap is not about rejecting it wholesale, but engaging in dialogue with it, 'bringing wreck' to its 'stereotypes about black womanhood'.[51]

Finally, feminists are supporting other women and girls in male-dominated areas of culture. For example, *Girl-wonder.org* 'is a collection of sites dedicated to female characters and creators in mainstream comics'. It aims 'to foster an attentive, empowered audience community and to encourage respect and high-quality character depiction within the industry'.[52] Spin-off projects included an anti-harassment project to make fan conventions safer spaces for all. Girls Rock! camp in the USA teaches girls from 8 to 18 to make music in a safe, supportive environment. In the UK, similar projects have been held, such as Ladies Rock! in Brixton, London, where thirty women formed bands, learned instruments, wrote songs and performed. At the Edinburgh Fringe Festival in 2009, female comics, increasingly marginalised in the comedy scene, organised a group photo of eighty women comedians to challenge their invisibility. In sport, the Women's Running Network was set up in 1998 to inspire women of all ages to run for fun and fitness. The Muslim Women's Sports Foundation began in 2001 to provide women with opportunities to participate in sports, generally in female-only environments. In Mumbai and Delhi, a project called Goal Girls garnered sponsorship from a major bank to provide netball training and life-skills training to teenage girls living in poverty.

Critiquing and interacting with culture

Feminists don't just moan about culture, they interact with it and challenge it directly. Aspiring feminist guy Jonathan McIntosh was watching *Twilight*, a film adaptation of a popular teen book about a relationship between teenager, Bella, and vampire, Edward. He explains:

> Over the course of the film Edward is in turns patronising, condescending and just downright creepy. He spies on Bella, he stalks her (for 'her own good'), he sneaks into her room to watch her sleep (without her consent) and even confesses to a deep, over-powering desire to kill her. [My friend and I] marvelled at how the film attempted to present this behavior as sweet and deeply romantic – and how the larger pop culture discussion continued that framing for millions of young Twilight fans. At several points during the film [we] found ourselves asking each other: 'What Would Buffy Do?'[53]

McIntosh went on to create a remixed version of the problematic scenes, replacing Bella's reactions with those of proto-feminist icon Buffy the Vampire Slayer. His video was an Internet hit, and thousands of viewers commented on how clearly it illuminated feminist concerns about *Twilight*.

This sort of interaction with culture typifies the activities of today's feminists, whether it's deconstructing an issue of *The Lady* for fun (blogger Cath Elliott), debating the meaning of Florence and the Machine's lyric 'A kiss with a fist is better than none', or blogging about a particular aspect of culture (feministmusicgeek. com). Pick any cultural genre and you'll find a feminist group engaging with it: Muslimah Media Watch analyse media reporting on Muslim women; Naomi M's blog *A Vagina Dentata* looks at bad science reporting as applied to gender; *The Bechdel Test Movie List* website reviews films according to cartoonist Alison Bechdel's famous test (a film passes if: (a) it has at least two women in it, (b) who talk to each other, (c) about something besides a man). Feminists question everything (in fact, some-times we secretly enjoy it). Some feminists take inspiration from organisations like Adbusters (which question not only the content of adverts but their very prevalence in our lives), and participate in 'culture-jamming' activities such as defacing billboards or putting up spoof ads.

This engagement with culture can start at any age. Ten-year-old feminist Ananya wrote an article for *The F Word* about magazines for girls:

> There are quite a few magazines available in the shops aimed at girls of around the ages of seven to 12. These magazines suggest that girls can only be interested in certain topics, e.g. fashion, celebrities and some pop stars selected by the magazines themselves. They also suggest that girls must not be interested in any school work and find it fun or be clever... I don't see why they can't be interested in both![54]

In the UK, the award-winning Pink Stinks campaign was set up by sisters Abi and Emma Moore. It aims to 'challenge the culture of pink which invades every aspect of girls' lives'. They explain:

> We believe that body image obsession is starting younger and younger, and that the seeds are sown during the pink stage, as young girls are taught the boundaries within which they will grow up, as well as narrow and damaging messages about what it is to be a girl... We will redress the balance by providing girls with positive female role models chosen because of their achievements, skills, accomplishments and successes.[55]

We've discussed earlier how representations of masculinity are problematic. Today's egalitarians are critiquing those stereotypes. Here's Alex Gibson, writing about men and feminism:

> The idea of men as stupid and sex-obsessed is an enduring generalisation that is allowed to flourish in – dare I say it – a much more brazen way than the stereotypes about women, mainly because no man ever stands up and says: 'Hey, that's sexist and it offends

me!' The problem is, while women are encouraged to reject the ludicrous ideas that are held about them, men are supposed to embrace them...

But guys, have you seen what we're supposed to be like? ...Men are often characterised as spoiled, helpless brats utterly unable to perform simple household tasks, too stupid to remember anniversaries and appointments and completely unable to understand these strange female creatures and their hysterical emotions. We're base brutes ruled by our overactive sex drives who simply can't help being crass and immature, because that is the way God made us... This is precisely the kind of ridiculous stereotype that, if applied to women, would be torn to shreds in intelligent debate. So why don't men object at being labelled emotional morons totally in thrall to their basest instincts?[56]

Other pro-feminist men questioning mainstream representations of masculinity include anti-sexist, anti-violence activist Jackson Katz, who lectures in the USA and develops educational videos which address issues of masculinity, and Michael Flood, founder of www.xyonline.net, an extensive collection of writings by pro-feminist men.

In India, The Pink Chaddi Campaign (aka the Corsortium of Pubgoing, Loose, and Forward Women) aimed to mobilise a 'strong protest against the recent attacks on women in the context of moral/cultural policing and religious intolerance, attacks that are escalating as women resist and fight back'. Organisers distributed flyers, organised a 'take back the night' march, posted pink chaddis (underwear) to offending organisations as a humorous form of protest, and arranged email campaigns, petitions and art exhibitions. One organiser commented:

I truly believe part of what we are achieving here is staking a claim for our shared culture. Not the fake, monolith, imaginary culture that the right-wing groups insist we have, but the real stuff. It is messy, complicated, wonderful. Each of us define Indian culture differently. No one is wrong, no one is more right. But why slug it out when we can have some fun? Let us go out and win back Indian culture, one chaddi at a time.[57]

Conclusion

As we've seen, feminists are challenging cultural sexism wherever they find it. Individually and collectively they are blogging, publishing magazines and starting bands. They recognise that there's plenty wrong with popular culture, especially its gender stereotypes and privileging of male talent. These make it ripe for feminist analysis and activism, and as central a concern for today's feminists as legal independence was for the women's liberation movement. In the next and final chapter we turn to our seventh and final priority, reclaiming feminism itself.

Take action!

1. Consider the music you buy, the authors you read, the sportspeople you watch and the artists you support. Make efforts to diversify your consumption.
2. Communicate your concerns about gender equality to the media industries: give feedback to advertisers; ask advertising regulators to improve their handling of complaints about sexism; ask for TV companies to commission programmes with more positive representations of women and men; ask your local cinema to show more films directed by women.
3. Undertake your own gender analysis of newspapers, adverts, TV programmes, or sports coverage and share the results.
4. Support feminist media: subscribe to magazines, attend festivals, or contribute to blogs or projects. Organise your own feminist film screening.
5. Reject lazy stereotypes about men and women that you hear in everyday life.

7

FEMINISM RECLAIMED

THE ISSUES we've covered are serious and wide-ranging. This brings us to our final demand, which is also our suggestion for a solution – a feminist revival, or an end to the backlash against feminism. It may seem odd to have a solution as a demand in itself. But the state of feminism itself was one of the issues that a substantial number of feminists we surveyed highlighted. Here, in their words, are some of their concerns:

- The question of what feminism is and why many women identify as 'not a feminist'.
- Spreading feminism.
- Encouraging people to consider feminism as a viable academic theory.
- Engaging women, men, boys and girls and communicating feminist ideals. Making feminism be seen and felt in the world.
- Misconceptions about feminism and its goals.
- Making feminism accessible to young people.
- Misrepresentation of what feminism is and that the battle still needs fighting.

- The way women today seem to think feminism is not needed any more – consciousness raising.
- Representation/inclusion of women of colour and non-Western women within mainstream Western feminism.
- How feminism is taught/represented in schools.
- Awareness (or lack of) among young women of the importance of feminism.
- That girls will grow up knowing feminism is important for them.

In general terms, their comments can be summarised as a desire for a larger, more visible, diverse and inclusive feminist movement, and an eagerness to ensure that more people – especially young people – are attracted to and empowered by it. In short, for even more of us to reclaim feminism.

To a large extent, we believe that a feminist resurgence is occurring, and we've hopefully given a taste of the movement's passion and vibrancy. But we want to build on what's already there and spread feminism to more people. As Bec Star wrote in *Starlette* zine 2 (*c.* 2001):

'Everyone is born feminist. It takes a lot of social conditioning to make people otherwise.' FEMALE, 17

> although the scene benefits girls by letting them know they are not alone and giving them inspiration, it cannot begin to change things, really change things, until it reaches more people.... Wouldn't it be great it modern feminist ideas and riot grrrl attitudes got through to those girls who choose to shut their eyes?

Why feminism?

But first, let's answer the question of why we need feminism. Why feminism – why can't people just try to address any of the issues we've mentioned as individuals?

First of all, on a personal level, feminism is a survival mechanism. It assures you that you have a right to live your life the way you want and imagine a brighter future for the world. It prompts you to question the status quo, rather than assuming that the way things are is the best they can be. Feminism assures you that you're not alone, that the problems you experience are shared by others, and that, as a woman or a gender non-conforming person, your concerns are important:

> Thank fuck for feminism, then. You can either go on feeling like the freak, insecure because you *just can't be like them*, even though you are told you are *supposed* to be like them. Or you can say 'fuck it' and just be who you are, because that's what makes you happy. And feminism kind of helps you foster that attitude. (MICHELLE, 23)[1]

But feminism isn't just about 'making us feel better'. It's about collective action. So, second, feminism encourages us to consider the wider impact of our actions. In other words, it's not just about us, but is about ending sexism and liberating *everyone* from centuries of oppression based on gender.

Third, feminism provides you with a support network for your interests and campaigns. It enables us to band together on issues we agree on. Someone who calls themselves a feminist will often have interests and concerns that span several key areas.

And, finally, feminism can move all the issues we've highlighted – issues that are interconnected and overlap – up the political agenda. It often seems that women's issues are considered a 'minority' issue – which is ridiculous, when women are 51 per cent of the population. To take some examples, when the Million Women Rise march to protest about violence against women occurred in London in 2008, around 5,000 women from all over the UK participated, one of the largest marches of women in recent years. There was no coverage from the mainstream media. As march volunteer Louise Livesey pointed out,

Around the same time, the press managed to cover 5,000 protestors at Aldermaston, a threatened protest outside the new Banana Republic store, organised by War on Want, two men scaling a crane to protest in favour of a referendum on the EU, five men climbing onto the roof of the Palace of Westminster to protest against a third runway at Heathrow and 250 pig farmers protesting about low meat prices. Spot something, well, unequal about this?[2]

Feminism enables us to link together the problems highlighted in this book and see them not as coincidences but as part of a wider pattern of sexism underpinning our entire culture – some might refer to this as patriarchy or attribute it to capitalism. Indeed, as we've been writing the chapters, it's been hard to decide how to split the themes up, since they seem to seep into one another. These issues are not accidental or individual problems – they are part of a pattern of structural inequality.

Discussions about whether the word 'feminism' should be ditched in favour of something with less negative baggage are, on the whole, a distraction. Feminism has a proud history and we've all benefited from it, and if we're too scared to use the word in case we offend people, we'll probably also be too scared to fight for the changes women need.

But if most people have feminist views, does it really matter whether they identify as feminists? We believe it does. Whilst we respect those who would rather not label themselves, there's something about embracing a belief system or identity, something about joining with others in a cause larger than ourselves, that inspires us to action. Individuals can do an enormous amount of good; but imagine the potential of a generation of women and men bred on the ideas of feminism who decide to act *together* to bring about the changes that are still necessary. Imagine the potential of a generation who, instead of taking feminism's work for granted, understand not just how far we've come but how far we still have to go, and dedicate themselves to closing that gap between the ideal and the real.

So if feminism is a solution, what's hindering it from growing? A large part of this, we feel, is feminism's negative image in the media and the myth that young people in particular don't care about feminist issues. We've proved this is a lie. As we hope we've shown, there are a large number of women and men who are embracing feminism, reclaiming it from the naysayers.

By drawing attention to these people and their thoughts and actions, we hope this book will inspire others to get involved, find out more, or just realise that they aren't alone. Let's look a bit more closely at the feminists we surveyed. More details can be found in the Appendix, but here are some highlights.

Our survey was targeted at UK feminists involved in new forms of feminism (mainly organisations, events and groups) that had arisen since 2000. As expected, the majority are female but with a promising number of men; moreover, over two-thirds think men can be feminists, and 90 per cent believe men should embrace feminism. Their ethnicity broadly reflects the make-up of the UK population. A staggering 62 per cent are in their twenties or under. They are highly educated, with 90 per cent having studied at degree or postgraduate level; this may reflect class issues prevalent in the wider feminist movement or the high proportion of individuals who heard about the survey online. The results should not be taken to reflect accurately the feminist movement as a whole; nevertheless, a few interesting results can be highlighted.

What makes people become feminists?

Some 70 per cent of our survey respondents started to identify as a feminist under the age of twenty. Additionally, just over half said that they had always been feminists and couldn't recall a specific time when they 'found' feminism. We asked those who could remember 'finding' feminism what sparked their interest. The results show a variety of reasons.

For many, reading feminist ideas and theories provided the spark:

> I read Naomi Wolf's *The Beauty Myth* when I was 18 and it made me realise that feminism was needed. Before then I didn't really think of myself as a feminist. (FEMALE, 26)

> Germaine Greer's *The Female Eunuch*. I read it when I was 19 and it changed my life. (FEMALE, 21)

> Just the internet. Reading the news and articles online, then finding blogs, and becoming more informed, and then suddenly realising 'hey! That's it! That's what I am, I'm a feminist!' And then learning from then on to question and analyse everything and not to take reports, stories, writing or anything about women at face value and search for any possible agenda or hidden meaning. (FEMALE, 27)

> Around the age of 14, I got sick of trying to fit into an extremely narrow beauty and 'girl' ideal and chose to go my own way. I started reading up on feminism and became a much stronger person, I realised that I did not have to fit into a stereotype of what a woman/girl is/should be/isn't/shouldn't be and do. (FEMALE, 24)

Others describe the joy of finally finding something to explain how they've always felt:

> I don't think my views have changed much – I think I had a 'feminist' attitude even before I knew what that was – but my actions certainly have changed, and along with that my interest and involvement in feminism has become a more significant part of my life and identity. (FEMALE, 27)

> I always had a sense growing up that something wasn't right. But as I grew up through my teens I slowly found out about feminist

thoughts/ideas and said 'yes! That's what I've been thinking all along!' (MALE, 23)

Some were influenced by negative experiences such as rape, domestic violence, harassment, or sexism in the workplace.

I was travelling alone on a late train when I was approached by a man who proceeded to try and accost me. The man had sat next to me on the nearly empty carriage and made it very difficult for me to move.... I eventually reported my anxiety to a male attendant ... who told me there wasn't much he could do. When I told him I was worried about waiting alone on the platform when I changed trains, he was extremely unhelpful and laughed at me when I asked if there would be anyone working at the station ... I eventually moved to a different part of the train and sat near a family, and then caught my next train quickly, but the man who accosted me paced the train for the remainder of the journey. Ever since then I have become extremely aware of the injustices woman face every day when reporting their fears or experiences of male violence. I used to think I could travel safely alone at night, and although I still do, I now carry a rape alarm and often alter my normal behaviour to ensure my personal safety. I have considered myself a feminist ever since, as it heightened my awareness and inspired me to participate in feminist activism. (FEMALE, 20)

At the age of 15, after a walk home from school on my own during which I was sexually/physically harassed by several different groups of males varying between the ages of 13–40+. I became a feminist that day in the hope that one day women would be able to walk on their own as freely and as confidently as men can. (FEMALE, 19)

In the 1970s I had a really good career, but found a lot of antagonism from men in the same industry, and at that time, there was no question of my being able to continue my career after childbirth. (FEMALE, 65)

Men often talk about having their eyes opened by a loved one:

I was always pro-equality but I was convinced over a period of time after I started going out with my rampagingly feminist girlfriend (who is now my wife). This view has been reinforced by both my work and having a daughter. (MALE, 31)

I had never been unfeminist (for want of a better word), but it was when I met my current partner who had just begun to articulate her feminism that she and I would discuss the issues together. We started becoming involved in online discussions in particular. (MALE, 25)

Others were raised feminist:

My parents were politically progressive, and very conscious of discriminating behaviour. Therefore I didn't recognise 'feminism' as a necessary issue. In that sense 'I can't remember a time when I wasn't a feminist' is more applicable. However since I was 15 or so I became more aware of inequalities between men and women and understood it to be a necessary political position. As a slight aside, this grew out of an annoyance with the casual homophobia throughout secondary school. (MALE, 21)

I 'found' feminism when I was 13, thanks to my wonderful father. (FEMALE, 26)

Quite a few found feminism through involvement with women's groups or organisations:

I joined a women's group in 1972 and it changed the ways that I thought about myself. I had previously read *The Second Sex* and *The Women's Room*. (FEMALE, 57)

Education was the most commonly mentioned reason for discovering feminism:

In my first year at university, we had a lecture in feminist criticism. I came into the lecture dreading it, as I didn't think I saw eye-to-eye with feminism, and, as my lecturer described it, I realised that I actually did. I went out of the lecture hall wanting to dance in the road and sing. It was amazing to know that I wasn't alone in how I conceived gender and its related trappings. ('OTHER', 21)

When I started to become aware of the way society worked when I was about 15. And then when I studied sociology at AS level and found I was the only one that found gender studies and women's rights interesting/relevant/important. I became more of a proud feminist when I met my current partner and had someone to talk to seriously about feminism. (FEMALE, 20)

At school (I went to a convent) when I was the only one in the playground arguing for a woman's right to choose against an angry mob of classmates who believed abortion was wrong, full stop. Many later changed their minds after seeing the 'Silent Scream' video (shown to us in an RE class) out of disgust at the tactics used by our teacher and SPUC to make them feel guilty about having sex. (FEMALE, 29)

[I] discovered feminism properly whilst at university, but had something of a 'lightbulb moment' at the age of 16 when my first bank statement arrived addressed me as 'Miss' – I realised I was being defined according to whether or not I was married to a man. (FEMALE, 24)

Overwhelmingly, the stories indicate that discovering feminism was a hugely empowering experience for most, if not all, of the people we surveyed.

The bravery of feminists

What makes feminists particularly admirable is that in a culture that sees feminism as a dirty word, embracing feminism can have negative consequences. We asked feminists if they had suffered any negative consequences as a result of being a feminist. Some 63 per cent of female

'Feminism makes society better for everybody. It should be taught in schools and its activists should be remembered and celebrated as heroes.' VERONICA, 36

respondents and 41 per cent of male ones said yes (are male egalitarians praised as progressive, while females are seen as 'strident'?) In this context, embracing a feminist identity is a brave thing to do.

The negative consequences suffered vary from ridicule to aggression, even occasionally physical attacks. Some of these comments are typical:

Derision and hostility from family, friends and acquaintances. Feeling depressed and frustrated most of the time about the lack of feminism in the world. Feeling like an outcast who has a shameful secret that I only dare to divulge under certain circumstances. Losing friends due to my beliefs. (FEMALE, 38)

People get embarrassed and look at the floor if I say I'm a feminist, e.g. at dinner parties! If they're men who don't understand feminism they'll say something snide like 'oooh is she going to beat us up then' or something equally stupid. (FEMALE, 24)

It really is the 'f-word', it has a big stigma attached to it, and people often react negatively, for example telling me to worry about 'more important things' etc. (FEMALE, 19)

My home country considers many 'feminist' ideals to be illegal. So there are legal consequences to being a feminist in many ways. (FEMALE, 26)

For some, the consequences go beyond a joke. Some feminists have received physical abuse or death threats; many who blog receive harassment on a daily basis (for example, threatening or abusive comments, including rape threats). Some women have given up publishing online due to the harassment, whilst some feminist websites have been specifically targeted by hackers.

For others, feminist activity, especially when combined with activism around race or other forms of discrimination, can lead to ostracism from their community or even, as a speaker at the 2009 Feminism in London conference recounted, the British

National Party outside their front door. Of course, for feminists in certain more conservative countries, activism can have very serious consequences, including beatings, prison or murder. Sudanese journalist Lubna Hussein is one example. In 2009 she and others broke Sudanese law by wearing trousers in public, and were arrested. Adamant that she was willing to be jailed rather than admit her 'guilt', she forced a trial to take place, raising international awareness of the tens of thousands of women flogged in Sudan for breaching the penal code each year.

This isn't intended to put people off feminism; far from it. We need more people to make it clear that such behaviour is not acceptable. We need to raise our voice and say how proud we are of these brave, inspiring women who just keep going, fighting for justice, whilst the rest of the world considers them a hilarious joke.

What do feminists do?

Throughout the book we've given lots of examples of feminists' activism. We asked feminists what sort of activities they take part in. A table indicating these activities – from lobbying MPs to rejecting beauty practices – can be found in the Appendix.

As we hope to have made clear, activism can take many forms. Chally, at the *Feminists with Disabilities* blog, writes:

> There are a lot of forms of activism ... and looking down one's nose at some of them is detrimental as well as being offensive to those of us working hard to make valuable contributions in any way we can.[3]

All acts of resistance are worthwhile, and none should be valued more highly than others. Barriers to participation in activism include money, time, having children, caring responsibilities, transport, confidence, disability and health problems; the 'more is better' attitude towards activism potentially excludes and alienates people who wish to do more but for whatever reason cannot. The inclusion of people with disabilities and health problems (physical or mental) is an issue the feminist movement hasn't fully addressed. Whether it's making venues for meetings accessible, providing sign-language interpreters at rallies, or just accepting that Internet activism and letter-writing is just as valid as marching the streets with a placard, changes need to take place to ensure that as many people feel able to engage in feminist activism without being judged on the quality and quantity of their contributions.[4]

As for concrete examples of activism, let's look at the UK feminist scene; different – and sometimes similar – activities will be taking place in countries all over the world. Today, what many would think of as 'traditional style' feminist activism (protests, rallies and marches) still occurs. Countless protests have been held about issues such as conviction rates for rape, lap-dancing clubs and lads' mags, the threatened stoning of a rape victim in Nigeria, the staging of Miss World in the UK, abortion rights, and the murders of sex workers in Ipswich, to name but a few. These rallies vary greatly in number, attracting between ten and a thousand people. The spirit of Greenham Common lives on at Aldermaston and Menwith Hill women's peace camps. The major national marches have been held in London, with Million Women Rise attracting around 5,000 women each year to make their voices heard about violence and rape.

When we turn to campaigning groups and single-issue organisations, listing them all would be a book in itself. Many organisations existing prior to 2000 are still going strong, such as The Fawcett Society, Justice for Women, Southall Black Sisters, Women Against Rape, Women for Peace, Women's Environmental Network, FORWARD, Campaign Against Domestic Violence,

Women in Black, Scottish Women Against Pornography, Feminists Against Censorship, and the Feminist and Women's Studies Association, to pick a few. However, since 2000 many more *new* campaigning groups have formed, and we've featured many of these throughout the book. Estimating the numbers involved in all these groups is difficult; membership is often fluid rather than official and some people belong to more than one group. However, some of these groups' membership reaches into the hundreds or even thousands.

Feminism still holds a vibrant place in UK universities, despite the closure of undergraduate women's and gender studies courses. Gender studies remains popular at M.A. and Ph.D. level, and feminist modules are available as options on most undergraduate degree courses in the arts, social sciences and humanities. The National Union of Students (NUS) Women's Campaign has been going for twenty years, and NUS women's officers are promoting women's rights in most universities. Student women's groups and feminist societies are also active in at least a dozen universities, many of them having been set up in the last few years. In the USA and elsewhere in Europe, women's studies undergraduate degree courses are well subscribed.

In the UK local networking groups for feminists have mushroomed. These groups' activities vary from discussion evenings, book clubs, social/networking events, to cultural events, feminist-themed gigs, and protests, campaigns and actions. Often connected via the Web as well as meeting locally, these groups tend to have a core of active members of around 10 to 50 with up to 1,000 on their wider mailing list. These groups are frequently dynamic; some cease to be active after a while, others split or relaunch and new groups are formed.

National networking takes place through events like the FEM conferences organised by activist Kat Banyard, Reclaim the Night and Million Women Rise marches and online via websites like *The F Word* and email 'noticeboards' for action and events such as UK Feminist Action.[5]

UK feminists have also created a vibrant alternative culture and media. *The F Word* receives 100,000 visits each month. The Grrrl Zine Network acts as a focal point for the prolific creators of feminist and pro-grrrl zines. There are many hundreds of feminist blogs with tens of thousands of readers; the 'Carnival of Feminists', a collaborative, regular summary of noteworthy feminist blog posts, was set up by a UK feminist blogger. New print magazines like *Subtext*, *Filament* and *Herstoria* have also emerged alongside feminist-influenced magazines like *Mslexia* and *Scarlet*.[6]

And then there is individual activism. Feminism is not 'me-ism', but if it can't first connect with the individual woman, then it's not going to take her into collective work to improve other women's lives. For this reason, our personal expressions of feminism must be supported. The diaries and blogs written in the solitude of our bedrooms, the zines where we tell our stories of abortions or sexual crises, and our inner frustrations when we walk past a group of men who leer at us, are all real, important aspects of our feminism. Sure, feminism should not just stop with ourselves: just as our lives connect with others, so feminism will affect what we do and who we do it for. The feminism that begins when we look in a mirror and wonder why we are comparing ourselves to whichever current celebrity is being held up as hot very often filters through to our home lives, schools, universities, workplaces, culture and across the globe.

Is this a movement?

So much for individuals. Can we describe this as a feminist move-ment? We think so. But it might not be as you imagine it or how it was in the 1960s or 1970s. Feminism today is often criticized for being too disparate, more disjointed than it used to be. But unlike in the USA, in the UK there was never a national feminist organisation directing the masses; feminist activity consisted of hundreds of small groups working on separate issues, coming together for the odd national conference. The emphasis was on democratic, non-hierarchical ways of organising. Indeed the scene was so disparate that a 1979 pamphlet, *Beyond the Fragments*, described feminism as 'different parts of a piece of cloth ... woven creatively and with *ad hoc* contact between the weavers, but without anyone having a master plan.'[7] It is not a particular failing of today's feminists that there is no membership card or special badge, just as it wasn't a failing in the 1970s. Only 16 per cent of our survey respondents agreed that 'feminism was better in the 1960s/70s'; 51 per cent were unsure or neutral and 33 per cent disagreed.

Another criticism levelled at today's feminist community is that there is no 'leader'. What people want, it seems, is a new feminist who's a household name mud-wrestling on *Newsnight* with Germaine Greer. The problem with this is the assumption that feminism's success necessitates having one or two media figureheads; the more famous those individuals are, the more successful feminism is. This is as misguided now as it was in the 1970s. Ask most British people to think of a feminist and they are most likely to name Germaine Greer, now over 70, or Andrea Dworkin, who died in 2005, both famous for producing powerful, groundbreaking polemics. But whilst they were incredibly important in putting forward new ideas, they didn't 'lead' feminism, and neither do feminist writers today. In fact, in today's celebrity-obsessed culture it's significant that most feminists are unconcerned with fame. When asked to name who inspires them, the feminists we surveyed were more likely to name their mother, their friends and grassroots activists than famous women like Greer. Rather than demonstrating feminism's failure, this is an amazing demonstration of feminism's success. It also represents willingness to accept that one person does not – and should not – represent feminism.

The other criticism of today's feminist movement is that feminists don't agree on everything. How can it be a movement if there is disagreement? But there is no progressive social movement where everyone agrees on everything, so it's disingenuous to single out feminism for particular criticism. Certainly, there are some significant disagreements within feminism, and this means that identifying 'the feminist' view on certain issues can be difficult. But almost 70 per cent of feminists we surveyed believe that the diverse range of opinions within feminism is a strength. Activist Loretta Ross, founder of the SisterSong Women of Colour Reproductive Health Collective in the USA, wholeheartedly agrees:

> I'm convinced that we're going to have to learn to unite people through diversity. Of opinion, of race, of gender, of sexual identity; we've just got to cross over all of these artificial boundaries that we who are oppressed live in. And figure out: how do we pull people together without imposing upon them 'group think.' Because, historically, we've organized social justice movements based on the premise that we would persuade everybody to agree with us. To build a human rights movement we're going to have to organise people based on the premise that everyone should not and will not agree with us, and how do we pull them together anyway? … The thing that I love about the women's movement is that no one can claim that we all belong to the same organization. We don't all agree…. The only thing I think feminists have in common is a commitment to end the oppression of women. Beyond that we are as diverse as they come. And yet I don't think anybody would hesitate to call us a movement because we are women with a lot of different ideas moving in the same direction. That to me is a movement.[8]

The majority of feminists we surveyed were optimistic about feminism's future, and – as we hope we've demonstrated – with good reason. Feminism is a vibrant, living movement with an inspirational past and present; let's be proud of it and reclaim it for ourselves.

Take action!

1. Read up on feminist issues; subscribe to a feminist magazine or blog, or set up your own.
2. Find a local feminist activist or networking group and take part. If there isn't one in your area, set one up!
3. Ask for feminist books to be stocked in your local, school or university library, or ask for them to be added to academic reading lists. Ensure that they are representative of global feminism and not just white, western, middle-class feminism.
4. Ask a feminist to speak at your organisation.
5. Reclaim the word 'feminist' as a badge of honour.

APPENDIX

SURVEY RESULTS

THE SURVEY was distributed in hard copy and online to people involved in manifestations of feminism which had formed in the UK since 2000, with a request that it be passed on to individuals involved with their activities. These included four conferences, events or festivals, over fifty local and national organisations, and web-based groups. All those who identify as feminist or pro-feminist were asked to complete the questionnaire and were assured of confidentiality and anonymity. A total of 1,265 people completed the questionnaire. Approximately two-thirds of respondents filled it in online; the rest filled in a hard-copy version.

Unless specified, all figures are given as percentages and apply only to those who answered the question, so all tables with percentages total 100; missing responses (where someone chose to skip a question) were excluded from calculations. Where 'free text field' is indicated, respondents were asked to write in their response (rather than choose from preset options). In cases where data are given below, responses were coded into categories we developed following data collection.

PART 1 **We would like to find out a bit more about the types of people who call themselves feminists or pro-feminists.**
Please tick the relevant box or write in your response as requested.

QUESTION 1.1 Do you identify as (tick one)

Female	91.0
Male	7.1
Other	1.4
Prefer not to say	0.6

QUESTION 1.2 Your age

Under 20	8.5
20–29	53.8
30–39	19.4
40–49	9.0
50–59	5.9
Over 60	3.4

Note: Some respondents ticked 'prefer not to say'; these have been excluded from the table. Minimum age: 15; maximum age: 81. Mean: 31, median: 27, mode: 23.

QUESTION 1.3   Ethnicity

White English/Welsh/Scottish/Northern Irish/British	81.0
White Irish	2.9
Other White	7.6
Mixed White and Black Caribbean	0.2
Mixed White and Black African	0.1
Mixed White and Asian	1.1
Other mixed/Multiple ethnic background	2.9
Indian	0.8
Pakistani	0.2
Chinese	0.3
Other Asian background	0.9
Black African	0.3
Black Caribbean	0.2
Any other Black/African/Caribbean background	0.3
Arab	0.4
Any other ethnic group	1.2

Note: free text field; answers were then categorised as above. Respondents who ticked 'prefer not to say' have been excluded from the table.

QUESTION 1.4   Sexuality (tick one)

Heterosexual	59.8
Lesbian/gay	10.5
Bisexual	20.2
Other	6.4
Prefer not to say	3.0

QUESTION 1.5   Religious or spiritual views

Buddhist	0.9
Christian (includes Quaker)	8.7
Jewish	0.6
Muslim	0.7
Alternative spirituality (including pagan, Wiccan, pantheist)	3.2
Other single religion (includes Hindu, Sikh, Bah'ai, Taoist)	0.3
Two or more religions	0.7
Atheist (including anti-theist, anti-religion)	39.4
Agnostic	15.7
Humanist	1.9
Spiritual/believe in deity(ies) but not religious	4.4
Two or more atheist/agnostic/humanist/none	2.1
Agnostic and one or more religion(s)	1.2
Spiritual/Pagan atheist	1.3
Formerly religious/spiritual (includes lapsed)	2.1
Unsure/open-minded	1.0
Other	0.8
None	15.0

Note: Free text field; answers were then categorised as above. Respondents who ticked 'prefer not to say' have been excluded from the table.

QUESTION 1.6   Highest level of academic education (including current studies)

GCSE or equivalent	2.5
A or AS level/Scottish Highers	7.3
Undergraduate/HND/Certificate of Higher Education	48.7
Postgraduate (inc. PG Cert/PGCE/MA/Ph.D.)	41.5

QUESTION 1.7   Have you ever undertaken any academic study on feminism or women's studies?

Yes	46.3
No	53.7

Note: 'Yes' answers include short modules covered in other academic subjects as well as formal feminism/women's studies courses.

QUESTION 1.8   If yes, please describe (free text)

QUESTION 1.9   Current location in UK

London	21.9
South East	13.0
South West	7.3
East of England	2.6
North West	8.7
North East	1.9
Midlands	13.7
Yorkshire and Humberside	10.9
Wales	2.9
Scotland	14.4
Northern Ireland	2.7

PART 2   Tell us about how you came to be a feminist

QUESTION 2.1   Please tick the statement which best reflects you

I can't remember a time when I wasn't a feminist	52.9
There was definitely a noticeable time in my life when I 'found' feminism	47.1

QUESTION 2.2   If you ticked 'there was definitely a noticeable time', please explain what sparked your interest?

Positive educational experience	157
Reading feminist books	104
Feminist friends/family/partner/colleagues	62
Internet feminism	55
General awareness of inequality	43
Positive experiences of feminist popular culture	40
Experiencing feminist groups/activism	33
Finding a name to describe beliefs in equality	27
Positive experiences in other (non-feminist) political groups	24
Working for women's/feminist organisations	24
Being brought up by feminist parents/carers	23
Negative experiences of popular culture	22
Negative educational experiences	21
Negative experiences of heterosexual relationships	20
Negative experiences at work	17
Negative experiences in your family	17
Experience of rape/sexual abuse	12
Having children/care responsibilities	12
Negative experiences of religion	9
Identification as lesbian/bisexual	8
Negative experiences in other (non-feminist) political groups	7
Other issues	63

Note: Free text field; answers were then categorised as above. Expressed as number of respondents who mentioned each 'spark', not percentages.

QUESTION 2.3   At what age did you start to identify as a feminist?

Under 20	70.1
20–29	26.6
30–39	2.7
40–49	0.5
50–59	0.1
60–69	0.1

QUESTION 2.4   What has been the biggest influence on your development as a feminist? (please pick one only)

Internet	21.0
Reading feminist books/magazines	15.8
Meeting other feminists	15.6
Brought up as feminist by parent/carer	16.0
Academic study	12.6
Other	19.1

PART 3 Tell us about your feminism

QUESTION 3.1 Do you particularly identify with any of the following types of feminism (tick all that apply)?

Feminism generally	614
Socialist	363
Academic	301
Liberal	296
Radical	251
Sex-positive	229
3rd-wave	188
Queer	172
Eco-feminism	163
Riot grrrl	162
Revolutionary	114
Lesbian	112
Pro-/male feminism	112
2nd-wave	91
Spiritual/religious	82
Trans-	53
Womanist	53
Black	40
Separatist	23
Another type	142

Note: Expressed as number of respondents who ticked each choice.

QUESTION 3.2   How important is feminism to you?
(please tick one)

Very important	75.7
Quite important	22.9
Quite unimportant	0.9
Not important at all	0.4

QUESTION 3.3   Please list the three feminist issues that most
interest or concern you

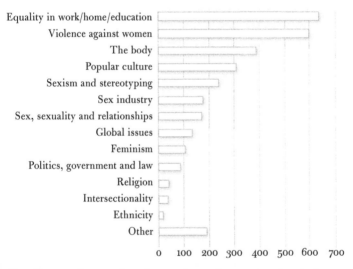

Note: Expressed as number of respondents who mentioned each theme.
Responses were analysed and categories developed based on the most
frequently recurring themes. Responses were then allocated to these themes.
For example, if someone mentioned one or more issue related to violence
against women (such as domestic violence, rape or honour violence), this
was coded under the major theme of 'Violence against women'. The figure
above shows the number of respondents who mentioned each major theme.
For example, 593 people mentioned violence. The topics we have grouped
the categories under were allocated by the researchers.

To show the specific issues or sub-themes raised by respondents, responses were then coded against any key words mentioned. For example, where a person said an issue they were concerned about was 'prostitution and pornography' this was coded under 'Sex industry' (as the major theme) and 'Prostitution' and 'Pornography' (two sub-themes).

The results below show the percentage of total survey respondents who mentioned any of the sub-themes listed. For example, 20.6 per cent of people mentioned rape/sexual abuse specifically, and 19.6 per cent mentioned violence against women in general terms (or another specific violence issue).

EQUALITY IN WORK, HOME AND EDUCATION

Equal pay	20.7
Job opportunities	17.2
Economic independence	3.0
Ending poverty	2.0
Education	4.3
Caring responsibilities	6.2
Housework	1.3
Equality general/other	11.6

VIOLENCE AGAINST WOMEN

Rape/sexual abuse	20.6
Domestic violence	8.9
FGM	0.9
Sexual harassment	2.1
Forced marriage	0.5
Violence against women general/other	19.6

THE BODY

Abortion	10.4
Reproductive rights	8.2
Body image/beauty ideals	7.7
Self-esteem/mental health	2.6

Motherhood	3.1
Body general/other	3.6

POPULAR CULTURE

Media representation and participation	12.4
Objectification	7.2
Sexualisation of popular culture	3.6
Feminist popular culture	0.4
Popular culture general/other	3.3

SEXISM AND STEREOTYPING

Ending sexism	2.5
Gender stereotyping	6.5
Gender socialisation	3.8
Sexist language	1.6
Men's attitudes	0.8
Masculinity	0.9
Bringing up children/young people	3.2
Stereotyping general/other	1.5

SEX INDUSTRY

Pornography	7.4
Prostitution/sex work	4.4
Trafficking	1.6
Lap dancing	1.2
Sex tourism	0.1
Sex industry general/other	2.2

SEX, SEXUALITY AND RELATIONSHIPS

Sexual double standard	0.9
Heterosexism/heteronormativity	0.8
LGB issues	1.1

Marriage/partnerships	2.3
Queer/trans/intersex	1.9
Sexuality other/general	7.2

GLOBAL ISSUES

Migration	0.7
Environment	0.6
Human rights	2.1
Capitalism/poverty/development	0.9
War	0.5
Global issues/general/other	6.0

OTHER ISSUES

Feminism	8.4
Intersectionality/intersecting oppressions (e.g. race, class, etc.)	2.8
Politics/government/law	7.0
Religion	3.3
Ethnicity/racism	1.1
Any other issues	15.1

QUESTION 3.4   How similar do you think the important feminist issues today are to those of the 1970s? (please tick one)

Very similar	23.3
Quite similar	62.1
Not very similar	12.9
Not at all similar	1.8

QUESTION 3.5   What do you understand the term 'feminism' to mean? (free text)

QUESTION 3.6   Do your friends share your feminist values? Please tick the statement that best applies to you

Most or all do	29.1
Some do	58.8
None or hardly any do	12.1

QUESTION 3.7   Have you experienced any negative consequences of embracing feminism?

Sex/gender	No	Yes	Unsure/ prefer not to say
Female	22.9	62.9	14.2
Male	42.6	41.5	15.9
Other	12.5	62.5	25.0
Prefer not to say	33.3	50.0	16.7

QUESTION 3.8   If yes, please describe (free text)

QUESTION 3.9   Who inspires you most as a feminist? (free text)

PART 4 **Please tell us what sort of feminist activities you are involved with**

QUESTION 4.1 From the list below, please tick any activities that you currently take part in

Challenge anti-feminist views I hear expressed	980
Make changes to my own lifestyle (e.g. reject certain beauty practices, clothing, behaviour)	817
Support pro-women businesses/ethical products	670
Seeking out and promoting feminist culture (books, magazines, music, etc.)	572
Blogging or internet activism	464
Writing to complain about issues	454
Write to or lobby my MP	402
Donate to feminist causes	378
Member of local feminist organisation(s) or group(s)	360
Discussion group, book group or consciousness-raising group	302
Member of national feminist organisation(s) or group(s)	291
Boycotts	289
Writing & publishing about feminist issues	272
Produce or read zines	232
Volunteering	225
Marching	225
Protests	223
Speak or write to the media/press	221
Speak to groups on feminist issues	205
Feminist performances (e.g. plays, comedy, art, music)	200
Attend festivals	177
Teaching about feminist issues	168
Mentoring	110
Organise festivals or conferences	106
Stickering or defacing advertisements	104
Other	102

Note: Number of respondents.

PART 5   Your view on UK feminism today

QUESTION 5.1   Based on your experience of feminism in the UK today, please read the following statements and indicate whether you tend to agree or disagree with each statement

	Tend to agree	Unsure/ neither agree nor disagree	Tend to disagree
The feminist movement today is too diverse to be effective	15.9	28.0	56.1
We need a set of goals that everyone can agree on	30.6	20.7	48.8
It would be wonderful if more people called themselves feminists	86.2	9.1	4.7
Too many people are calling themselves feminists who don't have feminist views	20.7	26.0	53.3
It's a good thing that feminism does not have any visible 'leaders'	39.4	27.6	33.0
It is more important to fight for political change than cultural change	8.2	29.0	62.8
Both cultural and political activism are important	95.6	1.7	2.7
Feminism today is too Internet-based	18.5	30.7	50.8
The Internet has been instrumental to today's feminist movement	70.7	25.0	4.4
There seem to be more feminist actions/ events/groups than five years ago	36.4	50.7	12.9
A resurgence of feminism is occurring in the UK	38.3	43.7	18.0
There is too much talking and not enough action	41.7	31.6	26.7

Women-only spaces are under threat and should be defended	48.1	32.9	19.0
Men should embrace feminism	89.8	7.0	3.2
Feminism should address men's concerns (e.g. deconstructing masculinity) as well as women's	66.5	16.7	16.8
I feel positively about the term 'third-wave feminism'	35.1	49.7	15.2
Feminism was better in the 1960s/1970s	16.3	50.7	33.1
I feel optimistic about feminism's future	59.8	24.8	15.4
Feminism is too white and middle class	47.8	29.2	23.0
The diverse range of opinions within feminism today is a strength	67.8	24.4	7.8

QUESTION 5.2   How well do you feel that current feminist groups/organisations/networks/online communities meet your needs? (tick one)

Very well	12.6
Quite well	56.3
Not particularly well	27.1
Not well at all	4.0

QUESTION 5.3   If there are other sorts of groups/organisations/networks/online communities that you would like to be join or to be formed, what are they? (free text)

QUESTION 5.4   Do you tend to find yourself working or
interacting with feminists who are:

Mainly your own age	30.9
A mixture of ages	48.1
Mainly of a different age from you	7.2
Do not interact with other feminists	8.5
Don't know/unsure	5.3

QUESTION 5.5   Why do you think this is? Please explain your
answer (free text)

QUESTION 5.6   Do you think men can be feminists?
(please tick one)

Yes	67.9
To some extent	25.5
No	4.9
Unsure	1.6

QUESTION 5.7   If you wish, please explain your answer
(free text)

NOTES

PROLOGUE

1. We gave people we interviewed the choice of whether they wanted us to include their real name or a pseudonym.
2. Libby Brooks, 'Ducking Weldon's Verbal Grenades', *Guardian*, 28 August 2009.

PREFACE

1. New research supports our observations about the negative tone of media discussions of feminism: Jonathan Dean notes that despite 'numerous affirmations of the new feminisms' in the broadsheets, 'a dominant discourse remains grounded in loss, or disappointment. A common narrative ... is that feminism has become swallowed up by a hedonistic popular culture, and/or that young feminists have got their political priorities wrong.' See J. Dean, 'On the March or On the Margins? Affirmations and Erasures of Feminist Activism in the UK', *European Journal of Women's Studies*, vol. 19, no. 3, 2012: 315–29; 319). Dean has written about the tendency we observed for people to consider something 'proper feminism' only if it conforms to certain characteristics (e.g. if it's radical, autonomous and independent of the state); see Jonathan Dean, *Rethinking Contemporary Feminist Politics*, Palgrave Macmillan, Basingstoke, 2010. Jaworska and Krishnamurthy's linguistic study of 2,728 articles in the British press between 1990 and 2009 shows that 'feminism receives little attention ... and there is a climate of negativity surrounding the term'. They add: 'There is also a noticeable "willingness" on the part of the press to report the

demise of feminism, or to treat it with a degree of irony (trivialisation). Moreover, feminism is not seen as a movement having wide social support, but is increasingly re-located to the domain of academia, literature and the arts, which are ... spheres open to only a small number of middle-class women' (Sylvia Jaworska and Ramesh Krishnamurthy, 'On the F word: A Corpus-based Analysis of the Media Representation of Feminism in British and German Press Discourse, 1990–2009', *Discourse & Society,* vol. 23, no. 4, 2012: 401–31; 424).

2. See Dean, *Rethinking Contemporary Feminist Politics*; Julia Downes, 'The Expansion of Punk Rock: Riot Grrrl Challenges to Gender Power Relations in British Indie Music Subcultures', *Women's Studies: An Interdisciplinary Journal*, vol. 41, no. 2, 2012: 204–37; Julia Long, *Anti-Porn: The Resurgence of Anti-Pornography Feminism*, Zed Books, London, 2012; Finn Mackay, 'A Movement of Their Own: Voices of Young Feminist Activists in the London Feminist Network', *Interface 3*, 2011: 152–79.

3. She compares press reports in four British and four American newspapers in the period 1968–82 with 2008. In 2008 (when we were beginning research for this book) Mendes noted that a good deal – at least half – of the articles were positive towards feminism. Kaitlynn Mendes, *Feminism in the News: Representations of the Women's Movement since the 1960s*, Palgrave Macmillan, Basingstoke, 2011).

4. *Cosmopolitan* magazine hosted the March 2012 debate at the Women of the World Festival at London's Southbank Centre.

5. Christina Scharff, 'Young Women's Negotiations of Heterosexual Conventions: Theorizing Sexuality in Constructions of "the Feminist"', *Sociology*, vol. 44, no. 5, 2010: 827–42.

6. Ellie Levenson, *The Noughtie Girl's Guide to Feminism*, Oneworld Publications, London, 2009; Jennifer Armstrong and Heather Wood Rudulph, *Sexy Feminism*, Mariner Books, New York, 2013.

7. www.netmums.com/home/feminism (accessed 25 February 2013).

8. Lisa Hallgarten, 'Forced Contraception of Jewish Ethiopian Women Is Tip of Global Iceberg', *Guardian*, 30 January 2013.

9. www.irinnews.org/Report/97352/Furore-in-Israel-over-birth-control-drugs-for-Ethiopian-Jews (accessed 25 February 2013).

10. www.motherjones.com/mojo/2012/02/most-european-countries-force-sterilization-transgender-people-map (accessed 25 February 2013).

11. www.channel4.com/news/prostitution-escort-agencies-students-sex-work (accessed 25 February 2013).

12. OECD, *Education at a Glance 2011: Highlights*, OECD, Paris, 2011, http://dx.doi.org/10.1787/eag_highlights-2011-en (accessed 24 February 2013).

13. Women's Budget Group, 'The Impact on Women of the Budget 2011', April 2011, p. 6, www.wbg.org.uk/index_7_282363355.pdf (accessed 8 February 2013).

14. Ibid., p. 2.

15. Natalie Bennett, 'Britain's Gendered Austerity', *Green European Journal* 2, 9 May 2012, www.greeneuropeanjournal.eu/britains-gendered-austerity (accessed 8 February 2013).

16. Jane Lethbridge, *Impact of the Global Economic Crisis and Austerity Measures on Women* Public Services International Research Unit, University of Greenwich, 2012, www.psiru.org/reports/impact-global-financial-crisis-austerity-measures-women.

17. See Randy Albelda, 'Gender Impacts of the "Great Recession" in the United States', in Maria Karamessini and Jill Rubery (eds), *Women and Austerity: The Economic Crisis and the Future for Gender Equality*, Routledge, London, 2013.

18. Randy Albelda and Christa Kelleher, 'Women in the Down Economy: Impacts of the Recession and the Stimulus in Massachusetts', 2010, http://works.bepress.com/randy_albelda/1 (accessed 1 March 2013).

19. Heidi Hartmann, 'Gender Implications of the Financial Crisis in the United States', Heinrich Böll Stiftung, 2009, http://boell.org/downloads/Heidi_Hartmann_Paper_Final.pdf (accessed 1 March 2013); Eva Sierminska and Yelena Takhtamanova, 'Job Flows, Demographics, and the Great Recession', in Herwig Immervoll, Andreas Peichl and Konstantinos Tatsiramos (eds), *Who Loses in the Downturn? Economic Crisis, Employment and Income Distribution*, Emerald, Bingley, 2011.

20. Heidi Hartmann, Jocelyn Fischer and Jacqui Logan, *Women and Men in the Recovery: Where the Jobs Are*, Institute for Women's Policy Research, Washington DC, 2012; Institute for Women's Policy Research, *Moderate Job Growth Continues for Women and Men: Revised Numbers Provide Brighter Picture of Recovery for Women*, Washington DC, February 2013.

21. Albelda, 'Gender Impacts of the "Great Recession" in the United States'.

22. Natalie Bennett, 'Britain's Gendered Austerity', *Green European Journal* 2, 9 May 2012, www.greeneuropeanjournal.eu/britains-gendered-austerity (accessed 8 February 2013). Jill Steans and Laura Jenkins, *All in This Together? Interrogating U.K. 'Austerity' through Gender Lenses*, report of the proceedings of a Symposium on the Gender Impacts of UK Austerity Measures, Department of Political Science and International Relations, University of Birmingham, April 2012, p. 6.

23. Ibid., p. 7.

24. http://pseudo-living.blogspot.co.uk/2012/05/intersect-confrence-2012.html (accessed 17 February 2013).

25. Working Families and Lancaster University Management School, *Working and Fathers: Combining Family Life and Work*, Working Families, London, 2011; Michael B. Wells and Anna Sarkadi, 'Do Father-Friendly Policies Promote Father-Friendly Child-Rearing Practices? A Review of

Swedish Parental Leave and Child Health Centers', *Journal of Child and Family Studies*, vol. 21, no. 1, 2012: 25–31; Esther Geisler and Michaela Kreyenfeld, 'Against All Odds: Fathers' Use of Parental Leave in Germany', *Journal of European Social Policy*, vol. 21, no. 1, 2011: 88–99.

26. Steans and Jenkins, *All in This Together?*, p. 20.

27. Ministry of Justice, Home Office and Office for National Statistics, *An Overview of Sexual Offending in England and Wales*, Statistics Bulletin, 10 January 2013, www.justice.gov.uk/downloads/statistics/criminal-justice-stats/sexual-offending/sexual-offending-overview-jan-2013.pdf (accessed 20 February 2013).

28. http://jezebel.com/5936160/the-official-guide-to-legitimate-rape (accessed 28 February 2013).

29. See www.guardian.co.uk/commentisfree/2011/jan/05/julian-assange-sex-crimes-anonymity. Wolf also wrote: '(Of course, as a feminist, I am also pleased that the alleged victims are using feminist-inspired rhetoric and law to assuage what appears to be personal injured feelings. That's what our brave suffragette foremothers intended!)', www.huffingtonpost.com/naomi-wolf/interpol-the-worlds-datin_b_793033.html (accessed 28 February 2013).

30. See http://jezebel.com/5713755/michael-moore-calls-assange-rape-case-hooey; www.guardian.co.uk/commentisfree/cifamerica/2010/dec/28/michael-moore-mooreandme-twitter (accessed 28 February 2013).

31. http://raffertyart.wordpress.com/2012/02/26/why/#comment-101 http://ore-addaily.blogspot.co.uk/2011/10/sexismsex-and-occupy-movement.html; Leela Yellesetty, 'No Place for Sexism at Occupy', *Socialist Worker*, 27 October 2011, http://socialistworker.org/2011/10/27/no-place-for-sexism-in-occupy (20 February 2013).

32. Laurie Penny, 'What Does the SWP's Way of Dealing with Sex Assault Allegations Tell Us about the Left?', *New Statesman*, 11 January 2013, www.newstatesman.com/laurie-penny/2013/01/what-does-swps-way-dealing-sex-assault-allegations-tell-us-about-left (accessed 25 February 2013).

33. Counting Women In, 'Sex and Power 2013: Who Runs Britain?', www.countingwomenin.org/wp-content/uploads/2013/02/Sex-and-Power-2013-finalv2.-pdf.pdf (accessed 25 February 2013).

34. Jennifer E. Manning and Colleen J. Shogan, *Women in the United States Congress: 1917–2012*, November 2012, Congressional Research Service, www.senate.gov/CRSReports/crs-publish.cfm?pid=%270E%2C%2APLS%3D%22%40%20%20%0A (accessed 1 March 2013).

35. *Women and the Arab Spring: Taking Their Place?*, FIDH, Paris, 2012.

36. Ibid., p. 80.

37. Carol Rumens, 'Pussy Riot's Punk Prayer Is Pure Protest Poetry', *Guardian*, 20 August 2012.

38. Maria Chehonadskih, 'What is Pussy Riot's "Idea"?' *Radical Philosophy*

176, November/December 2012, www.radicalphilosophy.com/commentary/what-is-pussy-riots-idea (accessed 13 February 2013).

39. Katja Richters, 'Pussy Riot: What the Church Really Said – and What Others Made of It', 9 November 2012, http://blogs.ucl.ac.uk/ssees/2012/11/09/pussy-riot-what-the-church-really-said-and-what-others-made-of-it.

40. 'Ukraine Is Not a Bordello', *Russia Today*, 14 December 2009, http://rt.com/news/ukraine-femen-sex-tourism

41. Sam Wilson, 'Ukraine's Femen: Topless Protests "Help Feminist Cause"', BBC News online, 24 October 2012, www.bbc.co.uk/news/world-europe-20028797 (accessed 20 February 2013).

42. Gianluca Mezzofiore, 'Aliaa Magda Elmahdy Egypt's Naked Blogger Joins Femen Protest against Mursi Constitution', *International Business Times*, 20 December 2012, www.ibtimes.co.uk/articles/417268/20121220/aliaa-magda-elmahdy-femen-egypt-constitution-nude.htm (accessed 20 February 2013).

43. http://christianfeministnetwork.com/about (accessed 11 February 2013).

44. Sariya Contractor, *Muslim Women in Britain: De-mystifying the Muslimah*, Routledge, London, 2012, p. 99.

45. Ibid., p. 106. Muhajababes = *Muhajaba* (one who practises hijab) + babes.

46. Jonathan Warren, Sharon Stoerger and Ken Kelley, 'Longitudinal Gender and Age Bias in a Prominent Amateur New Media Community', *New Media & Society,* vol. 14, no. 1, 2011: 7–27.

47. www.huffingtonpost.com/2012/12/28/potential-prostitutes-site_n_2376329.html (accessed 25 February 2013).

48. www.endviolenceagainstwomen.org.uk/data/files/End_Violence_Against_Women_Poll_Results.doc (accessed 25 February 2013).

49. www.endviolenceagainstwomen.org.uk/education (accessed 25 February 2013).

50. See http://50shadesisdomesticabuse.webs.com. A survey by the National Coalition for Sexual Freedom in the USA found that 33 per cent of BDSM practitioners – arguably more accustomed to openly discussing consent with sexual partners – reported having had their consent violated; https://ncsfreedom.org/images/stories/pdfs/Consent%20Counts/CC_Docs_New_011513/consent%20survey%20analysis.pdf (accessed 25 February 2013).

51. www.guardian.co.uk/news/datablog/2012/sep/07/gender-media-best-data-available?intcmp=srch; http://theopedproject.wordpress.com/2012/05/28/the-byline-survey-2011 (accessed 25 February 2013).

52. http://nomorepage3.wordpress.com (accessed 25 April 2013).

53. www.everydaysexism.com (accessed 25 February 2013).

54. http://indiawest.com/news/8406-indian-rape-protests-foretell-feminist-spring.html (accessed 25 February 2013).

55. http://onebillionrising.org (accessed 25 February 2013).

56. http://tigerbeatdown.com/2011/10/10/my-feminism-will-be-intersectional-or-it-will-be-bullshit (accessed 25 February 2013).

57. See for examples: www.newstatesman.com/lifestyle/2012/10/defence-caitlin-moran-and-populist-feminism; http://glosswatch.com/2012/10/23/intersectionality-worth-a-try-even-if-youre-a-total-tosser; http://black-feminists.org/tag/vagenda-magazine (accessed 25 February 2013). For an academic account of intersectionality see Leslie McCall, 'The Complexity of Intersectionality', *Signs*, vol. 30, no. 3, 2005: 1771–1800.

58. Sam Aziz, 'Reflection. "Kath Locke – A Historical Assessment"', Black Feminists Manchester, 18 April 2012, http://blackfeministsmanchester. wordpress.com (accessed 23 February 2013).

59. For more on this, see Angela Y. Davis, *Women, Race and Class*, Women's Press, London, 1982.; bell hooks, *Ain't I a Woman? Black Women and Feminism*, Pluto, London, 1982; Jennifer Nelson, *Women of Color and the Reproductive Rights Movement*, New York University Press, New York, 2003.

60. http://kafila.org/2013/02/20/dear-sisters-and-brothers-at-harvard (accessed 25 February 2013).

61. www.thefword.org.uk/features/2012/03/feminism_still (accessed 25 February 2013).

62. http://blackfeministworkinggroup.wordpress.com/2011/08/30/what-sistas-want-what-sistas-believe-black-feminist-twelve-point-plan.

63. Deborah M. Withers, 'Transgender and Feminist Alliances in Contemporary U.K. Feminist Politics', *Feminist Studies,* vol. 36, no. 3, 2010: 691–7.

64. Pamela Paxton, Melanie M. Hughes and Jennifer L. Green, 'The International Women's Movement and Women's Political Representation, 1893–2003', *American Sociological Review,* vol. 71, no. 6, 2006: 898–920; 916.

65. Mala Htun and S. Laurel Weldon, 'The Civic Origins of Progressive Policy Change: Combating Violence against Women in Global Perspective, 1975–2005', *American Political Science Review*, vol. 106, no. 3, 2012: 548–69.

INTRODUCTION

1. www.thefword.org.uk/comments/mar2001–oct2002 (accessed 28 November 2009).

2. Zoe Williams, 'Where Have All the Feminists Gone?', *New Statesman*, 16 January 2006.

3. Patricia Hewitt, Fabian Society New Year Conference, 2009, www.fabians. org.uk//images/stories/feminism_podcast.mp3 (accessed 28 November 2009).

4. 'Market-based Feminism', Editorial, *The Times*, 6 August 2009.

5. Deborah Orr, 'Who Would Want to Call Herself a Feminist?', *Independent*, 4 July 2003.

6. www.thefword.org.uk/comments/mar2001–oct2002 (accessed 28 November 2009).

7. Susan Faludi, *Backlash: The Undeclared War against Women*, Chatto & Windus, London, 1992.

8. www.cosmopolitan.co.uk/index.php/v1/Do_you_use_the_F-word %3F (accessed 6 July 2007).

9. Miranda Phillips, 'Teenagers on Family Values', in Alison Park, John Curtice, Katarina Thomson, Catherine Bromley and Miranda Phillips (eds), *British Social Attitudes: The 21st Report*, Sage, London, 2004; Rosemary Crompton, Michaela Brockmann and Richard D. Wiggins, 'A Woman's Place ... Employment and Family Life for Men and Women', in Alison Park, John Curtice, Katarina Thomson, Lindsey Jarvis and Catherine Bromley (eds), *British Social Attitudes: The 20th Report*, Sage, London, 2003.

10. Elizabeth A. Suter and Paige W. Toller, 'Gender Role and Feminism Revisited: A Follow-Up Study', *Sex Roles* 55, 2006: 135–46; 135.

11. www.womankind.org.uk/iwd-06.html (accessed 28 November 2009).

12. Lucy Ward, 'Girl Guides See a Future Blighted by Sex Bias and Pressure to be Thin', *Guardian*, 27 February 2007.

13. Jonathan Wynne-Jones and Andrew Alderson, 'Revealed: The Values, Habits and Role Models of Modern Women', *Daily Telegraph*, 19 November 2008.

14. Polly Toynbee, 'The Myth of Women's Lib', *Guardian*, 6 June 2002.

15. Shelley Budgeon, 'Emergent Feminist(?) Identities: Young Women and the Practice of Micropolitics', *European Journal of Women's Studies*, vol. 8, no. 1, 2001: 7–28.

16. Melanie Howard and Sue Tibballs, *Talking Equality: What Men and Women Think about Equality in Britain Today*, Future Foundation and Equal Opportunities Commission, London, 2003.

17. The term 'post-feminism' is used in different ways, but generally denotes the aftermath of second-wave feminism. It can mean that feminism is dead, feminism is no longer necessary because equality has been achieved, or that an anti-feminist 'backlash' pervades society. It's also used to signify young women's rejection of older forms of radical or socialist feminism in preference for an equal rights or 'power' feminism that enables them to keep the trappings of femininity. Occasionally it is used in academic theory to refer to postmodern or poststructuralist feminism. For Stacey, post-feminism is 'the simultaneous incorporation, revision, and depoliticisation of many of the central goals of second wave feminism'; see Judith Stacey, 'Sexism by a Subtler Name? Postindustrial Conditions and Postfeminist Consciousness in the Silicon Valley', *Socialist Review*, vol. 17, no. 6, 1987:

7–28; 8. See also Judith Stacey, *Brave New Families: Stories of Domestic Upheaval in Late-Twentieth-Century America*, 2nd edn, University of California Press, Berkeley, 1998; and Angela McRobbie, 'Post-feminism and Popular Culture', *Feminist Media Studies*, vol. 4, no. 3, 2004: 255–64.

18. Margaret Thatcher, in an interview in *Woman's Own*, 31 October 1987. Cited in Robert Andrews, *The New Penguin Dictionary of Modern Quotations*, Penguin, London, 2000, p. 419.

19. See Astrid Henry, *Not My Mother's Sister: Generational Conflict and Third-Wave Feminism*, Indiana University Press, Bloomington IN, 2004; and Leslie Heywood (ed.), *The Women's Movement Today: An Encyclopedia of Third Wave Feminism*, Greenwood Press, Westport CT, 2005.

20. In Canada, see Allyson Mitchell, Lisa Bryn Rundle and Lara Karaian (eds), *Turbo Chicks: Talking Young Feminism*, Sumach Press, Toronto, 2001. In the USA, see Henry, *Not My Mother's Sister*. Devoney Looser and E. Ann Kaplan (eds), *Generations: Academic Feminists in Dialogue*, University of Minnesota Press, Minneapolis MN, 1997, discusses generational differences between academic feminists. In Australia, see Virginia Trioli, *Generation F: Sex, Power and the Young Feminist*, Minerva, Port Melbourne, 1996.

21. Stacy Gillis and Rebecca Munford, 'Harvesting Our Strengths: Third Wave Feminism and Women's Studies', *Journal of International Women's Studies*, vol. 4, no. 2, 2003.

22. Stacy Gillis, Gillian Howie and Rebecca Munford (eds), *Third Wave Feminism: A Critical Exploration*, 2nd edn, Palgrave Macmillan, Basingstoke, 2007.

23. Thanks to Louise Livesey for helping us develop these ideas.

24. Zoe Williams, 'What Women Want', *Guardian*, 1 July 2003.

25. 'Feminism by Any Other Name', *Guardian*, letters, 3 July 2003.

26. For example, Angela McRobbie, 'Illegible Rage: Young Women's Post-feminist Disorders', lecture at the London School of Economics, 25 January 2007; Stacy Gillis and Rebecca Munford, 'Interview with Elaine Showalter', in Stacy Gillis, Gillian Howie and Rebecca Munford (eds), *Third Wave Feminism*; and Imelda Whelehan, 'Having It All (Again?)', paper at the ESRC *New Femininities* seminar, London School of Economics, 19 November 2004.

27. Anna Coote and Beatrix Campbell, *Sweet Freedom: The Struggle for Women's Liberation*, Blackwell, Oxford, 1982, especially pp. 24–6.

28. Germaine Greer, *The Whole Woman*, Anchor, London, 2000.

CHAPTER 1

1. Naomi Wolf, *The Beauty Myth: How Images of Beauty Are Used against Women*, Vintage, London, 1991, p. 13. See also Susan Brownmiller,

Femininity, Hamish Hamilton, London, 1984; and Sheila Jeffreys, *Beauty and Misogyny*, Routledge, London, 2005.

2. UNFPA *Thematic Fund for Maternal Health: Accelerating Progress Towards Millennium Development Goal 5*, United Nations Population Fund, New York, 2008.

3. www.endfistula.org (accessed 9 January 2010).

4. IPPF/UNFPA/Young Positives, *Change, Choice and Power: Young Women, Livelihoods and HIV Prevention*, International Planned Parenthood Federation, London/United Nations Population Fund, New York/Young Positives, Amsterdam, 2007.

5. http://seeingisbelieving.org.uk/about-us/latest-news/two-thirds-the-worlds-blind-are-women-or-girls (accessed 9 January 2010).

6. Sandra Lee Bartky, 'Foucault, Feminism and the Modernization of Patriarchal Power', in Rose Weitz (ed.), *The Politics of Women's Bodies*, 2nd edn, Oxford University Press, New York, 2003, pp. 33–4.

7. Nancy Etcoff, Susie Orbach, Jennifer Scott and Heidi D'Agostino, *Beyond Stereotypes: Rebuilding the Foundation of Beauty Beliefs – Findings of the 2005 Dove Global Survey*, StrategyOne, New York, 2006.

8. Laura Hurd Clarke and Meridith Griffin, 'Becoming and Being Gendered through the Body: Older Women, Their Mothers and Body Image', *Ageing & Society*, vol. 27, no. 5, 2007: 701–18; Maya A. Poran, 'The Politics of Protection: Body Image, Social Pressures, and the Misrepresentation of Young Black Women', *Sex Roles*, vol. 55, nos 11–12, 2006: 739–55; Sharlene Hesse-Biber, Patricia Leavy, Courtney E. Quinn and Julia Zoino, 'The Mass Marketing of Disordered Eating and Eating Disorders: The Social Psychology of Women, Thinness and Culture', *Women's Studies International Forum*, vol. 29, no. 2, 2006: 208–24; Bonnie Moradi, Danielle Dirks and Alicia V. Matteson, 'Roles of Sexual Objectification Experiences and Internalization of Standards of Beauty in Eating Disorder Symptomatology: A Test and Extension of Objectification Theory', *Journal of Counseling Psychology*, vol. 52, no. 3, 2005: 420–28; Rachel M. Calogero, William N. Davis and J. Kevin Thompson, 'The Role of Self-objectification in the Experience of Women with Eating Disorders', *Sex Roles*, vol. 52, nos 1–2, 2005: 43–50.

9. Winfried Rief, Ulrike Buhlmann, Sabine Wilhelm, Ada Borkenhagen and Elmar Brähler, 'The Prevalence of Body Dysmorphic Disorder: A Population-Based Survey', *Psychological Medicine*, vol. 36, no. 6, 2006: 877–85.

10. Natalie Wain, 'Size Zero: Chico Thinks It's Time to Get Curvy', *Daily Telegraph*, 10 October 2007.

11. Carol Byrd-Bredbenner, Jessica Murray and Yvette R. Schlussel, 'Temporal Changes in Anthropometric Measurements of Idealized Females and Young Women in General', *Women & Health*, vol. 41, no. 2,

2005: 13–30. See also 'SizeUK Announce Results from UK National Sizing Survey', 2004, www.fashion.arts.ac.uk/sizeuk.htm (accessed 15 January 2010).

12. Kate Fox, *Mirror, Mirror: A Summary of Research Findings on Body Image*, Social Issues Research Centre, Oxford, 1997.

13. American Psychiatric Association Work Group on Eating Disorders, Practice Guideline for the Treatment of Patients with Eating Disorders (revision), *American Journal of Psychiatry*, vol. 157, no. 1 (Suppl.), January 2000: 1–39; A. Keski-Rahkonen, H.W. Hoek, M.S. Linna, A. Raevuori, E. Sihvola, C.M. Bulik, A. Rissanen and J. Kaprio, 'Incidence and Outcomes of Bulimia Nervosa in a Nationwide Population-based Study', *Psychological Medicine*, vol. 39, no. 5, 2009: 823–31.

14. beat, *Has Fashion Got Its House in Order? Report from beat's Enquiry*, beat, Norwich, October 2007.

15. Joanna Bourke, 'Mini-skirt or Burka – My Choice', *The Times*, 8 March 2008; Jane Wheatley, 'If the Shoe Doesn't Fit…', *The Times*, 18 June 2007; Katha Pollitt, *Virginity or Death! And Other Social and Political Issues of Our Day*, Random House, New York, 2006.

16. Susie Orbach, *Bodies*, Profile Books, London, 2009, p. 90.

17. Kate Bellamy and Katherine Rake, *Money, Money, Money: Is the UK Still a Rich Man's World?*, Fawcett Society, London, 2005, p. 31; Jenny Westaway and Stephen McKay, *Women's Financial Assets and Debts*, Fawcett Society, London, 2007, p. 12.

18. Michael Atkinson, 'Exploring Male Femininity in the "Crisis": Men and Cosmetic Surgery', *Body & Society*, vol. 14, no. 1, 2008: 67–87.

19. www.consultingroom.com/statistics (accessed 9 January 2010).

20. Rachel Williams, 'Cosmetic Surgery and Treatments Set to Hit £1bn a Year', *Guardian*, 19 December 2007.

21. Bartky, 'Foucault, Feminism and the Modernization of Patriarchal Power', p. 28.

22. Fox, *Mirror, Mirror*.

23. zohra moosa, 'Objectification and Ethnic Minority Women', *StopGap: The Fawcett Society Magazine*, 2009, p. 13.

24. Orbach, *Bodies*, pp. 81–3.

25. Angela McRobbie, 'Notes on "What Not To Wear" and Post-feminist Symbolic Violence', in Lisa Adkins and Beverley Skeggs (eds), *Feminism after Bourdieu*, Blackwell, Oxford, 2004.

26. www.nowmagazine.co.uk/body/celeb_diets (accessed 10 March 2008).

27. Paula Black, 'Discipline and Pleasure? The Uneasy Relationship between Feminism and the Beauty Industry', in Joanne Hollows and Rachel Moseley (eds), Feminism *in Popular Culture*, Berg, Oxford, 2006.

28. Daniel Clay, Vivian L. Vignoles and Helga Dittmar, 'Body Image and Self-Esteem among Adolescent Girls: Testing the Influence of Sociocultural

Factors', *Journal of Research on Adolescence*, vol. 15, no. 4, 2005: 451–77; Kristine L. Lokken, Julianne Trautmann and Sheri Lokken Worthy, 'Examining the Links among Magazine Preference, Levels of Awareness and Internalisation of Sociocultural Appearance Standards, and Presence of Eating-disordered Symptoms in College Women', *Family and Consumer Sciences Research Journal*, vol. 32, no. 4, 2004: 361–81; Marika Tiggemann and Belinda McGill, 'The Role of Social Comparison in the Effect of Magazine Advertisements on Women's Mood and Body Dissatisfaction', *Journal of Social and Clinical Psychology*, vol. 23, no. 1, 2004: 23–44; Williams, 'Cosmetic Surgery and Treatments Set to Hit £1bn a Year'; Constanze Rossmann and Hans-Bernd Brosius, 'From Ugly Duckling to Beautiful Swan? On the Representation and Effects of Plastic Surgery on TV', *Medien & Kommunikationswissenschaft*, vol. 53, no. 4, 2005: 507–32.

29. Harry Wallop and Richard Fletcher, 'Women's Spending Is Pushing Up Clothes Cost', *Daily Telegraph*, 3 August 2007.

30. Elizabeth Wilson, *Adorned in Dreams: Fashion and Modernity*, 2nd edn, I.B. Tauris, London, 2003, p. 90.

31. ICM for Amnesty International, *Sexual Assault Research Summary Report*, Amnesty International, London, 2005.

32. Manal Omar, 'I Felt More Welcome in the Bible Belt', *Guardian*, 20 April 2007.

33. www.jcore.org.uk/sanitary.php (accessed 9 January 2010).

34. Luisa Marván and Claudia Escobedo, 'Premenstrual Symptomatology: The Role of Prior Knowledge about Premenstrual Syndrome', *Psychosomatic Medicine* 61, 1999: 163–7.

35. Sophie Laws, 'Who Needs PMT?', in Stevi Jackson et al. (eds), *Women's Studies: A Reader*, Harvester Wheatsheaf, Brighton, 1985.

36. Janice Delaney, Mary Jane Lupton and Emily Toth, *The Curse: A Cultural History of Menstruation*, 2nd edn, University of Illinois Press, Champaign, 1988.

37. Joseph A. Diorio and Jennifer A. Monro, 'Doing Harm in the Name of Protection: Menstruation as a Topic for Sex Education', *Gender and Education*, vol. 12, no. 3, 2000: 347–65.

38. www.beinggirl.co.uk (accessed 9 January 2010).

39. M. Fontes and P. Roach, 'Predictors and Confounders of Unprotected Sex: A UK Web-based Study', *European Journal of Contraception and Reproductive Health Care*, vol. 12, no. 1, 2007: 36–45.

40. Katie Buston, Lisa Williamson and Graham Hart, 'Young Women under 16 Years with Experience of Sexual Intercourse: Who Becomes Pregnant?' *Journal of Epidemiology and Community Health* 61, 2007: 221–5.

41. Wendy Fidler, 'Going Dutch', 2007, www.sec-ed.co.uk/cgi-bin-go.pl/features/article.html?uid=2375 (accessed 3 March 2008); George Monbiot,

'Face Facts, Cardinal. Our Awful Rate of Abortion is Partly Your Responsibility', *Guardian*, 26 February 2008.

42. Lester M. Coleman and Adrienne Testa, 'Sexual Health Knowledge, Attitudes and Behaviours: Variations among a Religiously Diverse Sample of Young People in London, UK', *Ethnicity & Health*, vol. 13, no. 1, 2008: 55–72.

43. Cicely Marston, Eleanor King and Roger Ingram, 'Young People and Condom Use: Findings from Qualitative Research', in Roger Ingram and Peter Aggleton (eds), *Promoting Young People's Sexual Health: International Perspectives*, Routledge, Abingdon, 2006, p. 34.

44. John Guillebaud, *Contraception: Your Questions Answered*, 4th edn, Churchill Livingstone, Edinburgh, 2004, p. 48.

45. S.A. Batchelor, J. Kitzinger and E. Burtney, 'Representing Young People's Sexuality in the "Youth" Media', *Health Education Research*, vol. 19, no. 6, 2004: 669–76.

46. www.fpa.org.uk/News/Press/Current/page914 (accessed 9 January 2010).

47. I. O'Sullivan, L. Keyse, N. Park, A. Diaper and S. Short, *Contraception and Sexual Health, 2004/05*, Office for National Statistics, London, 2005.

48. www.abortionrights.org.uk (accessed 9 January 2010).

49. UNFPA, *Thematic Fund for Maternal Health*.

50. www.abortionrights.org.uk (accessed 9 January 2010).

51. Caroline Davey, 'Sexual and Reproductive Health and Rights in the United Kingdom at ICPD+10', *Reproductive Health Matters*, vol. 13, no. 25, 2005: 81–7.

52. Lucy Ward, 'Two-signature Rule on Abortions Should Be Abandoned, Say Doctors', *Guardian*, 11 October 2007.

53. Joni Seager, *The Atlas of Women in the World*, 4th edn, Earthscan, Brighton, 2009, pp. 38–9.

54. Louise France, 'A Woman's Right? We'll Be the Judge of That', *Observer Woman*, October 2007.

55. Naomi Wolf, *Misconceptions: Truth, Lies and the Unexpected on the Journey to Motherhood*, Chatto & Windus, London, 2001.

56. NHS Information Centre *Maternity Statistics 2008–09*, 2009; Amelia Hill, 'Caesareans Linked to Risk of Infertility', *Guardian*, 2 April 2002.

57. Sheila Kitzinger, *Birth Crisis*, Taylor & Francis, London, 2006.

58. C.C. Carter, 'The Herstory of My Hips', in Alix Olsen (ed.), *Word Warriors: 35 Women Leaders in the Spoken Word Revolution*, Seal Press, Berkeley, 2007.

59. www.thefword.org.uk/blog/2007/09/hairy_anniversa (accessed 9 January 2010).

60. www.facebook.com/group.php?gid=2467246125&ref=mf (accessed 16 January 2010).

61. Cooperative Bank, *Ten Years of Ethical Consumerism: 1999–2008*, Cooperative Bank, Manchester, 2009.

62. www.facebook.com/group.php?gid=6059369109 (accessed 16 January 2010).

CHAPTER 2

1. Alison Phipps, 'Rape and Respectability: Ideas about Sexual Violence and Social Class', *Sociology*, vol. 43, no. 4, 2009: 667–83.

2. Naomi Wolf, *Promiscuities: A Secret History of Female Desire*, Chatto & Windus, London, 1997, p. 149.

3. Naomi Wolf, *The Beauty Myth: How Images of Beauty Are Used against Women*, Vintage, London, 1991, pp. 157–8.

4. Lily Allen, 'Not Fair', from the album *It's Not Me, It's You*, Regal, 2009.

5. Ariel Levy, *Female Chauvinist Pigs: Women and the Rise of Raunch Culture*, Pocket Books, London, 2005.

6. Rosalind Gill, 'Empowerment/Sexism: Figuring Female Sexual Agency in Contemporary Advertising', *Feminism & Psychology*, vol. 18, no. 1, 2008: 35–60; 35.

7. Email interview with Jess Smith, 11 October 2009.

8. Laurie Penny, 'Burlesque Laid Bare', *Guardian*, 15 May 2009.

9. Elizabeth M. Morgan and Eileen L. Zurbriggen, 'Wanting Sex and Wanting to Wait: Young Adults' Accounts of Sexual Messages from First Significant Dating Partners', *Feminism & Psychology*, vol. 17, no. 4, 2007: 515–41.

10. Jennifer Drew, 'Dysfunctional, Moi? The Myth of Female Sexual Dysfunction and its Medicalisation', *The F Word*, 2003, www.thefword.org. uk/features/2003/04/dysfunctional_moi_the_myth_of_female_sexual_ dysfunction_and_its_medicalisation (accessed 9 January 2010).

11. http://sexperienceuk.channel4.com/your-questions/im-15-and-still-a-virgin-but-im-pressured-everyday-by-people-taking-da-piss-but-i-want-it-to-mean-something-wat-should-i-do (accessed 28 November 2009).

12. V, 'Blood, Sweat and Tears', from the album *You Stood Up*, Island Records, 2004. Rachel E, 'Every Girl Wants a Stalker', *The F Word*, 2004, www. thefword.org.uk/features/2004/08/every_girl_wants_a_stalker (accessed 28 November 2009).

13. Channel 4, 'Study Shows Teens' Sexual Attitudes', 5 November 2008, www.channel4.com/news/articles/society/health/study+shows+teens+s exual+attitudes/2758142 (accessed 28 November 2009).

14. Jenna Jameson, interviewed by Bill O'Reilly on 'The O'Reilly Factor', Fox News, 2003.

15. http://sexperienceuk.channel4.com/protect-from-porn (accessed 28 November 2009).

16. Channel 4, *The Sex Education Show*, episode 1, 2008, http://sexperience-uk.channel4.com/sex-education/season-1/programme-1 (accessed 28 November 2009).

17. Andrea Dworkin, *Pornography: Men Possessing Women*, Women's Press, London, 1981.

18. Patricia Hill Collins, *Black Feminist Thought*, Unwin Hyman, London, 1990.

19. Jennifer Lynn Gossett and Sarah Byrne, '"Click Here": A Content Analysis of Internet Rape Sites', *Gender & Society*, vol. 16, no. 5, 2002: 689–709.

20. Nadine Strossen, *Defending Pornography*, Abacus, London, 1996.

21. www.cosmopolitan.co.uk/love-&-sex/Sex-advice-sex-tips/special (accessed 26 August 2009).

22. www.cosmopolitan.co.uk (accessed 26 August 2009).

23. Daniel Ottoson/ILGA, *State Sponsored Homophobia: A World Survey of Laws Prohibiting Same Sex Activity between Consenting Adults*, International Lesbian, Gay, Bisexual, Trans and Intersex Association, 2009.

24. Sue Jackson and Tamsyn Gilbertson, '"Hot Lesbians": Young People's Talk about Representations of Lesbianism', *Sexualities*, vol. 12, no. 2, 2009: 199–224.

25. 'Rosie and Kayleee: Gentlemen, Sit Back and Enjoy Britain's Sexiest New Double Act!', *Nuts*, IPC Media, 5–11 December 2008, pp. 58–64.

26. Judit Takács, László Mocsonaki and Tamás P. Tóth, *Social Exclusion of Lesbian, Gay, Bisexual and Transgender (LGBT) People in Hungary: Research Report*, Institute of Sociology, Hungarian Academy of Sciences, Budapest, 2008, pp. 35, 40, 50.

27. Action Aid, *Hate Crimes: The Rise of 'Corrective' Rape in South Africa*, Action Aid, London, 2009, p. 8.

28. Helsinki Citizens' Assembly – Turkey Refugee Advocacy and Support Program and ORAM (Organization for Refuge, Asylum and Migration), *Unsafe Haven: The Security Challenges Facing Lesbian, Gay, Bisexual and Transgender Asylum Seekers and Refugees in Turkey*, June 2009, p. 16.

29. Independent Asylum Commission, *Deserving Dignity: Third Report of Conclusions and Recommendations*, IAC, London, 2008.

30. Sam Dick/Stonewall, *Homophobic Hate Crime: The Gay British Crime Survey 2008*, Stonewall, London, 2008.

31. Adrienne Rich, 'Compulsory Heterosexuality and Lesbian Existence', in Barbara Charlesworth Gelpi and Albert Gelpi (eds), *Adrienne Rich's Poetry and Prose*, W.W. Norton, New York, 1995.

32. Deborah Siegel, *Sisterhood Interrupted*, Palgrave Macmillan, New York, 2007, p. 88.

33. www.jofa.org/about.php/advocacy/guidetojewis (accessed 16 January 2010).

34. BBC, 'Sharia police block women's rally', 19 January 2009, http://news.bbc.co.uk/1/hi/world/africa/7837512.stm (accessed 28 November 2009).

35. http://eroticacoverwatch.wordpress.com/2008/12/11/erotica-cover-watch-group-hug (accessed 28 November 2009).

36. http://malesubmissionart.com/post/177738968/a-skinny-short-haired-man-kneels-on-a-dirty-floor (accessed 28 November 2009).

37. http://malesubmissionart.com/post/168794536/a-naked-man-lays-on-a-bed-next-to-a-video-camera (accessed 28 November 2009).

38. http://girlwithaonetrackmind.blogspot.com/2006/07/addict.html (accessed 28 November 2009).

39. http://bitchyjones.wordpress.com/2007/11/19/i-am-a-dominant-slut (accessed 28 November 2009).

40. Dossie Easton and Janet W. Hardy, *The Ethical Slut*, 2nd edn, Celestial Arts, Berkeley CA, 2009.

41. Maurice Taylor and Seana McGee, *The New Couple*, HarperCollins, New York, 2001.

42. Bryan Safi, 'Lady Kisses', Current TV, 2009, http://current.com/users/bryan_safi.htm (accessed 28 November 2009).

43. Lynn, on behalf of Meem, 'Lesbian Movements: Ruptures and Alliances', LGBT Human Rights Conference of the Outgames 2009, Copenhagen, July 2009.

44. Janice D. Yoder, Rachelle L. Perry and Ellen Irwin Saal, 'What Good is a Feminist Identity? Women's Feminist Identification and Role Expectations for Intimate and Sexual Relationships', *Sex Roles*, vol. 57, no. 5–6, 2007: 365–72.

45. Amy K. Kiefer, Diana T. Sanchez, Christina J. Kalinka and Oscar Ybarra, 'How Women's Nonconscious Association of Sex with Submission Relates to Their Subjective Sexual Arousability and Ability to Reach Orgasm', *Sex Roles*, vol. 55, nos 1–2, 2006: 83–94.

CHAPTER 3

1. Finn Mackay, Reclaim the Night 2008 speech, London, 2008, www.ldnfeministnetwork.ik.com/p_FinnMackaySpeech.ikml (accessed 6 December 2009).

2. Mary C. Ellsberg, 'Violence against Women: A Global Public Health Crisis', *Scandinavian Journal of Public Health*, vol. 34, nos 1–4, 2006: 1.

3. Figures from London Feminist Network, www.ldnfeministnetwork.ik.com/p_General_RTN.ikml (accessed 1 January 2010); and Julia Stuart, 'Women and Crime: Fear in Suburbia', *Independent*, 11 December 2005.

4. HM Government, *Cross Government Action Plan on Sexual Violence and Abuse*, Home Office, London, April 2007.

5. Sylvia Walby and Jonathan Allen, *Domestic Violence, Sexual Assault and*

Stalking: Findings from the British Crime Survey, Home Office, London, 2004, p. 94.

6. www.amnestyusa.org/violence-against-women/stop-violence-against-women-svaw/rape-as-a-tool-of-war/page.do?id=1108239 (accessed 9 January 2010).

7. Jo Lovett and Liz Kelly, *Different Systems, Similar Outcomes? Tracking Attrition in Reported Rape Cases across Europe*, Child and Women Abuse Studies Unit, London, 2009.

8. Rape Crisis and Women's Resource Centre, *The Crisis in Rape Crisis*, London, March 2008.

9. ICM for Amnesty International, *Sexual Assault Research Summary Report*, Amnesty International, London, 2005.

10. http://dmhatingfemisfromhell.blogspot.com/2009/08/sharia-law-vs-daily-mail-law.html (accessed 9 January 2010).

11. www.dailymail.co.uk/home/search.html?searchPhrase=rape (accessed 15 December 2009).

12. Liz Kelly, Jo Lovett and Linda Regan, *A Gap or a Chasm? Attrition in Reported Rape Cases*, Child and Women Abuse Studies Unit, London, 2005, pp. 47–53.

13. Laura Stott, 'WPC's Blog: It's Shocking – Policing is Harder than Ever', *Sun*, 29 July 2009.

14. Rachel Williams, 'Postcode Lottery in Rape Convictions Getting Worse', *Guardian*, 10 June 2009.

15. http://news.bbc.co.uk/1/hi/england/london/7908003.stm (accessed 17 January 2010).

16. http://thecurvature.com/2008/02/23/why-ask-men-to-stop-raping-when-women-can-barricade-themselves-in-their-homes (accessed 9 January 2010).

17. www.badscience.net/2009/07/rape-a-non-correction-from-the-telegraph (accessed 9 January 2010).

18. www.badscience.net/2009/07/asking-for-it (accessed 9 January 2010).

19. Rebeeca Sherdley and Amanda Smart, 'Wife Stabbed in Explosion of Fury', *Nottingham Evening Post*, 18 July 2009.

20. Walby and Allen, *Domestic Violence, Sexual Assault and Stalking*, p. 12.

21. Home Office, *Crime in England and Wales 2008/09: Volume 1, Findings from the British Crime Survey and Police Recorded Crime*, London, 2009, p. 56.

22. Massachusetts Department of Public Health, *The Health of Lesbian, Gay, Bisexual and Transgender (LGBT) Persons in Massachusetts*, Massachusetts Department of Public Health, Boston MA, 2009, p. 11.

23. Nora J. Baladerian, 'Domestic Violence and Individuals with Disabilities: Reflections on Research and Practice', *Journal of Aggression, Maltreatment & Trauma*, vol. 18, no. 2, 2009: 153–61.

24. Russell P. Dobash and R. Emerson Dobash, 'Women's Violence to Men in Intimate Relationships: Working on a Puzzle', *British Journal of Criminology* 44, 2004: 324–49.

25. Home Office, *Homicides, Firearm Offences and Intimate Violence 2007/08*, 3rd edn, London, 2009, p. 12.

26. Michael S. Kimmel, '"Gender Symmetry" in Domestic Violence: A Falsely-framed Issue', in June Keeling and Tom Mason (eds), *Domestic Violence: A Multi-professional Approach for Health-care Practitioners*, Open University Press, Maidenhead, 2008, p. 34.

27. James Brandon and Salam Hafez, *Crimes of the Community: Honour-based Violence in the UK*, Centre for Social Cohesion, London, 2008, p. 37.

28. Ibid., p. 38.

29. Ibid., p. 33.

30. Ibid., pp. 21–6.

31. www.fco.gov.uk/en/global-issues/human-rights/forced-marriage-unit (accessed 17 January 2010).

32. Brandon and Hafez, *Crimes of the Community*, p. 18.

33. Seager, *The Atlas of Women in the World*, p. 24.

34. Rebecca Emerson Dobash and Russell P. Dobash, 'Violent Men and Violent Contexts', in R. Emerson Dobash and Russell P. Dobash (eds), *Rethinking Violence against Women*, Sage, London, 1998, pp. 152, 154.

35. For a useful discussion of the debates about gender symmetry or asymmetry in domestic abuse, see Kimmel, '"Gender Symmetry" in Domestic Violence'.

36. Dobash and Dobash, 'Violent Men and Violent Contexts'.

37. Margo Wilson and Martin Daly, 'Till Death Us Do Part', in Jill Radford and Diana E.H. Russell (eds), *Femicide: The Politics of Woman Killing*, Open University Press, Buckingham, 1992.

38. Dobash and Dobash, 'Violent Men and Violent Contexts', p. 144.

39. Tahira S. Khan, *Beyond Honour: A Historical Materialist Explanation of Honour Related Violence*, Oxford University Press, Oxford, 2006, p. 307.

40. Comment from 'LB', *The F Word*, www.thefword.org.uk/features/2005/04/take_back_the_streets (accessed 9 January 2010).

41. Martha J. Langelan, *Back Off! How to Confront and Stop Sexual Harassment*, Fireside, New York, 1993, p. 81.

42. http://noblesavage.me.uk/2009/09/14/seasons-of-safety (accessed 15 December 2009).

43. Langelan, *Back Off!*, p. 53.

44. Janice Raymond, 'Ten Reasons for *Not* Legalizing Prostitution and a Legal Response to the Demand for Prostitution', *Journal of Trauma Practice* 2, 2003: 315–32; Seager, *The Atlas of Women in the World*, p. 57.

45. C. Gabrielle Salfati, Alison R. James and Lynn Ferguson, 'Prostitute Homicides: A Descriptive Study', *Journal of Interpersonal Violence*, vol.

23, no. 4, 2008: 505–43.

46. Richard Littlejohn, 'Spare us the "People's Prostitute' Routine", *Daily Mail*, 18 December 2006.

47. Alys Willman, 'Safety First, Then Condoms: Commercial Sex, Risky Behavior, and the Spread of HIV/AIDS in Managua, Nicaragua', *Feminist Economics*, vol. 14, no. 4, 2008: 37–65.

48. Stephanie Church, Marion Henderson, Marina Barnard and Graham Hart, 'Violence by Clients towards Female Prostitutes in Different Work Settings: Questionnaire Survey', *BMJ* 322, 2001: 524–5; Graham Hart and Marina Barnard, '"Jump on Top, Get the Job Done": Strategies Employed by Female Prostitutes to Reduce the Risk of Client Violence', in Elizabeth A. Stanko (ed.), *The Meanings of Violence*, Routledge, London, 2003.

49. Jayne Arnott and Anna-Louise Crago, *Rights not Rescue: Female, Male, and Trans Sex Workers' Human Rights in Botswana, Namibia, and South Africa*, Open Society Institute, New York, 2009.

50. Church et al., 'Violence by Clients towards Female Prostitutes in Different Work Settings'; Hart and Barnard, '"Jump on Top, Get the Job Done"'.

51. Suzanne Jenkins, *Summary Report: Beyond Gender – An Examination of Exploitation in Sex Work*, Keele University, n.d., www.sexworker.at/phpBB2/download.php?id=479 (accessed 1 January 2010).

52. Paola Monzini, *Sex Traffic: Prostitution, Crime and Exploitation*, trans. Patrick Camiller, Zed Books, London, 2005, pp. 39–40.

53. Alexandra K. Murphy and Sudhir Alladi Venkatesh, 'Vice Careers: The Changing Contours of Sex Work in New York City', *Qualitative Sociology*, vol. 29, no. 2, 2006: 129–54; Tooru Nemoto, Mariko Iwamoto, Donn Colby, Samantha Witt, Alefiyah Pishori, Mai Nhung Le, Dang Thi Nhat Vinh and Le Truong Giang, 'HIV-Related Risk Behaviors among Female Sex Workers in Ho Chi Minh City, Vietnam', *AIDS Education and Prevention*, vol. 20, no. 5, 2008: 435–53.

54. Teela Sanders, *Sex Work: A Risky Business*, Willan, Cullompton, 2006.

55. Kathleen Barry, *The Prostitution of Sexuality*, New York University Press, New York, 1995, p. 35; see pp. 20–36 for a discussion of the emotional costs of prostitution.

56. Melissa Friedberg, 'Damaged Children to Throwaway Women: From Care to Prostitution', in Jill Radford, Melissa Friedberg and Lynne Harne (eds), *Women, Violence and Strategies for Action: Feminist Research, Policy and Practice*, Open University Press, Buckingham, 2000; Julia O'Connell Davidson, *Children in the Global Sex Trade*, Polity Press, Cambridge, 2005, pp. 45–52.

57. Kari Kesler, 'The Plain-Clothes Whore: Agency, Marginalization, and the Unmarked Prostitute Body', in Merri Lisa Johnson (ed.), *Jane Sexes It Up: True Confessions of Feminist Desire*, Thunder's Mouth Press, New York, 2002, pp. 237–8.

58. Eva Rosen and Sudhir Venkatesh, 'A "Perversion" of Choice: Sex Work Offers Just Enough in Chicago's Urban Ghetto', *Journal of Contemporary Ethnography*, vol. 37, no. 4, 2008: 417.

59. Belle de Jour, *The Intimate Adventures of a London Call Girl*, Orion, London, 2005.

60. Monzini, *Sex Traffic*, p. 34.

61. Devon D. Brewer, John J. Potterat, Stephen Q. Muth and John M. Roberts, 'A Large Specific Deterrent Effect of Arrest for Patronizing a Prostitute', *PloS ONE*, vol. 1, no. 1, 2006: e60.

62. Monzini, *Sex Traffic*, p. 15. See also Belinda Brooks-Gordon, *The Price of Sex: Prostitution, Policy and Society*, Willan, Cullompton, 2006, ch. 3.

63. Kevin Bales, 'Because She Looks Like a Child', in Barbara Ehrenreich and Arlie Russell Hochschild (eds), *Global Woman: Nannies, Maids and Sex Workers in the New Economy*, Granta, London, 2003, p. 215.

64. Maddy Coy, Miranda Horvath and Liz Kelly, *'It's Just Like Going to the Supermarket': Men Buying Sex in East London*, Child and Woman Abuse Studies Unit, London, 2007, p. 19.

65. Ibid., pp. 19–20.

66. International Organization for Migration, www.iom.int/jahia/Jahia/activities/by-theme/regulating-migration/counter-trafficking (accessed 9 January 2010).

67. Laura Agustín, *Sex at the Margins: Migration, Labour Markets and the Rescue Industry*, Zed Books, London, 2007.

68. Nick Mai, *Migrant Workers in the UK Sex Industry*, Institute for the Study of European Transformations, London Metropolitan University, 2009.

69. Jay G. Silverman, Michele R. Decker, Jhumka Gupta, Ayonija Maheshwari, Brian M. Willis and Anita Raj, 'HIV Prevalence and Predictors of Infection in Sex-Trafficked Nepalese Girls and Women', *Journal of the American Medical Association*, vol. 298, no. 5, 2007: 536–42.

70. Cathy Zimmerman, Mazeda Hossain, Kate Yun, Brenda Roche, Linda Morison and Charlotte Watts, *Stolen Smiles: A Summary Report on the Physical and Psychological Health Consequences of Women and Adolescents Trafficked in Europe*, London School of Hygiene and Tropical Medicine, London, 2006.

71. www.thefword.org.uk/blog/2009/06/london_flashmob (accessed 16 January 2010).

72. http://blog.blanknoise.org (accessed 15 December 2009).

73. www.spreadmagazine.org (accessed 15 December 2009).

74. For example, David Henry Sterry and R.J. Martin, *Hos, Hookers, Call Girls and Rent Boys*, Soft Skull Press, New York, 2009.

75. Stella and UQAM's Service aux collectivités, *Sex Work: 14 Answers to Your Questions*, Montreal, 2007.

76. Reported in *Ms* Magazine, Spring 2005: 33.

77. UK Network of Sex Work Projects, *Working with Sex Workers: Exiting*, UK Network of Sex Work Projects, Manchester, 2008.

78. Metropolitan Police, *The Attrition of Rape Allegations in London: A Review*, Metropolitan Police, London, 2007.

79. United Nations, 'Report of the Expert Group Meeting on Good Practices in Legislation on Violence Against Women', EGM/GPL/VAW, 2008, p. 24.

80. Raymond, 'Ten Reasons'.

81. www.catwinternational.org/about/index.php (accessed 15 July 2009).

82. Coy, Horvath and Kelly, *'It's Just Like Going to the Supermarket'*, p. 26.

83. International Center for Research on Women, *Success on the Ground: Reducing Child Marriage*, International Center for Research on Women, Washington DC, 2007.

CHAPTER 4

1. Commission of the European Communities, *Equality between Women and Men – 2008*, Brussels, 2008, pp. 13–14.

2. Kate Purcell and Peter Elias, *Seven Years On: Graduate Careers in a Changing Labour Market*, Higher Education Careers Service Unit, Manchester, 2004, p. 12.

3. Becky Francis, 'The Gendered Subject: Students' Subject Preferences and Discussions of Gender and Subject Ability', *Oxford Review of Education*, vol. 26, no. 1, 2000: 35–48.

4. Commission of the European Communities, *Equality between Women and Men*, p. 21.

5. Rachael Hawkins, The Experiences of Young Women in Science, *The F Word*, 2002, www.thefword.org.uk/features/2002/11/the_experiences_of_young_women_in_science (accessed 5 December 2009).

6. The gender gap in attainment is much smaller than the class gap, and variations in attainment by ethnicity are also wider than by gender. See Department for Education and Skills, *Gender and Education: The Evidence on Pupils in England*, DfES Publications, Nottingham, 2007, pp. 57–71.

7. J. Benetto, *Staying On: Making the Extra Years in Education Count for All Young People*, Equality and Human Rights Commission, London, 2009.

8. Wisrutta Atthakor, 'The Woman Engineer: Are We Really That Incompetent?', *The F Word*, 2009, www.thefword.org.uk/features/2009/07/the_woman_engin (accessed 5 December 2009).

9. Becky Francis, *Gender, Toys and Learning*, Roehampton University, 2008, www.roehampton.ac.uk/news/genderedtoys.html (accessed 10 December 2009).

10. Mark Brosnan, *Factors Predicting Attitudes and Success upon a Science/*

Engineering Project: Full Research Report, ESRC, Swindon, 2007.

11. Nicole M. Else-Quest, Janet Shibley Hyde and Marcia C. Linn, 'Cross-National Patterns of Gender Differences in Mathematics: A Meta-Analysis' *Psychological Bulletin*, vol. 136, no. 1, 2010: 103–27.

12. Data Service, 'Statistical First Release March 2009: Post-16 Education & Skills: Learner Participation, Outcomes and Level of Highest Qualification Held', 2009, www.thedataservice.org.uk/statistics/sfrmar09/summary.htm (accessed 10 January 2010).

13. Barry Fong and Andrew Phelps, *Apprenticeship Pay: 2007 Survey of Earnings by Sector*, Department for Innovation, Universities and Skills and BMRB Research, London, 2007, p. 25.

14. Alison Fuller, Vanessa Beck and Lorna Unwin, *Employers, Young People and Gender Segregation (England)*, Equal Opportunities Commission, Manchester, 2005; Becky Francis, Jayne Osgood, Jacinta Dalgety and Louise Archer, *Gender Equality in Work Experience Placements for Young People*, Equal Opportunities Commission, Manchester, 2005.

15. Equal Opportunities Commission, *Plugging Britain's Skills Gap: Challenging Gender Segregation in Training and Work*, Equal Opportunities Commission, Manchester, 2004.

16. Jyotsna Jha, 'Gender Equality in Education: The Role of Schools', presentation given at University of Nottingham, October 2008.

17. Robert O'Brien and Marc Williams, *Global Political Economy: Evolution and Dynamics*, 2nd edn, Palgrave Macmillan, Basingstoke, 2007, pp. 311–18.

18. Ibid., p. 289.

19. J. Elias, 'The Gendered Political Economy of Control and Resistance on the Shop Floor of the Multinational Firm: A Case-study from Malaysia', *New Political Economy*, vol. 10, no. 2, 2005: 203–22.

20. Seager, *The Atlas of Women in the World*, pp. 68–9.

21. Lin Lean Lim, *More and Better Jobs for Women: An Action Guide*, International Labour Organization, Geneva, 1996, p. 11.

22. Department for Work and Politics, *Households Below Average Income*, London, 2003, Table 7.9.

23. www.thefword.org.uk/blog/2009/10/new_anarcha_fem#comment40170 (accessed 5 December 2009).

24. TUC, *Closing the Gender Pay Gap: An Update Report for TUC Women's Conference 2008*, Trades Union Congress, London, 2007, p. 6.

25. Office for National Statistics, *Statistical Bulletin: Annual Survey of Hours and Earnings*, London, 12 November 2009.

26. Simonetta Longhi and Lucinda Platt (2008) *Pay Gaps across Equalities Areas*, Equality and Human Rights Commission, Manchester, pp. 20–24.

27. TUC, *Closing the Gender Pay Gap*, p. 17.

28. Fawcett Society, *Women and Money: A Briefing*, Fawcett Society, London, 2007.

29. Commission of the European Communities, *Equality between Women and Men*, p. 17.

30. Michael Buerk, 'It's Not Only Men Who Will Suffer in a Woman's World', *Financial Mail Women's Forum*, 28 August 2005.

31. Joan Acker, 'Hierarchies, Bodies, and Jobs: A Gendered Theory of Organizations', *Gender & Society*, vol. 4, no. 2, 1990: 139–58.

32. Christopher Uggen and Amy Blackstone, 'Sexual Harassment as a Gendered Expression of Power', *American Sociological Review* 69, 2004: 64–92.

33. Linda Wirth, 'Sexual Harassment', in Nancy E. Sacks and Catherine Marrone (eds), *Gender and Work in Today's World: A Reader*, Westview Press, Cambridge MA, 2004, pp. 269, 273–4.

34. Betty Eisenberg, 'Marking Gender Boundaries: Porn, Piss, Power Tools', in Sacks and Marrone (eds), *Gender and Work in Today's World*, pp. 291–2.

35. Uggen and Blackstone, 'Sexual Harassment as a Gendered Expression of Power'.

36. Celia Kitzinger, 'Anti-lesbian Harassment', in Clare Brant and Yun Lee Too (eds), *Rethinking Sexual Harassment*, Pluto, London, 1995.

37. Edith Wen-Chu Chen, 'Sexual Harassment from the Perspective of Asian-American Women', in Carol Rambo Ronai, Barbara A. Zsembik and Joe R. Feagin (eds), *Everyday Sexism in the Third Millennium*, Routledge, London, 1997.

38. Kathryn Hopkins, 'City Bankers "Regularly Offer Prostitutes to Clients"', *Guardian*, 14 October 2009.

39. TUC, *Closing the Gender Pay Gap*, p. 23.

40. www.statistics.gov.uk/cci/nugget.asp?id=1654 (accessed 6 December 2009).

41. Anne Phillips and Barbara Taylor, 'Sex and Skill', *Feminist Review* 6, 1980: 79–88.

42. Rosemary Crompton and Gareth Jones, *White-Collar Proletariat: Deskilling and Gender in Clerical Work*, Temple University Press, Philadelphia, 1984.

43. Peta Tancred, 'Women's Work: A Challenge to the Sociology of Work', *Gender, Work & Organization*, vol. 2, no. 1, 1995: 11–20.

44. Arlie Russell Hochschild, *The Managed Heart: Commercialization of Human Feeling*, University of California Press, Berkeley, 1983.

45. Commission of the European Communities, *Equality Between Women and Men*, p. 10.

46. Tracey Warren, 'Working Part-time: Achieving a Successful "Work–Life" Balance?', *British Journal of Sociology*, vol. 55, no. 1, 2004: 99–122.

47. Quoted in Cynthia Fuchs Epstein, Carroll Seron, Bonnie Oglensky and Robert Stone, 'Part-Time Work as Deviance: Stigmatization and Its

Consequences', in Nancy E. Sacks and Catherine Marrone (eds), *Gender and Work in Today's World: A Reader*, Westview Press, Cambridge MA, 2004, p. 164.

48. Catherine Hakim, 'Grateful Slaves and Self Made Women: Fact and Fantasy in Women's Work Orientations', *European Sociological Review*, vol. 7, no. 2, 1991: 101–21; and 'Five Feminist Myths about Women's Employment', *British Journal of Sociology*, vol. 46, no. 3, 1995: 429–55.

49. Sally Walters, 'Making the Best of Bad Job? Female Part-Timers' Orientations and Attitudes to Work', *Gender, Work & Organization*, vol. 12, no. 3, 2005: 193–216; 209.

50. For example, see Christine Delphy and Diana Leonard, *Familiar Exploitation: A New Analysis of Marriage in Contemporary Western Societies*, Polity Press, Cambridge, 1992.

51. Betty Friedan, *The Feminine Mystique*, Victor Gollancz, London, 1963.

52. C. Percheski, 'Opting Out? Cohort Differences in Professional Women's Employment Rates from 1960 to 2005', *American Sociological Review*, vol. 73, no. 3, 2008: 497–517.

53. Kimberley Fisher, Muriel Egerton, Jonathan I. Gershuny and John P. Robinson, 'Gender Convergence in the American Heritage Time Use Study (AHTUS)', *Social Indicators Research*, vol. 82, no. 1, 2007: 1–33; 18.

54. Scott Coltrane, 'Family Man', in Sacks and Marrone (eds), *Gender and Work in Today's World*, pp. 328–53.

55. Arlie Russell Hochschild with Anne Machung, *The Second Shift: Working Parents and the Revolution at Home*, Viking, New York, 1989.

56. Joel Waldfogel, 'Couch Entitlement: Surprise – Men Do Just as Much Work as Women Do', Slate.com, 16 April 2007, www.slate.com/id/2164268/pagenum/all/#p2 (accessed 6 December 2009).

57. Seager, *The Atlas of Women in the World*, pp. 70–71, 76.

58. Barbara Ehrenreich and Arlie Russell Hochschild, 'Introduction', in Barbara Ehrenreich and Arlie Russell Hochschild (eds), *Global Woman: Nannies, Maids and Sex Workers in the New Economy*, Granta, London, 2003.

59. L. Gulati, 'Asian Women Workers in International Labour Migration: An Overview', in Anuja Agrawal (ed.), *Migrant Women and Work*, Sage, New Delhi, 2006; Maureen C. Pagaduan, 'Leaving Home: Filipino Women Surviving Migration', in Sadhna Arya and Anupama Roy (eds), *Poverty, Gender and Migration*, Sage, New Delhi, 2006; Rhacel Salazar Parreñas, 'Perpetually Foreign: Filipina Migrant Domestic Workers in Rome', in Helma Lutz (ed.), *Migration and Domestic Work: A European Perspective on a Global Theme*, Ashgate, Aldershot, 2008.

60. Arlie Russell Hochschild, 'Global Care Chains and Emotional Surplus Value', in Will Hutton and Anthony Giddens (eds), *On the Edge: Living*

with Global Capitalism, Vintage, London, 2001, pp. 130–31.

61. Rhacel Salazar Parreñas, (2003) 'The Care Crisis in the Philippines: Children and Transnational Families in the New Global Economy', in Ehrenreich and Hochschild (eds), *Global Woman*, p. 47.

62. Ehrenreich and Hochschild, 'Introduction', p. 4.

63. J. Ginn and J. Sandall, 'Balancing Home and Employment', *Work, Employment and Society*, vol. 11, no. 3, 1997: 414–31; 429.

64. Emily Andrews, 'Sir Alan Sugar: Why I Have To Think Twice before Employing a Woman', *Daily Mail*, 9 February 2008.

65. Caroline Gatrell, *Embodying Women's Work*, Open University Press, Maidenhead, 2008, p. 15.

66. www.robogals.org.uk (accessed 10 December 2009).

67. Beyond Access, 'Developing Curricula for Gender Equality and Quality Basic Education: A Beyond Access Project Policy Paper', Institute of Education and Oxfam GB, London, 2003.

68. Janet Raynor, 'Educating Girls in Bangladesh: Watering a Neighbour's Tree?', in Sheila Aikman and Elaine Unterhalter (eds), *Beyond Access: Transforming Policy and Practice for Gender Equality in Education*, Oxfam, Oxford, 2005, p. 94.

69. Sheila Aikman and Elaine Unterhalter, 'Conclusion: Policy and Practice Change for Gender Equality', in Sheila Aikman and Elaine Unterhalter (eds), *Beyond Access: Transforming Policy and Practice for Gender Equality in Education*, Oxfam, Oxford, 2005.

70. www.navdanya.org/diverse-women-for-diversity (accessed 28 October 2009).

71. www.labourbehindthelabel.org/campaigns/urgent/desa (accessed 6 December 2009).

72. www.fawcettsociety.org.uk/index.asp?PageID=682 (accessed 6 December 2009).

73. Janet C. Gornick and Marcia K. Meyers, 'Creating Gender Egalitarian Societies: An Agenda for Reform', *Politics and Society*, vol. 36, no. 3, 2008: 313–49.

74. Isaac D. Balbus, *Marxism and Domination: A Neo-Hegelian, Feminist, Psychoanalytic Theory of Sexual, Politics, and Technological Liberation*, Princeton University Press, Princeton NJ, 1982, p. 312.

75. Amy Richards, *Opting In: Having a Child without Losing Yourself*, Farrar, Straus & Giroux, New York, 2008, pp. 194–200.

76. http://hugoschwyzer.net/2009/06/17/by-request-some-more-thoughts-on-feminist-fathering (accessed 6 December 2009).

CHAPTER 5

1. Marie-Claude Gervais, *Ethnic Minority Women: Routes to Power*, Government Equality Office, London, 2008.

2. www.ipu.org/wmn-e/world.htm (accessed 10 November 2009).

3. zohra moosa, *Lifts and Ladders: Resolving Ethnic Minority Women's Exclusion from Power*, Fawcett Society, London, 2009.

4. Azza Karam, 'Conclusion', in Julie Ballington and Azza Karam (eds), *Women in Parliament: Beyond Numbers*, International IDEA, Stockholm, 2005, p. 250.

5. United Nations, 'The Beijing Platform for Action: Women in Decision Making', 1995, para. 181, www.un.org/womenwatch/daw/beijing/platform (accessed 23 January 2010).

6. Bojana Stoparic, 'Climate Change is a Women's Issue', *Alternet*, 2006, www.alternet.org/story/38659 (accessed 25 January 2010).

7. *Ms* magazine, Winter 2008: 57.

8. London Assembly, Mayor's Question Time, 14 October 2009.

9. Julia Clark, Roger Mortimore and Katherine Rake, *Women's Votes: Myth and Reality*, Ipsos MORI/Fawcett Society, London, 2007, p. 15.

10. Azza Karam and Joni Lovenduski, 'Women in Parliament: Making a Difference', in Julie Ballington Julie and Azza Karam (eds), *Women in Parliament: Beyond Numbers*, International IDEA, Stockholm, 2005, p. 207.

11. http://twitter.com/leechalmers/status/4341271232 (accessed 15 December 2009).

12. www.ipsos-mori.com/researchpublications/researcharchive/poll.aspx?oItemId=969 (accessed 15 December 2009).

13. *Ms* magazine, December 2001/January 2002: 61.

14. www.ipu.org/wmn-e/classif.htm (accessed 27 October 2009).

15. Julie Ballington and Azza Karam, (eds), *Women in Parliament: Beyond Numbers*, International IDEA, Stockholm, 2005, p. 41.

16. Electoral Reform Society, *Women in Parliament: A Documentary*, London, 2008, www.wpradio.co.uk/mp3s/ERSwomenMPs.mp3 (accessed 8 March 2010).

17. Nirmal Puwar, *Space Invaders: Race, Gender and Bodies Out of Place*, Berg, Oxford, 2004.

18. Ballington and Karam, *Women in Parliament*, p. 38.

19. Fawcett Society, *Experiences of Labour Party Women in Parliamentary Selections Interim Findings*, London, n.d.

20. Rod Liddle, 'Harriet Harman is Either Thick or Criminally Disingenuous', *Spectator*, 8 August 2009.

21. http://mediamatters.org/research/200703150011 (accessed 10 November 2009).

22. http://tpmdc.talkingpointsmemo.com/2009/07/in-beer-summit-spoof-milbank-suggests-hillary-drink-mad-bitch-beer.php (accessed 10 November 2009).

23. www.feministing.com/archives/011077.html (accessed 10 November 2009).

24. Gervais, *Ethnic Minority Women*, p. 49.
25. http://news.bbc.co.uk/1/hi/world/europe/7862804.stm (accessed 10 November 2009).
26. Puwar, *Space Invaders*.
27. Ballington and Karam, *Women in Parliament*, p. 44.
28. Nadezhda Shvedova, 'Obstacles to Women's Participation in Parliament', in Ballington and Karam (eds), *Women in Parliament*, p. 35.
29. www.womenandthevote.com/devgovstats.html (accessed 10 November 2009).
30. Julie Ballingon, 'Introduction', in Ballington and Karam (eds), *Women in Parliament*, p. 26.
31. *Ms* magazine, Winter 2008: 28.
32. www.fawcettsociety.org.uk/index.asp?PageID=635 (accessed 10 November 2009).
33. Electoral Reform Society, *Women in Parliament*.
34. Drude Dahlerup, 'Increasing Women's Political Representation: New Trends in Gender Quotas', in Ballington and Karam (eds), *Women in Parliament*, p. 147.
35. *Ms* magazine, Winter 2008: 29.
36. One World Action, 'More Women More Power', 2008, p. 8, www.oneworldaction.org/more_women_more_power (accessed 28 March 2010).
37. www.womenintopolitics.org (accessed 10 November 2009).
38. www.thedowningstreetproject.com/services.html (accessed 10 November 2009).
39. http://edinburghfeministing.wordpress.com/2009/10/17/equality-vs-liberation (accessed 10 November 2009).
40. Chicago Anarcho-Feminists, 'Anarcho-Feminist Manifesto', *Siren: A Journal of Anarcho-Feminism*, vol. 1, no. 1, 1971.
41. http://nopretence.wordpress.com/2009/06/03/text-and-film (accessed 10 November 2009).
42. Cath Elliott, 'I'm Not Praying', *Guardian*, 19 August 2008.
43. Kathryn Feltey and Margaret Poloma, 'From Sex Differences to Gender Role Beliefs', *Sex Roles* 25, 1991: 181–3.
44. http://christianfeminist.blogspot.com; http://achristianfeministjourney.blogspot.com; Tamsila Tauqir, 'Spectrum Spirituality and Community Day', 27 June 2004, Rottingdean, www.safraproject.org/publications.htm.
45. Email interview with Caroline Ophis, 13 October 2009.
46. Benazir Bhutto, *Daughter of Destiny*, Simon & Schuster, New York, 1989.
47. Amina Wadud, *Qur'an and Woman: Rereading the Sacred Text from a Woman's Perspective*, Oxford University Press, New York, 1999, pp. 69–74.
48. Pamela Dickey Young, 'Experience', in Lisa Isherwood and Dorothea

McEwan (eds), *The A to Z of Feminist Theology*, Sheffield Academic Press, Sheffield, 1996, p. 61.

49. Sally McFague, *Models of God: Theology for an Ecological, Nuclear Age*, SCM Press, London, 1987.

50. Rita Gross, 'Buddhism after Patriarchy', in Paula M. Cooey, William R. Eakin and Jay B. McDaniel (eds), *After Patriarchy: Feminist Transformations of the World Religions*, Orbis Books, Maryknoll NY, 1991.

51. Valerie Saiving, 'The Human Situation: A Feminine View', *Journal of Religion* 40, 1960: 100–112; Rosemary Radford Ruether, *Sexism and God-Talk*, Beacon Press, Boston MA, 1983; Susan Brooks Thistlethwaite, *Sex, Race and God*, Geoffrey Chapman, London, 1990.

52. Delores Williams, 'A Womanist Perspective on Sin', in Emilie M. Townes (ed.), *A Troubling in My Soul: Womanist Perspectives on Evil and Suffering*, Orbis, Maryknoll NY, 1993.

53. Carol Christ, 'Why Women Need the Goddess', in Carol Christ and Judith Plaskow (eds), *Womanspirit Rising*, Harper & Row, New York, 1979; Carol Christ, *The Laughter of Aphrodite*, Harper & Row, San Francisco, 1987.

54. http://taslimanasrin.com/index2.html (accessed 10 December 2009).

55. Mary Daly, *Beyond God the Father: Toward a Philosophy of Women's Liberation* Beacon Press, Boston MA, 1973, p. 19.

56. Karen Pechilis (ed.), *The Graceful Guru: Hindu Female Gurus in India and the United States*, Oxford University Press, Oxford, 2004.

57. Office for National Statistics, Census, April 2001.

58. Email interview with Sonja White, 15 October 2009.

59. Rebecca Watson, 'Why Chicks Matter', talk given at Skepticon 2, Missouri State University, Springfield, Missouri, 20–21 November 2009.

60. Email interview with Anna Mavrogianni, 16 October 2009.

61. www.womenagainstfundamentalism.org.uk/index.html (accessed 19 October 2009).

62. Johann Hari, 'Why Should I Respect These Oppressive Religions?' *Independent*, 28 January 2009.

63. http://community.feministing.com/2009/07/feminism-with-my-faith.html.

64. Kate Dugan and Jennifer Owens, *From the Pews in the Back: Young Women and Catholicism*, Liturgical Press, Collegeville MN, 2009.

65. http://sophianetwork.typepad.com/sophia_network/about.html (accessed 26 October 2009).

66. www.mwnuk.co.uk (accessed 8 October 2009).

67. 'Women Only Jihad', *Dispatches*, Channel 4, 30 October 2006.

68. Suhraiya Jivra and Anisa de Jongj, *Sexuality, Gender and Islam*, Safra Project, 2003, www.safraproject.org/sgi-intro.htm (accessed 28 October 2009).

69. www.sikhnet.com/news/why-sikhs-need-more-female-granthis (accessed 28 October 2009).

70. www.sikhnet.com/news/strength-and-beauty-women-sikh-faith-and-gloal-community, http://fateh.sikhnet.com/s/WhyTurbans (accessed 28 October 2009).

71. Pythia Peay, 'Feminism's Spiritual Wave', *Utne*, March–April 2005: pp. 59–60.

72. Leela Fernandes, *Transforming Feminist Practice: Non-Violence, Social Justice and the Possibilities of a Spiritualized Feminism*, Aunt Lute Books, San Francisco, 2003, p. 11.

73. Peay, 'Feminism's Spiritual Wave', pp. 59–60.

74. http://gatherthewomen.org (accessed 23 October 2009).

75. Laurel Zwissler, 'Ritual Actions: Feminist Spirituality in Anti-Globalization Protests', in Chris Klassen (ed.), *Feminist Spirituality: The Next Generation*, Lexington Books, Lanham MD, 2009, pp. 161, 171, 167, 171.

76. Email interview with Caroline Ophis, 13 October 2009. See also www.barbieshakti.com (accessed 22 January 2009).

77. Giselle Vincett, 'Generational Change in Goddess Feminism: Some Observations from the UK', in Klassen (ed.), *Feminist Spirituality*, pp. 146–9.

78. Catherine Telford-Keogh, 'Queering Feminist Witchcraft', in Klassen (ed.), *Feminist Spirituality*, p. 40.

CHAPTER 6

1. C. Wright Mills, *The Sociological Imagination*, Oxford University Press, London, 1959.

2. Collette, 'Paper Dolls: Searching for Women Within Kerrang Magazine', *The F Word*, 2006, www.thefword.org.uk/reviews/2006/09/kerrang (accessed 12 December 2009).

3. Byron Hurt, *Hip Hop: Beyond Beats and Rhymes*, Media Education Foundation, Northampton MA, 2006.

4. Eisa Davis, 'Sexism and the Art of Feminist Hip-Hop Maintenance', in Rebecca Walker (ed.), *To Be Real: Telling the Truth and Changing the Face of Feminism*, Anchor, New York, 1995, p. 131.

5. Christina N. Baker, 'Images of Women's Sexuality in Advertisements: A Content Analysis of Black- and White-Oriented Women's and Men's Magazines', *Sex Roles*, vol. 52, nos 1/2, 2005: 13–27; 13.

6. Adrian Furnham and Twiggy Mak, 'Sex-Role Stereotyping in Television Commercials: A Review and Comparison of Fourteen Studies Done on Five Continents over 25 Years', *Sex Roles*, vol. 41, nos 5/6, 1999: 413–37.

7. Marcelo Royo-Vela, Joaquin Aldas-Manzano, Inés Küster and Natalia Vila, 'Adaptation of Marketing Activities to Cultural and Social Context:

Gender Role Portrayals and Sexism in Spanish Commercials', *Sex Roles* 58, 2008: 379–90.

8. Elza Ibroscheva, 'Caught Between East and West? Portrayals of Gender in Bulgarian Television Advertisements', *Sex Roles* 57, 2007: 409–18.

9. Angela McRobbie, 'Post-feminism and Popular Culture', *Feminist Media Studies*, vol. 4, no. 3, 2004: 255–64; 255.

10. Robert Goldman, *Reading Ads Socially*, Routledge, London, 1992, p. 130; Rosalind Gill, *Gender and the Media*, Polity Press, Cambridge, 2007, p. 88.

11. www.asa.org.uk/asa/focus/Live+Issue/Live+issue+Sexism+and+sensibil ity.htm (accessed 30 July 2009).

12. Mark Sweeney, 'Virgin Atlantic Ad Not Sexist, Rules ASA', *Guardian*, 9 February 2009.

13. Matthew Reisz, 'The Seven Deadly Sins of the Academy', *Times Higher Education Supplement*, 17 September 2009.

14. http://jezebel.com/5376250/4-anti+feminist-cliches-highlights-of-the-texas-t+shirt-saga (accessed 12 December 2009).

15. Annabelle Mooney, 'Boys Will Be Boys: Men's Magazines and the Normalisation of Pornography', *Feminist Media Studies*, vol. 8, no. 3, 2008: 247–65; 257.

16. Hadassah Nymark, '"Sexist" HomePride Ad Dodges Ban', *Campaign-live*, 20 May 2009, http://campaignlive.co.uk/news/906955/Sexist-Home-Pride-ad-dodges-ban (accessed 30 July 2009).

17. Katharina Lindner, 'Images of Women in General Interest and Fashion Magazine Advertisements from 1955 to 2002', *Sex Roles*, vol. 51, no. 7/8, 2004: 409–421; 409–10.

18. www.asa.org.uk/asa/focus/Live+Issue/Live+issue+Sexism+and+sensi-bility.htm (accessed 30 July 2009).

19. Lindner, 'Images of Women in General Interest and Fashion Magazine Advertisements', p. 409.

20. www.bristolfawcett.org.uk/MediaRepresentation.html (accessed 12 December 2009).

21. Anne and Bill Moir, *Why Men Don't Iron: The New Reality of Gender Differences*, HarperCollins, London, 1999.

22. Allan and Barbara Pease, *Why Men Don't Listen and Women Can't Read Maps*, Orion, London, 2001; *Why Men Lie and Women Cry*, Orion, London, 2002; *Why Men Don't Have a Clue and Women Always Need More Shoes*, Broadway Books, New York, 2004.

23. Edward O. Wilson, *Sociobiology: The New Synthesis*, Harvard University Press, Cambridge MA, 1975, p. 575.

24. Amy Adele Hasinoff, 'It's Sociobiology, Hon! Genetic Gender Determinism in Cosmopolitan Magazine', *Feminist Media Studies*, vol. 9, no. 3, 2009: 267–83.

25. John Gray, *Men Are from Mars, Women Are from Venus*, Thorsons, London, 1993, p. 10.

26. Lesley Rogers, *Sexing the Brain*, Phoenix, London, 2000, pp. 129–32.

27. www.thefword.org.uk/blog/2009/08/evolutionary_ps (accessed 12 December 2009).

28. Deborah Cameron, *The Myth of Mars and Venus*, Oxford University Press, Oxford, 2007, p. 92.

29. Ibid. p. 5.

30. Department for Children, Schools and Families, *Statistical First Release: Participation in Education, Training and Employment by 16–18 Year Olds in England*, London, 16 June 2009.

31. Naomi Haywood, Sharon Walker, Gill O'Toole, Chris Hewitson, Ellen Pugh and Preethi Sundaram, *Engaging All Young People in Meaningful Learning after 16: A Review*, Equality and Human Rights Commission, Manchester, 2009, p. vi.

32. Liz Atkins, 'Travelling Hopefully: An Exploration of the Limited Possibilities for Level 1 Students in the English Further Education System', *Research in Post-Compulsory Education*, vol. 13, no. 2, 2008: 195–204.

33. See Sherbert Research, *Customer Voice Research: Aspirations and the Children and Young People Segmentation*, Department for Children, Schools and Families, London, 2009.

34. Press release, 'The Geena David Institute on Gender in Media Releases New Findings: Males Outnumber Females by almost 3 to 1 in Films', http://womeninview.ca/articles/geena_davis.doc (accessed 10 January 2009).

35. University of Warwick, *New Performers Working Lives: A Survey of Leavers from Dance and Drama Schools*, University of Warwick, 2006.

36. Deborah Dean, *Age, Gender and Performer Employment in Europe*, University of Warwick, 2008, p. 30.

37. Sport England, *Active People Survey 2008/09*, Sport England, London, 2009.

38. Women's Sport and Fitness Foundation, *Barriers to Sports Participation for Women and Girls*, WSFF, London, 2008.

39. Women's Sports and Fitness Foundation, *Women's Sports Foundation Media Evaluation*, WSFF, London, 2006.

40. Women's Sport and Fitness Foundation, *Barriers to Sports Participation for Women and Girls*.

41. Diane Negra, 'The Feminisation of Crisis Celebrity', *Guardian*, 9 July 2008.

42. Finlo Rohrer, 'Does This Picture Make You Angry?' *BBC News Magazine*, 16 May 2008, http://news.bbc.co.uk/go/pr/fr/-/1/hi/magazine/7402907.stm (accessed 13 January 2010).

43. David Gauntlett, 'Media Celebrities and Young People's Aspirations: A Visual Research Project', paper at the Media, Communication and

Cultural Studies Association conference, University of Sussex, Brighton, 19–21 December 2003.

44. http://fugitivus.wordpress.com/stuff-what-boys-can-do (accessed 12 December 2009).

45. www.themuffia.co.uk/page6.htm (accessed 12 December 2009).

46. Debbie Stoller, *Stitch 'n Bitch*, Workman Publishing, New York, 2003, p. 7.

47. www.feministafrica.org/index.php/femrite (accessed 10 January 2010).

48. Clare Rudebeck, 'Are You Ranting? No, I'm Dancing', *Independent*, 27 August 2003.

49. http://blogs.myspace.com/index.cfm?fuseaction=blog.view&friendId=55779025&blogId=244192946 (accessed 10 December 2009).

50. www.guerillacabaret.com/aboutus.html (accessed 10 December 2009).

51. Gwendolyn D. Pough, *Check It While I Wreck It: Black Womanhood, Hip-Hop Culture, and the Public Sphere*, Northeastern University Press, Boston MA, 2004, pp. 186–7.

52. http://girl-wonder.org (accessed 10 January 2010).

53. www.wimnonline.org/WIMNsVoicesBlog/?p=1272 (accessed 10 January 2010).

54. Ananya, 'So, You Really Think We're Stupid, Do You?', *The F Word*, 2008, www.thefword.org.uk/features/2008/10/so_you_really_t (accessed 12 December 2009).

55. http://pinkstinks.co.uk (accessed 10 January 2010).

56. Alex Gibson, 'Why Men Should Care about Gender Stereotypes', *The F Word*, 2008, www.thefword.org.uk/features/2008/02/men_stereotypes (accessed 12 December 2009).

57. http://thepinkchaddicampaign.blogspot.com/2009/02/chaddi-campaign-what-next.html (accessed 10 January 2010).

CHAPTER 7

1. http://lonergrrrl.blogspot.com/2007/06/some-confused-meanderings-on-make-up. html (accessed 20 July 2007).

2. www.thefword.org.uk/blog/2008/08/new_feature_mil (accessed 10 January 2010).

3. http://disabledfeminists.com/?p=354 (accessed 10 January 2010).

4. Thanks to Rose Holyoak for additional thoughts on this.

5. http://uk.groups.yahoo.com/group/ukfeministaction (accessed 10 January 2010).

6. Jess McCabe, 'Leading from the Front Page', *Guardian*, 13 July 2007.

7. David Bouchier, *The Feminist Challenge*, Macmillan, London, 1983, p. 210.

8. Loretta Ross, Interview, *The F-Word* zine (California) 3, 2008.

FURTHER READING

Chapter 1

Boston Women's Health Book Collective (2005) *Our Bodies Ourselves: A New Edition for a New Era*, Simon & Schuster, New York.

Edut, Ophira (ed.) (2000) *Body Outlaws: Young Women Write about Body Image and Identity*, Seal Press, Berkeley.

Houppert, Karen (2000) *The Curse: Confronting the Last Taboo: Menstruation*, Profile Books, New York.

Kitzinger, Sheila (2006) *Birth Crisis*, Taylor & Francis, London.

Muscio, Inga (1998) *Cunt! A Declaration of Independence*, Avalon Group, New York.

Orbach, Susie (2009) *Bodies*, Profile Books, London.

Wolf, Naomi (1991) *The Beauty Myth*, Chatto & Windus, London.

Chapter 2

Baumgardner, Jennifer (2008) *Look Both Ways: Bisexual Politics*, Silverback Books, San Francisco.

Corral, Jill, and Lisa Miya-Jervis (2001) *Young Wives' Tales: New Adventures in Love and Partnership*, Seal Press, Berkeley.

Jensen, Robert (2007) *Getting Off: Pornography and the End of Masculinity*, South End Press, Cambridge MA.

Johnson, Merri Lisa (ed.) (2002) *Jane Sexes It Up: True Confessions of Feminist Desire*, Four Walls Eight Windows, New York.

Levy, Ariel (2006) *Female Chauvinist Pigs*, Pocket Books, London.

Tanenbaum, Leora (2000) *Slut! Growing Up Female with a Bad Reputation*, Harper Paperbacks, New York.

Walter, Natasha (2010) *Living Dolls: The Return of Sexism*, Virago Press, London.

Chapter 3

Brownmiller, Susan (1976) *Against Our Will: Men, Women and Rape*, Bantam Books, New York.

Friedman Jaclyn and Jessica Valenti (eds) (2008) *Yes Means Yes: Visions of Female Sexual Power and a World without Rape*, Avalon Publishing, New York.

Jeffreys, Sheila (2009) *The Industrial Vagina: The Political Economy of the Global Sex Trade*, Routledge, London.

Langelan, Martha J. (1993) *Back Off! How to Confront and Stop Sexual Harassment and Harassers*, Fireside, New York.

Sebold, Alice (2003) *Lucky,* Picador, London.

Waugh, Louisa (2006) *Selling Olga: Stories of Human Trafficking*, Weidenfeld & Nicolson, London.

Chapter 4

Ehrenreich, Barbara and Arlie Russell Hochschild (2003) *Global Woman: Nannies, Maids and Sex Workers in the New Economy*, Granta, London.

Hochschild, Arlie Russell (2003) *The Second Shift* [1989], Penguin, London.

Maushart, Susan (2002) *Wifework: What Marriage Really Means for Women*, Bloomsbury, London.

Richards, Amy (2008) *Opting In: Having a Child without Losing Yourself,* Farrar, Straus & Giroux, New York.

Seager, Joni (2009) *The Atlas of Women in the World*, 4th edn, Earthscan, Brighton.

Toynbee, Polly (2003) *Hard Work: Life in Low-pay Britain*, Bloomsbury, London.

Wilkinson, Richard, and Kate Pickett (2009) *The Spirit Level: Why More Equal Societies Almost Always Do Better*, Allen Lane, London.

Chapter 5

Benson, Ophelia, and Jeremy Stangroom (2009) *Does God Hate Women?* Continuum, London.

Fernea, E.W. (2002) *In Search of Islamic Feminism*, Bantam Doubleday Dell, New York.

Henig, Simon (2000) W*omen and Political Power: Europe since 1945*, Routledge, London.

Hunt, Helen LaKelly (2004) *Faith and Feminism: A Holy Alliance*, Pocket Books, New York.

Marcotte, Amanda (2010) *Get Opinionated! A Progressive's Guide to Finding Your Voice (and Taking a Little Action)*, Seal Press, Berkeley.

Slee, Nicola (2003) *Faith and Feminism: An Introduction to Christian Feminist Theology*, Darton, Longman & Todd, London.

Traister, Rebecca (2010) *Big Girls Don't Cry: Hillary Clinton, Sarah Palin, Michelle Obama, and the Year that Changed Everything*, Free Press, New York.

Chapter 6

Burton Nelson, Mariah (1996) *The Stronger Women Get, the More Men Love Football: Sexism and the Culture of Sport*, Women's Press, London.

Cameron, Deborah (2007) *The Myth of Mars and Venus: Do Men and Women Really Speak Different Languages?* Oxford University Press, Oxford.

Douglas, Susan J. (1995) *Where the Girls Are: Growing Up Female with the Mass Media*, Penguin, London.

Gill, Rosalind (2006) *Gender and the Media*, Polity Press, Cambridge.

Jervis, Lisa, and Andi Zeisler (eds) (2007) *Bitchfest: Ten Years of Cultural Criticism from the Pages of 'Bitch' Magazine,* Farrar, Straus & Giroux, New York.

Kilbourne, Jean (1999) *Can't Buy My Love: How Advertising Changes The Way We Think and Feel*, Touchstone, New York.

Piepmeier, Alison (2010) *Girl Zines: Making Media, Doing Feminism*, New York University Press, New York.

Chapter 7

Banyard, Kat (2010) *The Equality Illusion: The Truth About Women and Men Today*, Faber & Faber, London.

Baumgardner, Jennifer, and Amy Richards (2001) *Manifesta: Young Women, Feminism and the Future*, Farrar, Straus & Girroux, New York.

Brownmiller, Susan (2000) *In Our Time: Memoir of a Revolution,* Aurum Press, London.

Hernandez, Daisy, and Bushra Rehman (2002) *Colonize This! Young Women of Color on Today's Feminism*, Seal Press, Berkeley.

Kristof, Nicholas D., and Sheryl WuDunn (2009) *Half the Sky: Turning Oppression into Opportunity for Women Worldwide*, Knopf, New York.

Faludi, Susan (1992) *Backlash! The Undeclared War against Women*, Vintage, London.

Siegel, Deborah (2007) *Sisterhood Interrupted: From Radical Women to Grrls Gone Wild*, Palgrave Macmillan, New York.

Valenti, Jessica (2007) *Full Frontal Feminism: A Young Woman's Guide to Why Feminism Matters*, Seal Press, Berkeley.

INDEX

CPSIA information can be obtained
at www.ICGtesting.com
Printed in the USA
LVHW092334081221
705605LV00001BA/5